The Cosmic Common Good

The Cosmic Common Good

Religious Grounds for
Ecological Ethics

DANIEL P. SCHEID

OXFORD

UNIVERSITY PRESS

OXFORD
UNIVERSITY PRESS

Oxford University Press is a department of the University of
Oxford. It furthers the University's objective of excellence in research,
scholarship, and education by publishing worldwide.
Oxford is a registered trademark of Oxford University Press
in the UK and certain other countries.

Published in the United States of America by
Oxford University Press
198 Madison Avenue, New York, NY 10016, United States of America.

© Oxford University Press 2016

Portions of Chapter 2 appeared in Daniel P. Scheid's "Common Good: Human, or Cosmic?"
Journal of Religion & Society, Supplement Series 9: "The Greening of the Papacy," edited by
Ronald A. Simkins and John J. O'Keefe (2013): 5–15.

Portions of Chapters 2 and 9 appeared in Daniel P. Scheid's "Catholic Common Good,
Buddhist Interdependence, and the Practice of Interreligious Ecological Ethics," *Journal of
Inter-Religious Studies* 16 (2015): 72–80.

Portions of Chapters 5 and 6 appeared in Daniel P. Scheid's "Expanding Catholic Ecological
Ethics: Ecological Solidarity and Earth Rights," in *Religion, Economics, and Culture in Conflict
and Conversation* (College Theology Society Annual Volume 2010), eds. Laurie Cassidy and
Maureen O'Connell (Maryknoll, NY: Orbis, 2011), 196–216.

Lines in Chapter 8 from *The Bhagavad Gita* translated by Zaehner (1966) 469w from 1.1, 2.12,
2.7, 4.6–8, 5.18, 7.5–11, 9:3–5, 10:8, 10:32, 11:17–18. By permission of Oxford University Press
(www.oup.com).

Lines in Chapter 8 from *The Law Code of Manu* translated by Olivelle (2009) 390w from
4.1, 5.28, 5.30, 5.38–39, 5.45–46, 5.48–49, 5.52, 5.53, 8:15, 8:21, 8.285–286, 10.83–84. By
permission of Oxford University Press (www.oup.com).

Library of Congress Cataloging-in-Publication Data
Scheid, Daniel P.
The cosmic common good : religious grounds for ecological ethics / Daniel P. Scheid.
pages cm
Includes bibliographical references and index.
ISBN 978–0–19–935943–1 (hardback : alk. paper) 1. Human ecology—Religious aspects—
Catholic Church. 2. Human ecology—Religious aspects. 3. Ecotheology. I. Title.
BX1795.H82S33 2016
205'.691—dc23
2015016509

To Anna, in gratitude for making her home on this beautiful Earth with me, and for our beloved children Henry Daniel, Clare Susanna, and Eamon Patrick: may the cosmic common good shine more brightly in their lives as a result of the efforts our generation expends today.

Contents

Acknowledgments

THIS BOOK IS the result of many years of ruminating about theological ecological ethics. When I began theological studies, my driving focus was what I might be able to contribute to the preservation, sustainability, and well-being of our planetary community. Indeed, some of these chapters began over a decade ago as papers in coursework. It is an immense joy to see the various pieces of the puzzle cohere, even as I expect these ideas to develop in further dialogue with others for many years to come.

Of course, this book would not be possible without an extensive community of scholars, family, and friends who have supported me and sustained me. I am grateful beyond words and beyond measure to them all.

I offer my thanks to those who read drafts of various chapters and provided invaluable and constructive feedback, including James Bailey, Bede Bidlack, John Grim, Aimee Light, David Loy, Sarah MacMillen, Ryan McLaughlin, Christiana Peppard, Kathryn Getek Soltis, Mary Evelyn Tucker, Elisabeth Vasko, and Greg Zuschlag. I also thank those who assisted me with research, proofreading, and other tasks while they were graduate students at Duquesne University, including Lisa Hickman, Marita Hunchuck, Arlene Monteveccio, Joseph Smith, and Ann Vinski. I am thankful, too, to the many colleagues who made comments on versions of some chapters at conferences such as the American Academy of Religion, Catholic Theological Ethics in the World Church, College Theology Society, and the Society for Christian Ethics.

I am grateful to my colleagues at Duquesne University for their consistent support, and to the university for two grants: the Fr. Richard V. Paluse Mission-Related Research Award, which supported the research and writing of Chapters 2 and 3; and the Presidential Scholarship Award, which enabled me to complete the final draft of the book.

Thank you to Theo Calderara and everyone at Oxford University Press for their support and assistance in bringing this book to fruition.

My mentors at Catholic Theological Union and Boston College guided me through my interests in comparative theological ecological ethics and helped me hone my particular theological vision. They have modeled how to combine careful and thoughtful scholarship with a search for wisdom and compassion for those who suffer. I remain indebted to Robert Schreiter, C.PP.S., Thomas Nairn, O.F.M., Stephen J. Pope, Francis X. Clooney, S.J., Lisa Sowle Cahill, James Keenan, S.J., and David Hollenbach, S.J.

Writing a book on cosmic flourishing has certainly taught me the importance of humility, and it evokes in me boundless gratitude to my family and friends who made it possible by encouraging me in countless ways. Thank you to my parents John and Nancy Scheid and my extensive network of family, who first taught me and who continue to teach me about the importance of the common good and flourishing in relationship to others. Thank you to my friends, who have become a second family to me and buttress me with their joy and confidence. And my sincerest and deepest thanks to my wife, Anna Floerke Scheid, for her love, inspiration, humor, and patience. I am blessed to have Anna not only as a wife and partner but also as a fellow theological ethicist and intellectual companion. She has accompanied me through my entire academic career, and I would not be the person or theologian I am today without her.

Fitting with my proposal for a cosmic common good, I offer this book for the various communities to which I belong:

For all my fellow creatures and our mutual happiness in God,

For the Earth and for the sustainable and resilient flourishing of its many beings,

For the immediate families of which I am blessed to be a part,

And most especially for my nearest family members: my wife, Anna, and our children Henry Daniel, Clare Susanna, and Eamon Patrick.

Introduction

TWO THOUGHT EXPERIMENTS will help to situate my proposal for an interreligious cosmic common good. First, imagine for a moment that humanity makes an unprecedented advancement in optical technology. A powerful telescope boasts a lens that not only can locate a "goldilocks" planet where life is possible, but it can now provide crisp and detailed images from thousands of light years away, of the sort we now enjoy of planet Earth. Imagine further that this telescope captures images of a planet teeming with life: thriving vegetation; myriad creatures of imaginable and unimaginable sorts and shapes; moving creatures that creep, crawl, fly, run, and swing; ecosystems and landscapes of color and complexity, beauty and opportunity, where creatures interact in relationships marked by cooperation, strife, and flexible stability. Humanity erupts in celebration: Earth is not alone in the universe! The resplendent power of life and its fascinating articulations exist elsewhere than on Earth, perhaps in many places yet to discover. There is no indication of a species comparable to *Homo sapiens*, which exhibits signs of self-conscious and rational behavior. It is an adolescent Cenezoic Earth, a planet before intelligent life has emerged. "Eden," as some have taken to call it, is utterly remote, and even with advanced space transportation, no human visitation is feasible. Our interaction with this planet is limited strictly to observation and learning, to wonder and appreciation. How might such a discovery alter humanity's sense of who we are in the universe, or of our role on Earth? Does it shift our relationship to our planetary home, or to the creatures with whom we share it? Does Earth become less magical and wondrous, or even more so? Imagine finally that a year after this Earth-shattering discovery (in the sense that it upends our view of Earth's uniqueness), there is another: we witness an asteroid plummeting into Eden, much more destructive than the one that annihilated the dinosaurs on Earth, and it nearly guarantees the end of all planetary life. How do we react? No human or self-conscious life has been lost. Yet might we still see this as a tragedy, as a desperate loss for us, and for the cosmos as a whole?

A second thought experiment, this time drawing on personal memory: recall a place and a setting where you have been when you experienced the vitality of the "more than human world,"[1] the presence and dynamism of diverse life forms, or the elemental powers of the Earth. Perhaps you are standing beside the ocean, hearing its deafening roar, feeling the windy salt air surround you, watching minnows, fish, crabs, and all kinds of marine life dart about. Or you are hiking a path up a mountain, watching the valley recede in view and perceiving how the river, the grasses, the trees, and the animals fit into a unified whole, one that pulsed with life before your arrival and will continue after you have left. Or you are walking in a nearby urban park and witness oaks, elms, pines, and entangling vines create a shelter and refuge for birds, chipmunks, and deer. Despite the conspicuous evidence of human influence, you feel yourself entering a realm that is theirs as much as yours, in which their pursuits and struggles both precede you and persist beyond you. In all of these ways, perhaps you sense that you have encountered another world, in which nonhuman creatures actively engage in a life and create a place of dwelling that is not subsidiary to the merely human world. Imagine your reaction when you find out that this setting and these creatures have experienced severe degradation or ruin. What has been lost? What has been lost in you? Does your response change whether this destruction was the result of natural processes, the rising influence of human presence, or human indifference to the consequences of their choices?

These two images express briefly the vision of the cosmic common good: a worldview that experiences the nonhuman or more than human world as the fullest setting for human life, and experiences the vitiation of the nonhuman world as a loss for the greater community of which we are a part. Some people may experience these two thought experiments as alienating: I feel small and insignificant beneath the depths of space, beside the ocean, atop a mountain, alone in a forest. Yet for many, and I would suggest for most people throughout human cultural and religious history, there is instead a sensation of expansion and belonging, of a release from the narrow confines of self-enclosure. The cosmic common good acknowledges and recognizes the reality of the utility of the nonhuman world; all creatures use each other for survival. But it also celebrates the goodness of nonhumans and the life-supporting contexts in which they dwell, for what and who they are, for who we are when we are with them, and that only together are we truly "us."

As the book proceeds, keep in mind these two images, of places densely packed with life, creatures interacting, cooperating, striving, consuming, and growing. What is the moral vision required to truly behold and understand this world and our place in it? What is the good to be celebrated, the loss to be mourned, when we shift our vision to the living and now imperiled Earth?

The Cosmic Common Good

I

The Cosmic Common Good
as a Ground for Interreligious
Ecological Ethics

I. Imperiled Earth and Religious Responses

The Earth, "our common home," is imperiled.[1] With increasing clarity, we observe the extent and the variety of ways in which the systems on Earth that generate and maintain an unparalleled diversity of life are threatened. Indeed, their very viability has come into question. These challenges are both global and local: they must be understood as threats that affect the entire planet, such as climate change, ocean acidification, and diminishing biodiversity; yet the shape that these problems take also fluctuates dramatically according to local and concrete conditions. Climate change may bring droughts or increased flooding, loss of biodiversity occurs not only through loss of habitat but also through the incursion of invasive and non-local species, and air and water quality improves in some privileged locations even as the stress on ecosystems globally intensifies: the Earth upon which human existence depends is in distress.[2] Indeed, no ethical issue encapsulates the increasingly interconnected contemporary world better than the ecological crisis. Over the course of the twentieth century, the world was slowly introduced to the possibility that human products and lifestyle choices could fundamentally alter the patterns of life for non-human creatures.[3] In response, ecological awareness has blossomed, permeating world cultures. Countless works have outlined the various kinds of ecological threats that endanger the Earth and the precise factors and fluctuating conditions of these ecological threats, and many have proposed a wide array of possible solutions. This is no longer the province of specialized scientists but a concern that transcends and spans academic disciplines.[4] We know something is wrong, and we are struggling to respond.

This book represents one response to this ecological crisis, rooted in the Catholic theological tradition but critically engaging other religious traditions as well. Theological traditions have a pivotal role to play for two reasons. First, as many religious leaders have argued, the ecological crisis is also a moral crisis.[5] Our recurrent inability to curb or even to address ecological threats like climate change is more than a policy failure, an economic conundrum, or a challenge to develop more advanced and sophisticated technology. It also represents a moral failure. Though science and politics play an important role, the proper response to imperiled Earth must include a renewed ethical vision. In my own Catholic tradition, recent popes have become ardent and vociferous proponents of environmental concern. In *Laudato Si'*, Pope Francis describes the ecological crisis as a "sign of the ethical, cultural and spiritual crisis of modernity" (119), and so we must penetrate "to the ethical and spiritual roots of environmental problems, which require that we look for solutions not only in technology but in a change of humanity; otherwise we would be dealing merely with symptoms" (9). We need a "broader vision of reality" (141) and a "renewal of humanity itself" (118). Therefore Francis calls for a "bold cultural revolution" (114), namely the development of a truly "ecological culture" that can provide "a lifestyle and a spirituality" that sees all reality as interconnected and thus might enable us to re-envision humanity's proper role on Earth (111).

The second reason that religious traditions are paramount for addressing ecological crises flows from the first: they have long been central in addressing ethical concerns and contributing to a vision of what humanity is and can be. Pope Emeritus Benedict XVI suggests the Catholic Church is an "expert in humanity,"[6] while Francis proposes that "the rich heritage of Christian spirituality, the fruit of twenty centuries of personal and communal experience, has a beautiful contribution to make to the renewal of humanity." Indeed, Francis points to the rich insights that all religions can make, and he urges dialogue among them "for the sake of protecting nature, defending the poor, and building networks of respect and fraternity."[7] Since the root of the ecological crisis is a faulty, sinful conception of the human person and her role in creation, so a theological redefinition of the human person and her good is an essential component of crafting a long-term, truly sustainable solution to the ecological crisis. The task of the theologian is not necessarily to endorse specific policy proposals, but to draw on the riches of a millennia-old tradition (and traditions) in order to provide the seeds of a global cultural renewal. The world's religious traditions are invited to contribute to nurturing new patterns of human-Earth relationship dedicated to a sustainable flourishing for all creatures.

I.1. Ecology and Religions: Anthropocentrism and Its Discontents

While I affirm the great potential for a productive relationship between religious traditions and the environmental movement, there has been historically a more ambiguous relationship between them that continues to shape how religions perceive and respond to the ecological crisis. Religions have always had an ecological dimension in the way they ground humans in nature's rhythms,[8] but their relationship to the modern environmental movement is more contentious. Up until the mid-twentieth century, environmentalism in the United States was understood by two broad approaches, *conservationism* and *preservationism.* Conservationists recognized that natural resources are not limitless, and so they aimed to ensure their long-term availability for future generations. Gifford Pinchot (1865–1946), the first chief of the US Forest Service, is the classical representative: "Without natural resources life itself is impossible. From birth to death, natural resources, transformed for human use, feed, clothe, shelter, and transport us. Upon them we depend for every material necessity, comfort, convenience, and protection in our lives. Without abundant resources prosperity is out of reach."[9] The second approach is typified by naturalist John Muir and the origins of the Sierra Club, and this movement had the initial goal of preserving the beauty of nature both for its own sake and for humanity's aesthetic enjoyment.

By the 1960s, however, a new strain of environmentalism emerged: *protectionism.*[10] Spurred on by the publication of Rachel Carson's *Silent Spring* (1962), the burning of the Cuyahoga River in Cleveland (1969), and the plight of endangered species, people became increasingly concerned about humanity's destructive capacity, and so the focus became protection, defending the Earth and nonhuman species from human beings' excessive contamination and profligate killing. Environmentalism moved from "*conserve* nature *for* human *use*" and "*preserve* nature *for* human *appreciation,*" to "*protect* nature *from* human *abuse.*"

More importantly, environmentalists diagnosed the cause of the problem as anthropocentrism and the presumption that nature has solely instrumental value. Anthropocentrism places the human at the center of moral consideration and as the only intrinsically worthwhile creature, for whom all other creatures are made. By contrast, nature possesses only instrumental value, as it contributes to human needs.[11] For some environmentalists, therefore, humanity is the problem, and reducing the human presence and returning to nature is the solution. Indeed, for some, nature has become the primary sacred reality to which humanity must submit.[12] Leaders of the environmental movement, never that rooted in traditional religions anyway, then "framed their agenda in increasingly secular or even anti-Christian terms."[13] Some groups (such as Earth First!) even adopted pagan symbols as a way to express their break from traditional religion, and some Christians retaliated by dismissing environmentalism outright.[14] Christian churches feared the effects of this kind of environmentalism and saw it as essentially anti-Christian. It attacks the human, unduly elevates nature, and eclipses God.

Christianity was early on identified as thoroughly anthropocentric and therefore at the root of this crisis.[15] Christian theologians responded in a variety of ways in order to demonstrate how Christianity can support ethical non-anthropocentrism and the intrinsic value of creation. They re-examined and reinterpreted scriptural passages and core theological doctrines, from the meaning of the incarnation of Jesus Christ to the activity of the Spirit in creation, and in doing so have formed a multifaceted and potent response. Activists have built relationships with environmental groups and have established collective projects, and the bond between religion and ecology is now strong.[16] They demonstrate the myriad ways in which religious traditions can indeed be a guide for nurturing a sustainable Earth ethic.

Mary Evelyn Tucker and John Grim, leaders in the field of religion and ecology, argue that religion has ways of grounding, orienting, nurturing, and transforming human communities. Religions offer cosmologies, stories that give humans a sense of the whole, that bind "peoples, biodiversity, and place together,"[17] and enable them to narrate the larger mystery that surrounds them.[18] Religious ecologies flow from them; they are "functional cosmologies that express an awareness of kinship with and dependence on nature for the continuity of all life."[19] Religious ecologies become ways of "orienting humans to the universe, grounding them in the community of nature and humans, nurturing them in Earth's fecund processes, and transforming them into their deeper cosmological selves."[20]

After forty years of work, religious ethicists are now revisiting the centrality of the cosmological question, and some suggest moving beyond the debate surrounding anthropocentrism versus geocentrism and nature's intrinsic versus instrumental value.[21] Willis Jenkins offers the categories of soteriology and grace for articulating a different approach to ecological ethics. Ecologies of grace, rather than cosmologies of nature's goodness, provide a more secure platform for Christians to engage ecological ethics because they conjoin caring for Earth with the core of religious practice, namely salvation.[22] Recently, Jenkins has warned against the "cosmological temptation" for doing ecological ethics. Effective ethics tend to be more pluralist and require a variety of contextually driven responses, rather than a "top-down" approach in which a theorist provides a vision of the world and hopes that ethical choices follow.[23] Jenkins and others are right that cosmological approaches are certainly not the sole contribution that religious ethicists can make.

At the same time, Jenkins acknowledges the abiding pragmatic value of cosmologies for guiding religious responses.[24] Especially in the Catholic Church, cosmological interpretations of humanity's relationship to God and to creation have proven fruitful for reorganizing themes of religious life, liturgy, and efforts to build a sustainable and just world.[25] Moreover, many organizations that draw on the Catholic Church's social teaching on the value of life, itself grounded in cosmological views of the person, have begun to adopt environmental themes, including Catholic Relief Services (CRS)[26] and the Catholic Campaign for Human Development (CCHD).[27]

The enduring vitality of religious cosmologies suggests that theologians still need to voice a definitive answer to the basic questions of humanity's role on Earth and in the cosmos[28] and of the value of nonhuman creatures.

To do so, I propose a cosmological ethic: the cosmic common good.[29] A cosmological approach lends itself to building bridges between religious traditions, for whom worldviews and ethics remain indissoluble. The dialogue I establish between a Catholic worldview and other religious traditions depends on the overriding context of cosmological worldviews and their ecological promise.[30] Moreover, I argue that the cosmic common good can also respond to Jenkins's proposal that ecological ethics be cast in terms of soteriology. Thus a cosmological dialogue, while not the only possible approach to an imperiled Earth and the call to do justice to both Earth and humanity, remains pertinent.

The cosmic common good provides a ground for and solidifies (1) an ethical non-anthropocentrism, in which humans are part of a greater whole; (2) both the instrumental and intrinsic value of nonhuman nature; and (3) a connection between the ends of religious practice and the pursuit of this common good. These broad parameters will find different expressions as they are thickened through the particularities of various religious traditions.

II. Twofold Approach: Catholic Social Thought and Other Religious Traditions
II.1. Part One: A Catholic Cosmic Common Good

This book approaches the question of what kind of ethics an imperiled Earth needs by conjoining two distinct but compatible methodological approaches. I begin this ethical renewal from the perspective of Catholicism, and specifically from the tradition of reflection on social issues known as Catholic social teaching[31] and Catholic social thought.[32] Though it has roots in Christian Scripture and is present in some manner throughout the theological traditions of the Church, Catholic social teaching proper begins in 1891, with the publication of *Rerum Novarum* by Pope Leo XIII. Today there are multiple papal social encyclicals and scores of documents from local bishops' conferences around the world that make up Catholic social teaching. From the beginning, Catholic social teaching has sought to apply core theological principles regarding the dignity of the human person and her intrinsically social nature to emerging problems of modern society. Leo XIII and subsequent popes responded to times of great social upheaval, and they strove to forge a properly Catholic and Christian understanding of the human person in relationship to society. They formulated and highlighted Catholic perspectives on social goods and evils, from the proper role of government and the scope of private property to colonialism and war. In this way, Catholic social teaching is grounded in a vision of the reign of God that is not fixed to particular historical contexts, yet is capable of growth in order to articulate principles that can meet a variety of social concerns and across shifting cultural contexts. Catholic social thought has utilized and ramified this heritage and has applied it to a host of diverse contexts and issues.

In Part One of this volume, I draw on the work of the many popes, bishops, and theologians who have used various principles of Catholic social thought to address ecological crises to argue that these principles, once extended and reoriented in a fully ecological and non-anthropocentric direction, form a suitable ground upon which to build a healthier human-Earth relationship.[33] In particular, it is from this expansive vision of the common good that I derive my proposal for the cosmic common good. A Catholic cosmic common good and related concepts of Earth solidarity and Earth rights frame my approach to Catholic ecological ethics. Of course, one could simply propose analogous concepts of the common good, solidarity, and rights that apply to nonhuman creation and bear different names. Yet creating terms applicable only to nonhuman nature serves to reinforce the sharp divide between humans and nature that ecological theologians have been striving to deconstruct. Moreover, drawing on and expanding concepts deeply rooted in Catholic social thought gives the reformulated terms a gravitas that they might not otherwise have. This additional moral weight is deserved based on the scope and severity of the ecological crisis. The global forces that imperil Earth and the planetary common good pose a danger that justifies retrieving and revising the traditions of the common good, solidarity, and rights so as to increase protections for the planetary common good. I hope to demonstrate that the extensions that I and many others have proposed are justified and necessary, and that this provides a consistent approach to ecological concerns based on Catholic social thought.

Of course, this does not begin to explore all the possible intersections between the Catholic intellectual tradition and ecological ethics, nor does my appeal to particular theologians within the Catholic tradition such as Augustine and Aquinas exhaust their potential contributions to a rigorous Catholic ecological ethic. Instead, I aim to do something more constrained and limited: an approach to ecological ethics through the principle of the cosmic common good. This book therefore proposes that revised principles from Catholic social thought—in particular the principle of the cosmic common good—can orient human responsibility toward humanity's fuller participation in a wider web of creation and thus can become a unifying framework for ecological ethics.

By calling the cosmic common good a "ground" for ecological ethics, I mean that it can function as a foundation and bedrock for further work, but I select the term "ground" deliberately. A foundation provides a solid and secure base upon which to build, and it may result from human labor or may occur naturally through nonhuman cosmic processes. Ground, however, is an organic foundation, upon which living creatures depend. An ethical ground is not only a basis for life; it is a living metaphor itself. In this way the cosmic common good does not refer to the cosmos (and more locally to the Earth) as a mere theoretical or metaphorical base. Instead, it is a principle that strives to return us to a living reality. The cosmic common good reminds us that every aspect of humanity's biological, cultural, and even spiritual lives are emergent properties that spring forth from and are inextricable from the ground of Earth. Moreover, "ground" also carries theological connotations of mysterious and divine depths. Lutheran theologian Paul Tillich famously defined God as the "ground and power of being."[34] In a similar way, I configure the cosmic common good as a grounding metaphor that points to the sacred depth dimension of the cosmos.[35] The cosmic Earth is the ground where God and the human meet. There is no sufficient human encounter with God, the ground and the power of being, without the Earth as ground.

In a similar way, I envision Catholic social thought as a kind of garden of ideas that have given fruit to the reflection of Catholics and non-Catholics alike. Like a garden, Catholic social thought is not a fixed and static tradition but a living reality, which provides a genetic heritage that can give birth to a new kind of ethical reflection. This neologism (or nearly so) is a conscious attempt to avoid the popular metaphor of "mining the tradition for its resources."[36] I am painfully aware that mining can produce dividends but can also be ecologically toxic. Mining can weaken and erode a tradition, just as it can weaken and erode the Earth. Rather, I attempt to develop, organically, from the soil of Catholic social thought, indications of ways that the Catholic tradition may be pruned so that it might bear more fruit (John 15:1–3).

II.2. Part Two: The Cosmic Common Good and Interreligious Ecological Ethics

Equally important, I believe that the cosmic common good can establish a common ground with other religious and theological traditions, and indeed that dialogue is necessary for a robust comprehension of each tradition's expression of the cosmic common good. Thus in Part Two I bring this expanded vision of Catholic social thought into dialogue with other religious traditions.[37]

Since much has been done to describe the ways in which various religious traditions might guide us to a more sustainable human-Earth relationship, I seek to place these contributions into constructive dialogue. I maintain that the cosmic common good can be a thoroughly Catholic concept, rooted in a Christian tradition devoted to the God of Jesus Christ. Yet its basic tenets are flexible enough that it can find resonance across multiple traditions that do not share the same theological and theocentric foundations. The cosmic common good springs from many religious grounds and so is well attuned to speak to diverse forms of religious ecological ethics and hopefully aid in addressing global ecological concerns.

Thus in the latter half of the book, I identify and explore cognates to a Catholic cosmic common good in non-Christian traditions, specifically Hindu, Buddhist, and American Indian traditions. This kind of interreligious dialogue, which as I explain later is more properly defined as comparative theology, is necessarily partial and merely preliminary. It does not propose to exhaust the possibilities for an interreligious ecological ethic, but it does hope to show that such a common ground can be reasonably proposed and supported.

This book therefore employs a twofold approach: a systematic presentation of how certain principles of Catholic social thought might be expanded in order to address ecological concerns; and a critical dialogue between these principles and non-Christian religious traditions in a way that challenges and expands these principles further. In other words, I aim (1) to extend Catholic social thought ecologically, and (2) to extend Catholic ecological ethics comparatively.

My vision of the cosmic common good is rooted in and stems from the Catholic Christian tradition, but it is also a solid ground for ecological ethics with roots in multiple religious traditions, and each tradition expresses it in various ways. The broad features of a Catholic cosmic common good can dialogue critically with non-Christian traditions in order to develop an interreligious theological vision for a sustainable ecological ethic. Each tradition that I engage becomes its own ground for the cosmic common good as well, which in turn expands my initial articulation of a Catholic cosmic common good. The cosmic common good reflects and unifies multiple religious grounds for ecological ethics and so bears the potential to be, as Francis describes, the "broader vision of reality" that sees all things as interconnected, the source for an "ecological culture" that might lead to "a renewal of humanity itself."

III. Outline of Chapters

My exploration of Catholic social thought and ecological ethics begins in Chapter 2 with the principle of the common good. I first outline the background and history of this principle in Catholic social thought. Then I explore the justifications, scientific and theological, for why Catholic social thought ought to promote a cosmocentric ethic that envisions the well-being of humanity as bound up with the flourishing of an intrinsically valuable cosmos, leading to reformulated principles of creaturely dignity and cosmic participation.

Chapter 3 looks to classical sources to enrich a Catholic cosmic common good, namely St. Augustine and St. Thomas Aquinas. I identify in their theologies of creation a fivefold cosmic common good: the ultimate good of creation to glorify God; the good of individual creatures pursuing their own perfections; the good of creatures for other creatures; the good of a diversity of creatures; and the good of the order of creatures. By looking to Augustine and Aquinas, I hope to demonstrate that the notion of a cosmic common good has significant roots in Christian theologies of creation, and that properly understood in a Christian context, the cosmic common good represents a theocentric valuation of all creation.

Chapter 4 focuses on cultural historian and "geologian" Thomas Berry, C.P., whose articulation of the evolutionary cosmic story as told by modern science has profoundly influenced contemporary eco-theologians. Berry underscores the importance of narrative, specifically the cosmos's history, as an essential component of understanding the cosmos's intrinsic goodness. For Berry, this narrative describes a threefold nature of every creature that signifies its contribution to the common good: differentiation, subjectivity, and communion. Together, these demonstrate how a Catholic cosmic common good represents a thoroughly cosmocentric valuation of creation.

The chapters on classical and modern contributions to a Catholic cosmic common good do not represent an exhaustive treatment of what Augustine, Aquinas, and Berry contribute to ecological ethics; nor do they purport to offer a systematic analysis of their theologies of creation. These chapters are markers, indicators of how the cosmic common good finds its roots in the Catholic tradition and what features of their theology the cosmic common good might include. As such, I do not enter into critical debates regarding any of these thinkers, or argue that these features are the only contribution to ecological ethics they may make.

With this foundation, Chapters 5 and 6 look into how other principles of Catholic social thought should be extended to correspond to the cosmic common good and to address properly the scope of ecological degradation. Chapter 5 examines the principle of solidarity in Catholic social thought, assessing its features as a virtue and outlining the dimensions of the virtue of Earth solidarity. Chapter 6 focuses on Catholic social thought's tradition of human rights and the justifications for extending rights to nonhumans before offering my own list of Earth rights. These two chapters attempt to capture, through the lens of Catholic social thought, the dual aims of love and justice for creation: What kind of affective dispositions should a Catholic cosmic common good cultivate? What concrete responsibilities and limits does a Catholic cosmic common good impose?

Chapters 2 through 6 synthesize a comprehensive ecological ethic framed through revised principles of Catholic social thought. The chapters in Part Two engage the second aim of this book: testing out the validity and boundaries of the cosmic common good in non-Christian religious traditions and seeing how this dialogue impacts a Catholic cosmic common good. Part Two begins, in Chapter 7, with a brief explanation of comparative theology, its methods and purposes, and why I limit myself to particular dimensions of each religious tradition. Similar to Chapters 2, 3, and 4, the next three chapters are merely indicators of how the cosmic common good finds resonance in other religious traditions. I hope that these preliminary investigations initiate a deeper and more rigorous dialogue between and among these traditions, as well as branching out to test this ground with other traditions.

In Chapter 8 I look to Hindu traditions and the principle of dharmic ecology. As depicted in the *Bhagavad Gītā*, Hindu dharma presents an alternative theocentric orientation of the cosmic common good in a way that confirms and diversifies a Catholic cosmic common good. Moreover, dharma focuses on the good of the *ātman* (self) and extols an ethic of *ahiṃsā* (nonviolence) and vegetarianism. Yet by including all living creatures in the scope of this *ātman*, dharmic ecology suggests that an *ātmanocentrism* poses a more intense rejection of anthropocentrism than even a Catholic cosmic common good attains.

Chapter 9 explores the Buddhist tradition and its principle of *pratītyasamutpāda*, translated as dependent origination or interdependence. Buddhist traditions offer a helpful contrast to my Christian articulation of the cosmic common good: they are non-theistic, avowing no Creator or supreme deity. So while the Christian may understand the common good to be thoroughly theocentric, a Buddhist counterpart will have no God to whom the whole is directed. While the Hindu principle of the *ātman* undermines human uniqueness, the Buddhist principle of interdependence *anatta* (no self) underscores creaturely commonality by depicting the radical dependence of all beings on each other.

Finally, Chapter 10 looks to indigenous traditions, specifically those of American Indians, and to two concrete religio-cultural practices of the Lakota. An indigenous tradition represents a critical dialogue partner for a Catholic cosmic common good: indigenous peoples are often seen as paragons of ecologically friendly cultural and religious traditions; even more importantly, they help expose the potentially oppressive and hegemonic tendencies of articulating a common good for all species and peoples, regardless of cultural differences. The Lakota ethic of balance with "all our relations" reiterates central components of the cosmic common good, while also injecting key warnings about how Western Christians understand the common good.

Each conversation with other religious traditions confirms, broadens, and challenges a Catholic cosmic common good in distinctive ways. Hindu dharmic ecology demonstrates how a thoroughgoing theocentrism can be combined with a broader category of dignity and a stronger ethic of solidarity. Buddhist interdependence underscores cosmological holism and its integral place in religious practice, but also presents a non-theistic universe. An American Indian ethic of balance with all our relations introduces spatiality as a lens to articulate human planetary belonging, a lens that also exposes histories of systemic violence.

Thus Part One argues that an expanded principle of the common good—the cosmic common good—presents the foundation for a coherent Catholic ecological ethic. As such, it includes and incorporates other facets of Catholic social thought, such as solidarity, rights, and the preferential option for the poor. Part Two extends this by arguing that the cosmic common good provides a bridge to other religious traditions, which have principles that are not identical, but that bear a family resemblance to a Catholic cosmic common good. The cosmic common good is an authentic way of ecologically reorienting Catholic social thought to respond to ecological issues that also resonates with other religious traditions. Deeper engagement with these other religious traditions will allow a Christian vision of the common good to be enriched and extended in unanticipated but fruitful ways.

The cosmic common good is an ambitious proposal. Each chapter deserves greater scrutiny and could indeed be its own book. I sketch the possibilities for various cosmic common goods not as a definitive conclusion but as an invitation to generate greater interreligious dialogue and cooperation on an issue that demands extensive and immediate action. Each chapter, I hope, is the beginning of a longer conversation. The cosmic common good emerges as a feasible ground for interreligious ecological ethics; it is the soil from which a truly "ecological culture" might emerge, returning humanity to a healthier and sustainable relationship to the planet and the cosmos to which we belong.

PART ONE

*A Catholic Cosmic
Common Good*

A Catholic Cosmic Common Good

OVERVIEW AND PROSPECTS

CATHOLIC REFLECTION ON the problems of ecological degradation, though a relatively recent development, has grown so significantly in just a few decades that "care for God's creation" is now one of the principal themes of Catholic social thought.[1] In this chapter I home in on what I consider to be the keystone principle of Catholic social thought on ecological ethics: the common good.

I begin by describing the general features of the common good and human dignity in Catholic social thought, as well as related principles of participation and subsidiarity. I present a particular conception of the relationship between the common good and human dignity as a form of holism, which emphasizes their complementarity and reciprocal nature. Next, I draw out scientific and theological justifications why Catholic teaching on ecological ethics should embrace a broader and nonanthropocentric common good: the cosmic common good. Finally, I conclude with an overview of the features of a Catholic cosmic common good.

I. The Common Good and Human Dignity in Catholic Social Thought

The common good and human dignity have a central place in Catholic social thought. Indeed, all the principles of Catholic social thought rest on the primacy of human dignity and the common good. In some construals, human dignity is the cornerstone, and other principles, including the common good, flow from it. For example, *The Compendium of The Social Doctrine of the Church*, the Catholic Church's official synthesis of Catholic social teaching, names the dignity of the human person as central: "The whole of the Church's social doctrine, in fact, develops from the principle that affirms the inviolable dignity of the human person."[2]

Human dignity is the bedrock of the common good, and any social structure that undermines human dignity is also antithetical to the common good.

An equally valid and perhaps superior approach, however, may be to begin with the common good rather than human dignity. The *Compendium* avers that the human person is fundamentally social and lives in a world of increasing interdependence. Yet as Todd Whitmore contends, by beginning primarily with the dignity of the person prior to her sociality, these accounts of Catholic social thought seem to echo Western philosophers like John Locke and Thomas Hobbes, who posit an individual detached from society. So Catholic social thought looks "more like classical liberal social thought" than it should.[3] Human dignity is based on our being made in God's image, but for Christians, God is a Trinity and intrinsically relational, giving sociality an even deeper theological underpinning. Failing to depict humanity as being made in the image of a relational God "robs the claim concerning the social nature of the person of its theological push and further reinforces any tendency toward individualism."[4] Beginning with the common good is a more theologically justified way to uphold the essentially social nature of human dignity and is a sounder basis for Catholic social ethics than a principle of purely individual dignity.

Thus I begin with the common good, and I understand the relationship of dignity and the common good in terms of parts and wholes. The common good and human dignity function together dynamically: the principle of human dignity affirms the essential goodness and inviolable dignity of each and every human person, while the common good affirms the essentially social nature of the human person, such that a human being cannot fulfill her vocation or achieve her happiness apart from others. Human dignity affirms the intrinsic, inherent, and inalienable dignity of every human person, who is both a whole and a part that belongs to something greater; and the common good affirms the intrinsic, inherent, inalienable dignity of the whole, composed of intrinsically dignified parts.

I.1. The Common Good

In Catholic social thought, the common good stresses the importance of maintaining a proper order in society so that a community and all its members can flourish. The classic definition stems from *Gaudium et Spes*: "[The common good is] the sum of those conditions of social life which allow social groups and their individual members relatively thorough and ready access to their own fulfillment."[5]

The "conditions of social life" include both private and communal goods. On the one hand, the common good can include those material goods that every individual requires, such as the human need for food, water, shelter, and clothing. These goods are "common" in the sense that the needs they meet are shared by others. The common good also includes a set of physical goods that belong to the whole as a whole, such as water and air. It is good for the community as a whole when the basic needs of each member are met. At the same time, the common good is much more than the mere aggregate or collectivity of individual goods. Rather, the common good also includes some goods that cannot be achieved except in community. David Hollenbach compares this communal dimension of the common good to the notion of public goods in economic theory. A public good must be "non-rivalrous in consumption," meaning that one person's use does not reduce another's use. And a public good must be non-excludable, meaning that persons cannot reasonably be prevented from using it.[6] Thus the common good includes goods required by individuals, such as food, clothing, and housing, but also goods that exist only when they exist in common, such as education and access to culture, transportation, and the freedom of communication and expression.

Public goods do not quite capture the fullness of the common good in a Christian theological framework, however. Hollenbach argues that the common good includes not only non-rivalrous and non-excludable goods, but also the personal dimensions of relationship, affection, and even love that binds societies together. The good of a human person includes her relationships; it "exists 'between' persons in the relations that make them who they are."[7] There can be no individual good—biologically, emotionally, socially—without a community in which that individual lives. Thus social life is necessary to meet some basic individual needs, and a certain utility of social relationships is natural. More than the mere compilation of those utilities, the common good includes the full social, intellectual, and spiritual flourishing of persons. All the varied ways in which we share our lives with others are not merely a means to individual flourishing, but "are aspects of flourishing itself."[8] Thus the common good speaks to living conditions that enable individuals to meet needs they cannot meet on their own, as well as realize "non-instrumental values that can only be attained in our life together."[9] The common good is the organic context in which each member of the community is enabled to achieve her good, which can only be done through relationship to others.

This vision of the common good is a form of holism, which privileges the identity of the whole as a whole, rather than as the mere combination of various components or subordinate to its parts. There is a dynamic relationship between the person and the community, even an "interpenetration" of the good of the person and of the culture, which enables that good to emerge.[10] The operative metaphor for the common good is not a machine, composed of myriad interchangeable parts, but a body in which each part has an important role and an intrinsic connection to the whole. Each human person is a whole comprising many parts, who then organically belongs to and exists as a member of a greater whole. The common good emphasizes not just the commonality of goods that persons need but the goodness of the whole, as a whole. Theologically, the common good signifies that God seeks the well-being of the whole in addition to the well-being of each person, and not just because a healthy community can better enable persons to achieve their own personal good. The essentially social nature of the person precludes a rendering of the common good as merely the conditions that allow persons as individuals to flourish. Rather, the common good affirms the presence of a good that transcends yet also includes the well-being of the individual part. The community to which persons belong has its own flourishing and health (or sickness), which is distinct from the good of the persons who belong to it, and which redounds to the benefit (or ill) of each member of the community. Each part is affected by the good of the whole and truly flourishes only when the whole flourishes as well.

In return, each member has a responsibility to contribute to the common good, as a duty corresponding to her membership in the community.[11] The common good is weakened, and the true good of the person is vitiated, when someone takes a good that belongs to the whole and appropriates it to herself for her own, private good. Pope Francis also employs part-whole imagery to understand the common good. "The whole is greater than the part, but it is also greater than the sum of its parts. ... Nor do people who wholeheartedly enter into the life of a community need to lose their individualism or hide their identity; instead, they receive new impulses to personal growth."[12]

The common good and human dignity strengthen, rather than oppose, each other. The Catholic vision of the common good repudiates any call for an individual or group to be harmed for the benefit of the rest. It does not erase the individual on behalf of a collective goal. Rather, the common good is concerned with the well-being of both the individual and the whole, and it seeks to mitigate tensions between them or the temptation to sacrifice one for the benefit of the other. Each part is a different part and more truly a part (the part it was meant to be by God) when it recognizes its participation in the whole. Each whole is different and more truly the whole it was meant to be by God when it upholds the dignity of each part. The inherent dignity of each part challenges a collectivism or totalitarianism that would swallow or crush the part; the inherent dignity of the whole challenges an individualism or separatism that would isolate the part from the whole and even set its flourishing against that of the whole.

The common good asserts indissoluble connections between every individual, and because of this interdependency the good of the individual can only emerge from within a healthy and vibrant social community. The preservation of this common good is a prerequisite to maintaining the social stability and personal freedom necessary to develop one's relationship with God. The common good, therefore, offers two indispensable principles: first, it provides a vision of wholeness and speaks to the interconnectedness of life. We are united because we all participate in God's love and derive our being from God. One's personal happiness is inextricable from the flourishing of the group to which one belongs. Second, the common good is an ethical precept that guides individual behavior on behalf of the community. It therefore motivates action to safeguard this good, ideally not only because it is indispensable for one's own flourishing, but also because it mirrors God's love for all people and God's desire for us to be in unity.

Catholic social thought's understanding of the human person and her relationship to society stands in contrast to that envisioned by liberal political philosophies. While the Catholic vision is more organic, liberal traditions tend to view the person as detached and autonomous from the society in which she finds herself. Michael Sandel calls this "the unencumbered self," a person with no fundamental obligations to others.[13] In turn, liberalism's common good is best represented by an ordering of social relationships that allows each person to pursue her own individual good, as long as that pursuit does not hinder another from his. By beginning with a holistic conception of the common good, Catholic social thought can challenge a restrictive understanding of its social teaching that elevates human dignity and relegates the common good to a secondary or aggregatory function. Catholic social thought envisions a fabric of human relationality, such that a truly flourishing human being cannot be extricated from the social bonds that form her and remain part of her good.

I.2. Human Dignity

The principle of human dignity constitutes the counterpart to the common good. The human person is made in the image and likeness of God (Genesis 1:26), and as such bears a unique relationship to God that confers an inviolable dignity to him or her. The human person is of infinite and intrinsic worth; whatever instrumental value a person may have for what he can contribute to society and to others, he also always possesses intrinsic value, based solely on his relationship to God. Human beings may be unequal in certain ways, in their differing intellectual or emotional capacities, their social or economic influence, or their access to basic goods. Not that all of these inequalities are acceptable or unavoidable—Francis tweeted that "inequality is the root of social evil."[14] Yet in their possession of basic dignity, all human beings are essentially equal to one another. Based on this fundamental equality, Catholic social thought affirms that some forms of inequality are sinful. Thus all human beings are entitled to be free from abuse and exploitation. They are never to be used simply as tools or as resources, but are always to be treated as subjects and ends in themselves. Humans cannot lose this dignity, regardless of the inhumane treatment to which they are exposed, or the inhumane actions they perpetrate.[15]

The principles of the common good and human dignity form a reciprocal relationship with each other: the common good fosters the dignity of every person, and each person attains her flourishing only in community with others. In this way, these two principles form a mutually supportive vision for Catholic social ethics: each human being is equal in dignity to others, and the common good is grounded on this equal dignity.

I.3. Participation

Three other principles of Catholic social thought further elucidate this dynamic between the common good and human dignity. Participation is the lynchpin that reinforces the mutuality and reciprocity between the common good and dignity. A person, by himself or in association with others, "contributes to the cultural, economic, political and social life of the civil community to which he belongs."[16] Participation speaks to the fundamental right and duty of every person to contribute to the common good. As a right, participation highlights the injustice in any barrier that prevents someone from contributing to the common good, whether deliberate or inadvertent. As a duty, participation forbids persons from concentrating on their individual or family well-being such that they ignore the health and well-being of the community.[17] Participation speaks to the dynamic relationship between part and whole: the whole does not subsume the part because it is a whole only through the active involvement of every part; and the part does not fulfill herself until she participates in the whole. Participation enables each part's ability to contribute to the common good, and ensures that the common good is secured by the active involvement of each part to the extent that they are able.

I.4. Subsidiarity

Subsidiarity also helps to explain how we are to pursue the common good. Subsidiarity is a social principle that calls on people to collaborate with each other in various kinds of social groupings to accomplish differing common goods, from direct and immediate to broad and complex ones, and all directed to a higher common good. As a political and economic principle, subsidiarity argues for decentralization and for larger and more distant bodies of decision-makers to become involved only to assist and augment the efforts of smaller and more local institutions. It suggests that those who are closest to a situation or problem are in the best position to address it, and so we ought to "rely as much as possible on those solutions (and bodies of decision-making) that are closest to the people affected and that employ the smallest groupings and mechanisms that are still effective."[18] Stated negatively, higher levels of government should never supplant the freedom of lower ones or intervene in their affairs unless absolutely necessary, and then only in order to help them help themselves. Viewed more positively, larger and more remote institutions should provide assistance through economic and institutional support. Subsidiarity works to enable each part and each community of parts to participate and to fulfill their collective roles in the greater common good.

Subsidiarity is not only political, however, but a statement of how civil society (or any larger collective group) functions. The common good involves economic, social, ecological, and cultural realities, and each of these dimensions contributes to forging the bonds between persons and the common good. Humans are social and operate in different spheres according to a variety of relationships—family, work, neighborhood, church, avocations—all of which should be directed to the common good. Principal and foremost among these intermediate institutions is the family, which explains the explicit focus on the family in Catholic social thought. The spheres are distinct and semi-autonomous, and each functions according to its own logic. In this sense, each has its own internal common good. Yet due to the intrinsic sociality of the human persons who animate these groups, they cannot be fully separated. The health of one sphere can and will affect the well-being of others, either through the way it impinges upon the well-being of its members, or as it affects the functioning of these other aspects of social life. Properly ordered, these sub-spheres do not interfere with each other but mutually support each other by enhancing the common good. These various spheres of activity are intermediate social institutions, creating the social fabric of a society and helping to organize the greater social common good in a multifaceted and multifactorial fashion.

The principle of subsidiarity offers another example of the way in which Catholic social thought positions itself in distinction to political theories of liberalism and collectivism. Since liberals—in which both major political parties of the United States are included—begin with an autonomous individual who only belongs to society and the state through personal choice, they ignore other vital forms of human associations. Democratic Party liberals turn to the state to solve social problems, while Republican Party liberals seek freedom from the intervention of the state into otherwise private affairs and so prefer to address social concerns through personal initiatives. Some theologians who begin with the principle of human dignity as a foundation make a similar assertion regarding the primacy of the person over the state. When the common good and subsidiarity are conceived as political principles in terms of the state and governmental power, it is clear that the person is superior to the state.

By contrast, subsidiarity is a way of regulating the healthy interactions of various intermediate associations as they contribute to the common good. Civil society, or social life, is thus a much broader term than the state, and subsidiarity much more than a political principle about the proper range of government. The person as a member of the community is not superior to the community, since the community is conceived as a social reality comprising multiple persons actively participating in a variety of intermediate institutions geared toward the common good. Subsidiarity is therefore concerned not only with state intervention into the public sphere, but also with how various social spheres interact with each other. It objects to any sphere of life intervening into another, such as government interference with religious practice, or economic interests dictating political life. Subsidiarity also rejects the excessive intervention by larger and distant institutions into more local ones, such as a large chain store pushing out smaller businesses through unfair competitive practices.[19] Participation and subsidiarity help to highlight the true dignity of the person as a cherished member of the community, but also the reality of the good of the whole, which is more than the aggregate of happy and flourishing persons. Participation speaks to the need for each member to be an active contributor to the common good, and subsidiarity attempts to safeguard the good of each intermediate sphere against other spheres, lest the participation of those subgroups in the common good also becomes compromised.

I.5. The Universal Destination of Goods

Finally, the universal destination of goods demands the socially responsible use of property. In *Gaudium et Spes*, the second Vatican council contended that "God destined the earth and all it contains for all men and all peoples so that all created things would be shared fairly by all mankind under the guidance of justice tempered by charity."[20] God created the Earth and its goods for the benefit of all human beings. The "common purpose" of created things is to satisfy the needs of all humanity. While the universal destination of goods allows for private property, it also relativizes it by stressing the priority of the human family above private interests. The Earth is a common gift to be used for the good of all God's children. St. John Paul II even declared private property to be under a "social mortgage," meaning that no one can claim exclusive right to any property since it belongs first to society.[21]

I.6. The Common Good: A History of Expansion

Catholic social teaching strives to articulate timeless moral principles, rather than offering a concrete political and economic agenda that forges a confident "third way" between the errors of liberalism and collectivism.[22] Thus principles like the common good, human dignity, participation, and subsidiarity do not outline specific policy proposals, but rather moral guidelines that aid in the evaluation of particular proposals. Still, there is a dynamism to this body of teaching that enables it to respond to concrete social conditions and to grow in its understanding of that timeless moral order. Indeed, modern Catholic social teaching itself emerged out of a particular historical context, namely the social dislocation and tumult that followed in the wake of the industrial revolution. The teaching on the common good exemplifies this pattern of development. Originally, the common good was limited to citizens within a single *polis*. In *Rerum Novarum*, Leo XIII spoke of the common good in terms of nation-states and the rights of individuals within them. Seventy years later, in *Pacem in Terris*, John XXIII expanded the common good to refer to the entire human family. The common good must no longer be limited to nation-states, because "one of the principal characteristics of our time is the multiplication of social relationships, that is, a daily more complex interdependence of citizens."[23] In a way, the common good of the nation state is understood via subsidiarity to be an important component of the global common good. More recently, Francis invokes the planet Earth to stress the oneness of the human family: "We love this magnificent planet on which God has put us, and we love the human family which dwells here, with all its tragedies and struggles, its hopes and aspirations, its strengths and weaknesses. The earth is our common home and all of us are brothers and sisters."[24] A global common good prompts the question: On what grounds and in what ways should Catholic social thought and the principles of the common good and dignity be expanded and ecologically reoriented to meet the needs of Earth, "this magnificent planet" and "our common home"?

II. Catholic Social Thought and the Cosmic Common Good

The common good is a natural fit for Catholic ecological ethics given its long-standing place in Catholic tradition and its obvious applications to environmental problems. Since the common good emphasizes the relationship of part to whole, it corresponds well to the ecological principle of interdependence. Just as oppression and dehumanization in a society affect the well-being of all citizens and indeed the entire human family, so too does pollution or degradation affect the good of the whole and impact every member of that ecosystem, regardless of who introduced it.

Initially, official Catholic social teaching on ecology, like Catholic social teaching in general, was generally anthropocentric. Environmental degradation was perceived primarily as a threat to the human beings whom it affects, most particularly the poor. Thus Earth's common good is the biospheric integrity that serves humanity. Donal Dorr, who revised the title of his summary of Catholic social teaching from *Option for the Poor* to *Option for the Poor and the Earth* in order to call for an expansion of Catholic social thought to include nonhuman creation,[25] offers a searing rebuttal of this approach in papal teaching on ecology. He notes that John Paul II and Benedict XVI both espoused a "nuanced anthropocentricity"[26] that enjoins humanity to respect natural limits inscribed in creation by God and offers no justification for human exploitation. Despite these strengths, both fail to adopt the Earth-centered or cosmos-centered approach that he identifies as the way forward for Catholic social thought and Christian theology today.[27]

Dorr notes two reasons for their reluctance to move from an enlightened anthropocentrism to a geo- or cosmocentric consciousness: first, a concern that it might undermine the transcendence and reality of God; second, that it places the human person on the same level as the rest of creation and thus denies human uniqueness, which could reduce human dignity and responsibility. In short, we might lose sight of the truth about God and of the human person.[28] Catholic teaching does uphold the superior value and uniqueness of the human person, but it also affirms that humans are part of a larger whole that has its own dignity and integrity and deserves its own respect. Given the elevated status of humanity, must the common good of the Earth exist strictly for human well-being?

Admittedly, there remain legitimate concerns about an ecologically oriented common good. The traditional principles of Catholic social thought, as we have seen, presume the equal dignity of the human person, made in the image of God and modeled after the interpersonal communion of the divine Trinity. As such, the common good—and as we shall see, related principles of solidarity and rights—connotes the potential for a mutual and transformative relationship between equals that culminates in interpersonal and reciprocal love and care. Can we responsibly think of the common good, dignity, solidarity, and rights in terms of humanity's relationship to the Earth? It is unclear how nonhuman nature could share in our lives as equals or love us in return, even by analogy. The common good, solidarity, and rights are to be expressed through respect, care, and self-sacrifice, yet humans are resigned to use and even kill nonhuman creatures in order to sustain human life. Moreover, broadening these categories to include nonhuman creation could fundamentally shift or even pervert their meaning to the point that they no longer provide clarity on moral issues related to interhuman ethics. More problematically, altered meanings of the common good, solidarity, and rights could perhaps dilute their force and diminish global concern for the human good. Echoing Dorr, any such expansion must not lose sight of the transcendence of God and the dignity of the human person.

I maintain that the future of Catholic social thought is better represented by the broader and more inclusive common good—the cosmic common good—which in a Catholic frame remains decidedly theocentric and which incorporates and even strengthens the human common good. There is ample precedent for a cosmic common good in the hierarchical magisterium.

Drawing from St. Francis of Assisi and his "Canticle of the Creatures," Pope Francis insists that the Earth is more than just a resource but is indeed "a sister with whom we share our life and a beautiful mother who opens her arms to embrace us." He stresses that humans "are not disconnected from the rest of creatures," but instead are linked with them by "unseen bonds and together form a kind of universal family, a sublime communion which fills us with a sacred, affectionate, and humble respect." Just as St. Francis called nonhumans sisters and brothers, Francis speaks of a "universal fraternity." Francis hints at the reciprocal nature of the common good and dignity, contending that since all creatures are connected, "each must be cherished with love and respect, for all of us as living creatures are dependent on one another."[29]

Decades earlier, John Paul II enjoined respect for life and cosmic order: "Theology, philosophy and science all speak of a harmonious universe, of a 'cosmos' endowed with its own integrity, its own internal, dynamic balance. This order must be respected."[30] The US Catholic Bishops highlighted the importance of the "planetary common good,"[31] and they argued that "working for the common good requires us to promote the flourishing of all human life and all of God's creation."[32]

Moreover, I detect among most Catholic theologians an emerging consensus that indeed an ecologically oriented cosmic common good represents an authentic and urgently needed articulation of Catholic social thought. They turn to various rationales or grounds to justify such an expansion: scientific, looking at evolution, ecology, and extinctions; and theological, based especially on the doctrine of creation and human dignity. I do not purport to defend these arguments in full, but simply indicate the most influential grounds among theologians for why the cosmic common good has deep and fertile roots in the Catholic tradition.

III. Scientific Grounds for the Cosmic Common Good
III.1. Evolution

The cosmic common good offers a more adequate theological response to the scientific account of humanity's place in the universe, in three ways. First, theologians look to the modern scientific description of the evolutionary development of life as a key source for ecological ethics.[33] Modern science describes a universe of astounding creativity and traces back the myriad life forms on Earth to a singular cosmic beginning, more popularly referred to as the "Big Bang." The evolutionary development of life on Earth, and eventually the emergence of *Homo sapiens sapiens*, signifies that all life on Earth and all creatures in the cosmos are fundamentally related. To be human is not merely to be a creature among others; it is to be related, in one's very genes, to countless life forms, chemical reactions, and physical processes, both past and present. Evolutionary and biological sciences indicate that human beings are kin to all the creatures we encounter on Earth, and indeed all these past, present, and future life forms have their origin in galactic and cosmic processes that span billions of years.[34]

The historic cosmic development that has yielded the emergence of all Earthly life is not merely a matter of scientific description but bears profound religious and ethical import.[35] John Hart notes that humans are recent arrivals in the 13.7-billion-year history of the cosmos and the 4.6-billion-year history of Earth. We are "complexified stardust," genetically related to all life on Earth.[36] John Feehan points to evolution as proof that "all life is one family," and so "the ripples of consanguinity must extend to all creatures," with all the ethical implications that entails.[37] Elizabeth Johnson affirms and celebrates Darwin's achievement in establishing extensive connective links between human beings and all other creatures: "A community of descent is the hidden bond that ties together all living beings in to one narrative of life and earth stretching over millions of years. Darwin's theory uncovers the inner affinity of all organic beings to one another, rather than their merely external relations."[38] Stephen Scharper and Andrew Weigert argue that Catholic social thought ought to follow the example of Thomas Berry and understand our role as humans within a greater story of cosmic unfolding. Catholic social thought needs an Earth-grounded hermeneutic that can offer a cosmological basis for ethics and thus shift humanity's collective self-understanding and relationship to the cosmos.[39] Leonardo Boff argues explicitly for a cosmic common good, and he bases this in part on the new emerging scientific paradigm of the universe. "The common good is not that of humans alone, but is rather that of the whole cosmic community." The particular common good of the human community thrives only through harmony with the cosmic common good.[40] Only an ethical framework that draws on the full scope of the evolutionary development of this kinship can be an adequate response. The cosmic common good presents a more honest assessment of humanity's place within this cosmos, which is massive in space and time.

III.2. Ecology

The evolutionary development of life leads to a second ground for the cosmic common good, namely the condition of ecological interdependence among creatures. Evolutionary theory posits a historical interconnection among creatures, while the ecological sciences argue that every creature is continually shaped and conditioned, to some extent, by the creatures and general contexts that surround it. John Grim and Mary Evelyn Tucker define biophysical ecology as the "empirical and experimental study of the interactions of living and nonliving components of an ecosystem through energy flow and nutrient cycling."[41] While many scientists may understand ecosystems and nature generally as a kind of factory and thus employ a purely quantitative approach, theologians generally turn to a more holistic understanding of ecology and therefore draw ethical implications from it. Humans are related to other Earthly creatures and to the cosmos itself not simply by dint of our historical roots, but by the everyday interactions that we depend on for our survival and flourishing: food, water, air, shelter, and even psychological and spiritual well-being. If any of these creatures and their flourishing are worthwhile, and we would certainly place our own human welfare in this category, then it is worthwhile and necessary to look at the great common good without which our individual or our collective human flourishing would not be possible. At the same time, Catholic theologians must not perpetuate a false and non-scientific sense of a primeval "balance in nature" that sees the Earth as essentially stable and routine, but must now understand ecosystems[42] "to be dynamic, open, complex systems, impacted by human actions, in ways that can be dramatically altered and within which there are limits to adaptability."[43]

The science of ecology speaks in terms of dynamic and systemic wholes, focusing not on creatures in isolation but on the relationships among them, and theologians have drawn from this scientific fact a host of theological and ethical implications. Russell Butkus and Steven Kolmes conclude that Earth's natural processes are not simply part of humanity's common good, but instead the common good must be "applied as an inclusive principle" that embraces the biophysical world and "embodies the entire commonwealth of creation."[44] A common good limited strictly to human beings makes little sense in light of ecological interdependence. They name sustainability as a new way to understand justice in Catholic social thought and to integrate ecological justice into traditional forms of human justice.[45] Reflecting on the *Compendium*, Scharper and Weigert similarly claim that the doctrinal understanding of the common good must be global and biospheric, not merely local or ecosystemic.[46] Likewise, human dignity must include more than social and interpersonal goods. Dignity starts with healthy air, water, and earth. The current ecological moment, they argue, compels Catholics and all humans to ask what it means to be human.[47] They urge Catholics "to extend the scope of understanding of 'personal dignity' and 'common good' to include all."[48] Jame Schaefer also draws on the evolutionary and ecological sciences to argue for a greater sense of human relatedness to nonhuman creation and calls on humans to value other creatures intrinsically, to understand how they relate to each other, and to value these interrelationships.[49]

The relationship between the evolutionary and ecological sciences and the development of a theologically sound ecological ethic is complex and contested. Lisa Sideris, for example, has critiqued a host of theologians for their unsubstantiated use of evolutionary theory and the biological sciences: "Ecotheologians do not pay enough attention to suffering in the allegedly scientific model of nature they construct."[50] Sideris charges that while many claim to derive their ecological ethics of interdependence and care from scientific analyses of nature and from evolutionary theory in particular, their science tends to be pre-Darwinian, such that "the darker side of Darwin's theory is downplayed or omitted."[51] Contrary to theological depictions of harmony, balance, and codependent evolution, Sideris argues that true evolutionary theory portrays "a fierce, competitive struggle for food, shelter, and mates. . . . The processes of evolution appear unpredictable and wasteful; if organisms 'relate' to one another at all, they do so primarily in terms of eating and being eaten."[52]

While Sideris is right that much of the relatedness between creatures in various habitats consists of predation and death, it nevertheless remains true that the good of any individual creature or species is not immune to the well-being or degradation of other creatures or of the habitat that supports them. For any creature or species, the well-being of some other set of creatures must be of concern, even if these other creatures are eventually destroyed and consumed. Whether or not this interdependence bears ethical weight for how human beings treat nonhuman creatures, as I and these other Catholic theologians argue it does, there is still good reason to validate and affirm the conditions that make human life possible and worthwhile. We have not yet necessarily moved to affirming the good of other creatures for their own sake, but we can certainly recognize the ecological embeddedness of human life and the impossibility of improving human welfare to the disregard of the rest of Earth.

III.3. "Eaarth": Planetary Breakdown and Human Responsibility

The aforementioned evolutionary and ecological grounds provide compelling scientific reasons that a plausible theological ecological ethic should affirm a broader common good, yet there is a third and more pressing justification: it is more properly the awareness of the vulnerability of these ecological systems to severe impairment and the looming threat of planetary breakdown and extinction due to human action and inaction that impel the search for a new approach to ecological ethics.

Perhaps, then, the most pressing evidence from science today that Christians must account for in their ecological ethics is not the theories of evolution and ecology, but the evidence that human beings are radically altering and devastating life on Earth.

Observers struggle to comprehend the magnitude of what is happening and properly name this new moment in the Earth's history. Some geologists propose declaring an end to the Holocene epoch (roughly the last 11,000 years) and renaming our present time as the "Anthropocene" epoch, to take its place among other time periods of massive planetary scale.[53] For the first time, a distinct geological time frame would be the result of choices made by a particular species, rather than just natural forces. Environmental activist Bill McKibben has recently coined the term "Eaarth," with the extra "a" standing for "extra awful": "Global warming is no longer a philosophical threat, no longer a future threat, no longer a threat at all. It's our reality. We've changed the planet, changed it in large and fundamental ways."[54] Thus a true "ecological awareness," or the call for "ecological conversion"[55] as encouraged by Francis and St. John Paul II, is not merely the awareness of the goodness of nature or of nonhuman creatures, but of the good of the ecological interdependences that sustain our lives and the recognition that these bonds are being strained and broken. A degraded Earth reconfirms that it is no longer acceptable to separate the human common good from that of other creatures. Human activity reaches to every corner of the planet, attenuating any sense of a "nature" untamed and untouched by human beings.[56] Citing evidence of DDT in penguins in Antarctica, Holmes Rolston III argues that "the 100% natural system no longer exists anywhere on Earth."[57]

Those who attempt to reflect on the ways in which humanity is reshaping the planet search for ethical terms that adequately address the scope and scale of human activity and of the interdependence between humans and other living creatures. Elizabeth Johnson highlights McKibben's work and explains, "The human species has become a geophysical force capable of raising the planet's temperature ... the planet on which humans have thrived for 10,000 years, 'the sweetest of sweet spots' that enabled successful farming and civilization's great cities to take shape, no longer exists. It may look familiar enough, but since the late 1960s the planet has reached a tipping point toward profound changes with dire consequences for other species."[58] William French notes that the environmental movement presents us with an understanding of previously unimaginable concerns, from climate change to ocean disruption to extensive habitat loss and species extinction. For French, "the recognition of the massiveness of contemporary environmental concerns calls forth attention to the categories of the 'planet,' the 'human species,' and, thus, the common good of humanity and all life-forms that share the sustaining power of the Earth."[59] Francis too contends that "doomsday predictions can no longer be met with irony or disdain. We may well be leaving to coming generations debris, desolation and filth." Thus "the gravity of the ecological crisis demands that we all look to the common good."[60]

Any reasonable theology must attend to a realistic picture of the world, and the ecological sciences increasingly provide substantial support for a broader, non-anthropocentric, and cosmic common good: humanity's and the Earth's miniscule place in the 14-billion-year history of the universe; our biological co-evolution with other Earth creatures; our radical dependence on Earth and its ecological systems for our biophysical and psycho-spiritual survival; and the manifold ways that these goods are under attack by human beings. All scientific evidence calls us to expand the common good of creation beyond a typically anthropocentric human common good so that care for the Earth includes care for nonhuman creatures directly, and for themselves.

IV. Theological Grounds for the Cosmic Common Good
IV.1. A Theocentric Doctrine of Creation

Beyond these scientific grounds, there are two key theological reasons for affirming a Catholic cosmic common good. The first sheds light on the evolutionary and ecological grounds as well: the doctrine of creation.[61] The cosmic common good is rooted in and is more consistent with an authentically Catholic and theocentric theology of creation. There is a convincing rationale for linking the cosmic common good to a theology of creation: focusing on creation focuses us on the Creator and decenters humanity. J. Milburn Thompson, for example, draws on the theme of companionship articulated by Michael and Kenneth Himes to argue that the "companionship model enlarges the common good to include all of creation. It can recognize a special role for humanity, but it gives the natural world a genuinely intrinsic value."[62] Creation, then, is the theological common ground for the common good. The doctrine of creation not only establishes a common bond between human beings and all other creatures, but it also gives the cosmos its divine context. It is theocentric, placing God and God's interests firmly in the center of reality and value. While the Christian tradition affirms a major moral difference between humans and other creatures, still the underlying theological truth remains one of a shared foundation of depending on and belonging to God.

The "Gospel of Creation" is the cornerstone of Francis's ecological vision. Forsaking God as Creator easily leads humans to pose themselves as Lord over the Earth and to claim the right to use it as they wish: "The best way to restore men and women to their rightful place, putting an end to their claim to absolute dominion over the earth, is to speak once more of the figure of a Father who creates and who alone owns the world." Affirming God as Creator reveals that "the ultimate purpose of other creatures is not to be found in us. Rather, all creatures are moving forward with us and through us towards a common point of arrival, which is God." Rather than "nature," which can be seen as a system external to humans that can be manipulated, creation is "the order of love," a gift of the Father, "a reality illuminated by the love which calls us together into universal communion." Indeed, "even the fleeting life of the least of beings is the object of his love, and in its few seconds of existence, God enfolds it with his affection."[63]

An anthropocentric common good is therefore weaker on the independent goodness of creation, and indeed weaker in its theocentrism. A cosmic common good is more adequate to the goodness and scope of creation, which posits a paradigm in which nonhumans have intrinsic value because they emanate from God's love. Studying the theology of creation allows us to perceive a common good that includes not only humans but also everything that exists. A Catholic cosmic common good, rooted in a theology of creation, offers an ethical construct that motivates concern for nonhumans, both because nonhuman nature serves human needs and because it is inherently good and loved by God for its own sake as creation. Recalling my thought experiment in the Introduction, should humans be concerned about the extinction of a species when that extinction does not impact human well-being? On the contrary, a cosmic common good offers a rationale for why such concern is theologically justified, which is a better reflection of each creature's intrinsic goodness. The cosmic common good is a more theocentric ecological ethic, which is consistent with a robust Creator-centered theology of creation. Rather than risking the loss of the transcendence of God, raising up the goodness of nature and positing a cosmic common good confirms it. While there certainly remain tensions within the cosmic common good over how to reconcile competing interests, the cosmic common good gives us a way to understand human flourishing within a broader theocentric context where creation does not exist merely for human well-being but for God's purposes as well.

IV.2. The Doctrine of Human Dignity

The cosmic common good also offers a more honest and accurate assessment of human dignity within the order of creation. As we saw above, Catholic social thought often rests on the twin pillars of the common good and human dignity. A common good that is cosmic can accommodate a robust human dignity;

indeed, it is more true to the human person than the model of "human as consumer" that a purely anthropocentric model encourages, and thus offers a better defense of human dignity. The greatest danger today to human dignity is not the notion that human beings should see themselves as part of a greater whole of creation, but the "technocratic paradigm," which encourages the myth of "unlimited material progress" and promotes extreme and "compulsive consumerism."[64] Limiting the common good to human flourishing alone leads not only to an impoverished theology of creation but also to a defective defense of human dignity. Indeed, at stake in how we address ecological devastation is our human dignity itself.[65]

Thus Catholic social thought ought to embrace the cosmic common good, which broadens humanity's horizons beyond mere human well-being and inculcates a theocentric perspective that sees creation and the human person in a more realistic perspective. I do not believe that such an emphasis would diminish the place or role of the human person. On the contrary, the cosmic common good stresses humanity's intrinsic and even elevated dignity within a community of creatures who possess intrinsic dignity. In a theocentric doctrine of creation, dignity must be creaturely, not merely human. Humanity's true vocation is not a manager of Earth's resources for ourselves, but a responsible agent capable of safeguarding the well-being of intrinsically valuable creatures. Humanity's place in creation need not be central in order to be dignified or even to be seen as greater in dignity than other creatures. The cosmic common good therefore represents a better defense of creaturely dignity, human and otherwise, as well as a theocentric ecological ethic rooted in a properly theological understanding of creation. A Catholic cosmic common good emphasizes the centrality of God, the goodness of creation, and humanity's dignified and privileged but contextualized role within the story of creation.

V. Why a Cosmic Common Good?

Thus far I have argued for a cosmic common good, a common membership in something that includes all creatures, human and nonhuman alike, and that there is a "good" that can be identified that pertains to this common whole. Yet one may ask, why use the descriptor "cosmic" to capture the scope of this common good and of this community? After all, to what extent can human beings purport to impact the well-being of other creatures on a truly cosmic scale? While other more potentially humble terms such as an "environmental," "ecological," "planetary," or even "Earthly" common good have validity, this book chooses as its focus the *cosmic* common good as the most adequate ethical formulation given the scientific and theological grounds discussed earlier, in three ways.[66]

V.1. Scientific Grounds

First, the cosmic common good provides the most realistic and inclusive possible framework for thinking about humanity and our proper place in the universe. A cosmic common good, rather than Earthly, offers the best account for the scope of evolutionary and ecological interrelatedness and the expansive context, both spatial and temporal, in which all creaturely good occurs.

Moreover, while human activity has a minor, even negligible role in the cosmos, there are two additional ways in which it is meaningful to speak of ecological issues in a cosmic sense. First, humanity's presence in the solar system grows steadily: as a species, we have sent satellites out beyond the farthest planets; we have landed robots on Mars and are actively planning for a colony within decades; and the amount of "stellar junk" orbiting just beyond Earth's atmosphere continues to accumulate. Renowned physicist Stephen Hawking voices the opinion of many when he encourages humans to begin planning to make journeys beyond this solar system, if we wish to perdure as a species.[67] Our impacts and certainly our ambitions already exceed the planet and even the solar system, and it is fitting that our moral vision reflect this.[68]

Second, a cosmic common good helps us understand not only humanity's role within the cosmos, but Earth's role in the cosmos itself. A sustainable and flourishing Earth community is not only significant for humans and future generations, and not only for all other creatures on Earth, but indeed it has bearing for the flourishing of the cosmos as a whole. To our knowledge, no other planet in the universe bears anything near the diversity and complexity of life we encounter here on Earth, let alone intelligent life. If astronauts discovered the simplest form of molecular life on another planet, it would garner international attention, yet we pay little consideration to the boggling florescence of life on Earth and its current precariousness. Again, a cosmic common good represents the most adequate framework for thinking through ecological concerns and understanding the full dimension and cosmic import of an imperiled Earth.

V.2. Theological Grounds

Second, a Catholic cosmic common good finds its theological roots in the goodness of God, and has as its focus the totality of being created by the good God. Only an ethical formulation that captures the fullness of God's creation seems adequate, and here even a planetary common good seems too narrow. As John Paul II contends, the Greeks referred to the natural world as *cosmos*, "alluding precisely to the order which distinguishes it."[69] For Christians, another term for creation is "cosmos." The cosmos stands for all that has been created and ordered by God, and indeed "the whole cosmos gives thanks to God."[70] As we shall see in

Chapter 3, for Aquinas it requires the entire creation to reflect the infinite pleni-
tude of God. Employing an ethical vision of the cosmos is the most adequate and
most theologically justified formulation given the all-encompassing nature of the
Christian doctrine of creation.

Despite this long-held doctrine of creation that affirms the goodness of all
creatures and Francis' repudiation of modern anthropocentrism,[71] there remains
among many Catholics a lingering anthropocentrism. A critical component of
reshaping Catholic moral vision is erasing the fiction that humanity can stand
apart from other creatures and can separate human flourishing from the Earth's
well-being, or that nonhumans earn moral consideration due to their utility as
instruments of human development. We need a vision of ethics that puts back
in view the full connectedness between humanity and Earth. A cosmic approach
to the common good therefore constitutes the strongest antidote to anthropocentrism and is the best defense of a realistic human dignity.

The terms "environmental" and "ecological," however construed, remain inadequate to describe the inclusive common good described earlier. An ethical framework ought to direct us to something real that we have real contact with, such as
the cosmos, rather than an abstract and ambiguous concept like the environment
or ecology. Worse, an ethic of the "natural environment" emerges as a dangerous
linguistic fallacy, as if the ethics of the "environment" can be quarantined away
from other ethical concerns. Indeed, the problems of ecological degradation and
escalating climate change have alerted us that this is not one political or ethical
problem among many, but the new horizon for all ethical activity, even as it poses
a fundamental challenge to the practice of ethical reflection itself.[72] Ultimately, an
ethic of the common good must not ground humanity in the abstraction of the
environment or an ecology, but return us to the soil of our human existence as
members of the planet Earth, the ground on which we stand.

Then why not simply an "Earth ethics"?[73] The cosmic common good strives to
articulate the most expansive possible context for ethical reasoning. Though an
ethic geared for the flourishing of Earth is certainly superior to an ethic focused
on humanity's natural environment, a cosmic ethic is even better suited to refram-
ing human anthropocentrism. Even an Earth-based ethic may not be sufficiently
powerful to counteract anthropocentric habits: it is "our" Earth, humanity's
planetary home.

Instead, the term "cosmos" is meant to highlight the context that has no single
center other than God; it raises up as worthy of our reflection those stellar locales
that add nothing to human well-being and indeed the vast stretches of space that
lie entirely hidden from human view. The horizon for our moral reasoning must
certainly move beyond humanity, but it need not stop at the end of the Earth's atmosphere; if, in a Christian framework, the horizon must stretch to God, then a concern for a cosmic common good seems best suited to do so. A focus on the cosmos

emphasizes our human identity not only as Earthly creatures but as galactic and cosmic ones as well. If there perdures a tendency to select humans apart from all other creatures, then perhaps the most adequate response is a moral framework that broadens the moral parameters as widely as possible. The best overall context for pondering ecological (or any) ethics is one that best accounts for every dimension of our creaturely existence, and that existence, one of "universal communion," is cosmic.[74]

While the descriptor "cosmic" in appendage to the common good may seem grandiose, I think it remains important for stretching human vision to the utmost horizon. In addition, the notion of a cosmic common good proposes a principle that obtains not just for humanity's responsibility to Earth, but that can be understood as a metaphysical reality. That is, this ethical foundation, in its barest principles, holds true for any intelligent life form that may exist apart from us, and it will hold true indefinitely. Whether the Earth continues to support human life or not, and whether the human community can learn to live within the context of the wider Earth community, or if it outstrips the Earth's limits and undermines the flourishing of itself and countless other species, creatures gifted with intelligence and the capacity for purposive action have the responsibility to promote the flourishing of other creatures and to safeguard the conditions under which a diversity of life may flourish.

V.3. The Cosmic Common Good as a Unifying Interreligious Ethical Framework

Third, focusing on the cosmic common good offers a point of contact and a bridge to other religious traditions, as well as secular ones.[75] As Francis demonstrates, a Christian may understand the cosmos as synonymous with creation. Indeed, some Christians conceive of and promote ecological awareness and environmental responsibility as "care of creation." As valuable as this is—and indeed I also root a Catholic cosmic common good in a Christian theology of creation—I seek an ethical principle that can span multiple religious traditions, whose conceptions of God and creation may differ widely, or which may be non-theistic. From the vantage point of these traditions, an Earth-based ethic, while honest about the limits of humanity's power, also appears too finite and narrow. An ecological ethic grounded in the goodness of the cosmos is a more fruitful category for dialogue with non-Christian traditions.

Thus my formulation of the cosmic common good bears much similarity with John Hart's "creatiocentric" ethic. Creatiocentrism understands the Creator and the biotic and abiotic creation as interrelated. It differs from anthropocentrism, since humanity is part of the biotic creation and is dependent on abiotic creation; from cosmocentrism, since this fails to balance a view of the cosmos with a view of the local commons, which is the site of our engagement with creation; from geocentrism, since this must expand even beyond a planetary vision; and from theocentrism, since this isolates God in Godself from God as Creator.[76] A creatiocentric ethic conjoins God as creator to cosmos as creation.

Still, the cosmic common good may provide a better formulation. First, it offers a point of contact with traditions that are non-theistic or do not avow a Creator. While I invest cosmos with a decidedly theocentric (and even Christocentric) identity, I believe "cosmos" need not be necessarily theocentric, or that it require belief in the same *theos*. The vision of an ordered universe, whose order and constituent parts are worthwhile, and whose order when threatened requires moral action, can transcend theological and cultural boundaries. It does not command universal assent; it will not answer the concerns of every ethical tradition. As Paul Knitter argues, there may be no globally accepted meta-narratives, but there are meta-problems like climate change that require the action of the whole planet and therefore provide the motive for interreligious dialogue,[77] and I believe the cosmic common good forms the optimal common ground for an interreligious, ecological ethic. Second, the cosmic common good poses the most thorough rebuke of modern anthropocentrism and best nurtures "that sublime fraternity with all creation which Saint Francis of Assisi so radiantly embodied."[78] Creation should not be reduced to an instrumental value, whether as a source of resources or as a conduit to the divine.[79] The cosmic common good stretches our horizons to their utmost.

Therefore, the cosmic common good has a dual role: it is both a Catholic and Christian theological and ethical principle, but it is also flexible enough to serve as a term that may resonate and amplify in other traditions. As the cosmic common good functions in a Catholic and Christian worldview, it is theocentrically cosmocentric: it espouses a cosmocentrism, which argues that the center of value is the cosmos itself, and that all creatures have an intrinsic value. Yet it is also theocentric, centered on God by linking the well-being and goodness of the cosmos to its origin in a loving and providential God. A Catholic cosmic common good introduces a distinctively theological emphasis on the primacy of the cosmos in divine intentions, while other cosmic common goods may espouse cosmological holism in differing ways.

VI. Features of a Catholic Cosmic Common Good

The cosmic common good has great potential for articulating an ethical non-anthropocentrism that grounds the intrinsic value of creatures, the instrumental value of creatures, and the overriding importance of their shared life together. It will reflect the insights of evolutionary, ecological, and environmental sciences; in Christian soil it will remain faithful to the Triune Creator, while for other traditions it will reflect a cosmic view of human identity. I propose the following features of a Catholic cosmic common good.

VI.1. A Theocentric Cosmic Common Good

In a Catholic Christian worldview, the cosmic common good is theocentric. A Catholic cosmic common good is derived from the goodness that God imparts to creation and is directed back to the Creator as the purpose for its existence.[80] God is the absolute cosmic common good, for which all things exist, while the integrity of cosmic dynamics and the sustainability of Earth's manifold and interconnected ecosystems represent the internal cosmic common good. As it resonates in other traditions, the cosmic common good is a non-anthropocentric cosmocentrism. The human being, though elevated in dignity, is not the sole purpose of other creatures' existence, and she must be understood to exist both for God and as a member of the ordered cosmos, not apart from or despite it.

VI.2. The Cosmos as Commons

The cosmic common good is also cosmocentric, stressing the cosmic identity of every creature. We dwell in widening circles, not as citizens, but as family members. Human beings are not just essentially communal and social, but also essentially planetary and cosmic creatures as well. John Hart elaborates on the cosmos as "commons." The "commons" signifies a space and context for mutual flourishing, such as a school or village commons, where people gather to procure both bodily and social nourishment. The commons emphasizes not only physical proximity but also the dimension of a shared life together, a place in which people both sustain their bodies and form relationships.[81]

While the cosmos might be its own kind of commons, for most of us our experience of sharing our lives with others must be more immediate. Thus our local bioregion or ecosystem is our more direct experience of the cosmic commons, the "local cosmos."[82] The cosmic common good then allows both a macroscopic and cosmic perspective, as well as a microscopic and local view, emphasizing the shared life of humanity with all other Earthly creatures in the real spaces where this life occurs. We can call the cosmos, the Earth, and the nearby local cosmos of our particular bioregion, our home. We belong to the various wholes in "the world of which we are a part,"[83] and the creatures who dwell there as well are part of our shared life.

VI.3. The Intrinsic Value of Creatures/Creaturely Dignity

Catholic social thought must situate humans within the cosmic common good, and human dignity within a broader category of creaturely dignity. Each creature has its own essential goodness, as a creature of God, and its own value just in being what it is, apart from how it might benefit other creatures. While human beings may be the only Earth creature who can value themselves self-consciously, value itself is imparted by God. This intrinsic value is twofold: (1) its value to God, in being what it is; (2) its value to itself, whether or not it is self-consciously aware of this valuation or not.

VI.4. Differentiated Dignity

A Catholic cosmic common good maintains a hierarchy of value between creatures. Creaturely dignity equally applies to all creatures, but it does not impart equal dignity. Human beings remain, for all the reasons attested to in the Catholic tradition, the most noble and valuable of Earth's creatures who are permitted to use nonhumans to sustain their lives, as well as to grow in the knowledge of God. Yet an elevated dignity for human beings still recognizes an essential dignity in other creatures. Parts of varying qualities can still form an integral whole, and creatures with more esteem and dignity are not more noble—and indeed they are less so—through the diminution, degradation, or elimination of less esteemed creatures.

VI.5. The Intrinsic Value of Diversity

Drawing from both ecosystem sciences and a theology of creation, a Catholic cosmic common good attests to the intrinsic value of a diversity of species. The Catholic tradition has often asserted the greater goodness of the totality of creatures and their mutual ordering within the universe as a whole. There is no contradiction in saying that some things exist for others and also for the universe's perfection.[84] Diversity lends greater stability to ecosystems and the Earth as a whole, and it better represents the creativity of the Creator.

VI.6. Cosmic Participation

The social principle of participation can now be described in a cosmic sense, as the way that each creature and species of creatures participate in the pattern of cosmic evolutionary development, in Earthly ecosystems, and in their own relationships to God. Just as the human common good is meant to encourage and enable human beings to participate in human society, cosmic participation points to the need for human beings to allow and to enable nonhuman creatures to participate in the cosmic common good. Cosmic participation lends an ethical valence to the ontological doctrine of existence via each creature's participation in God.[85] Participation for humans in society will of course involve multiple more levels of complexity, including political, economic, and cultural dimensions that are not applicable to nonhumans. Cosmic participation outlines a basic ontological foundation to the validity and goodness of all creaturely participation in the cosmic common good.

VI.7. Cosmic Subsidiarity

Subsidiarity can also now be conceived cosmically. Subsidiarity provides a rich and layered vision of human society that mediates between the extremes of liberalism and collectivism. Similarly, cosmic subsidiarity reminds human society of its embeddedness in varying biophysical and cosmic systems and points to the importance of these dynamics in forging political decisions. Many theologians have argued persuasively that subsidiarity should be shifted away from politically defined boundaries and should recognize instead our bioregional and ecosystemic identities.[86] More than this, though, cosmic subsidiarity also speaks to the importance of thinking in terms not just of the cosmos but of the intermediate collectives whose interconnected activities together help make up the common good. Just as Catholic social thought frowns on an excessive intervention of one sphere of human social life into another sphere, cosmic subsidiarity explains why excessive intervention of human activity into nonhuman lives and ecosystems is a violation of their right to cosmic participation. Humans ought to value ecosystems for their common good and learn to see themselves as citizens of ecosystems, rather than conquerors.[87] Decisions in the human community must be decentralized and made at the most possible local level, and similarly, judgments that impact planetary sustainability and functioning must not be centralized in such a way that they only encompass the human common good.

VI.8. The Instrumental Value of Creatures

In Chapter 1, I touched on the neuralgic issue in ecological ethics of the status of nonhuman creatures and the categories of intrinsic value versus instrumental value. The cosmic common good seeks to uphold and balance both the intrinsic and instrumental value of creatures. Larry Rasmussen observes the complexity of understanding intrinsic and instrumental value, noting how intrinsic value cannot end with the individual in him/her/itself but must also include the widening spheres of community to which the individual belongs.

There is inherent value in an individual creature, but also in that creature as part of a greater whole. Creatures are "not 'themselves' except as belonging to communities that create and sustain them."[88] Hence Rasmussen argues for a kind of "blended value," an ecological sense of value, "a systemic interweaving of value beyond the distinctions of inherent and instrumental, a value for which we do not yet have the name because we do not yet have the narrative and cosmology."[89] The cosmic common good strives to express that blended value and to provide the cosmology that defends that value with different supporting narratives in various religious traditions; it expresses the simultaneous presence of both intrinsic and instrumental value and the cosmic character of creatures who flourish as they belong to ever widening communities. All creatures possess instrumental value, based on their role within an ecosystem or as participants in cosmic dynamics. Competition and predatory dynamics may mean that a creature with intrinsic value is used instrumentally by another, but it never loses its intrinsic value.

Thus the cosmic common good includes "common goods," the use of some creatures by others for their sustenance, whether arising through natural processes or through human ingenuity.[90] Finite goods, though they belong to the community as a whole, are also meant to be used by individual creatures as they are needed and so should be made available to them.

VI.9. The Universal Destination of All Creaturely Goods

Earth necessitates a certain amount of death and decay in order for life to persist and flourish. A Catholic cosmic common good recognizes that creatures are instrumentally valuable, but here the utility is not simply directed to humans. The classical formulation of the universal destination of goods in Catholic social thought reinforces the mentality of human domination, of nonhumans as simply goods at the service of the human polis. The various common goods of the Earth belong to the entire human family. This intensifies an ethical anthropocentrism by introducing an anthropocentrifugalism: not only are humans at the center of creation, but all other creatures are rendered as "goods," destined to flow toward them.

Instead, the cosmic common good stresses that the goods of the Earth, including the innovations and improvements brought about by humans, must be directed to nonhuman creatures as well. Rather than a uni-directional flow of utility, the universal destination of goods is multi/omnidirectional and includes all creaturely goods. Humans are valuable to each other, creatures are valuable to each other, and the strands of usefulness extend in every direction to form a vast network or web of dependencies and utilities, all of which form part of the planetary and the cosmic common good. These goods are not only common to all human beings but also belong to the biotic community and to future generations as well. In cases of conflict, humanity's elevated dignity may mean a preference for human interests and the priority of human use of nonhuman creatures, but this is by no means absolute. In the context of imperiled Earth, there are good reasons to argue for an increasing reversal of the flow of instrumental use. In a Christian and theocentric framework, the primary instrumentality of each creature and the universe as a whole is as it exists for God and divine purposes.

VI.10. Respect for the Order of Creation

A Catholic cosmic common good strives to represent a blending of intrinsic and instrumental value, and so it affirms the intrinsic value of the instrumental ordering of creation. The cosmos is the holistic web in which intrinsic/instrumental values among and between creatures plays out. It affirms not only creaturely dignity, but the dignity of the various wholes to which creatures belong. For humans this will include all the various levels of human society, but it also includes those biophysical wholes of which we are a part: ecosystems, bioregions, Earth, and cosmos. It calls for the inclusion of the Earth as a whole, its multifarious ecosystems, and the myriad plants, animals, and creatures that live in them within the circle of moral consideration. These are all the different kinds of orders we encounter, and they are all part of the one great ordered whole of the cosmos. This is typical of a Catholic "both/and" theological approach: it includes both a concern for holistic systems as well as for the individual creatures that populate them. The cosmic common good attempts to balance what at times are two conflicting and divergent camps within ecological ethics: those concerned with "ecocentric holism," which focuses on the common good of the whole, such as Aldo Leopold's "land ethic";[91] and those who advocate a "biocentric individualism," which pays attention to the well-being of individual living creatures.[92] Following Catholic social thought on the human person and the common good, expanded principles of the cosmic common good, Earth solidarity, and Earth rights must strive to balance both poles of these concerns, not allowing either pole to swallow or suffocate the other. Francis claims that ecosystems "have an intrinsic value independent of their usefulness. Each organism, as a creature of God, is good and admirable in itself; the same is true of the harmonious ensemble of organisms existing in a defined space and functioning as a system."[93] As Jame Schaefer argues, the goodness of creation must be attributed to (1) the cosmological-biological process, (2) the diverse natures of creatures, (3) the relationships between entities, and (4) the interactions among creatures that contribute to the overall common good. At each level of complexity (individual creatures, species, ecosystems, the entire Earth biosphere, and the cosmos) resides both intrinsic and instrumental goodness, to each other and to the higher level to which they contribute.[94]

VI.11. The Good of the Variegated Dimensions of Creation

Finally, I suggest that a Catholic cosmic common good and its approach to intrinsic/instrumental valuation can help us understand the goodness of creation in five different kinds of places, which will become more apparent as we move to classical and contemporary theologies of creation. It creates a fabric that knits these various human experiences with nonhuman creation into a coherent whole.

1. First, it highlights the importance and value of the cosmos as a whole. It encourages a sense of holism, and it offers a proper context for the Earth as a whole.

2. Second, it offers a perspective on wild Earth, and the outermost stretches of the cosmos. The term "wilderness" is problematic because it can create a sense of nature that is oppositional to human presence.[95] Still, a Catholic cosmic common good emphasizes the importance of creatures and locations that are removed from normal human interactions and social exchanges. From Alpha Centuari and remote corners of the universe to those stretches of Earth that seem foreboding and overtly hostile to human presence, the cosmic common good affirms that these are part of the whole to which we belong. It can encourage humans to see goodness and value where before perhaps only emptiness was perceived.

3. Third, it encourages us to see the goodness of domesticated Earth as well. That there may be a non-anthropocentric goodness in pristine nature, in the stars, or in an unpopulated, wild setting is not hard to imagine; to perceive the goodness of creation and the hand of the Creator in our backyards, potted plants, and city parks is perhaps more challenging. A Catholic cosmic common good stresses the intrinsic value of nonhuman creatures who dwell in thoroughly anthropocentric settings and live under human control.

4. Fourth, it helps us address the goodness of degraded Earth and damaged ecosystems. In what way can we speak of value, intrinsic or instrumental, in areas impacted or ruined by environmental disaster? How do we understand land contaminated irreparably by nuclear waste or pollution, or the floating islands of plastic and garbage in our oceans that have begun to create their own ecosystem?[96] Degraded Earth and impoverished creatures represent a "negative contrast experience," in which a situation of intense suffering has the critical epistemological power to alert us to the truth.[97] When we feel sorrow

at the ugliness of a damaged landscape or the suffering of nonhumans, we recognize the presence of some kind of evil and injustice.[98] These experiences have a privileged epistemological power to reveal the concrete reality and truth of the cosmic common good and the dignity of all creatures.

5. Finally, a Catholic cosmic common good may give humans perspective on destructive Earth, the forces of cosmic and planetary change that threaten us individually or potentially collectively. These are necessary parts of the cosmic dynamic that has supported and allowed any planetary and cosmic good we discover to emerge.[99] Taken together, the cosmic common good provides a template for addressing human relatedness to variegated dimensions of nonhuman creation and describes our various human encounters with the cosmos.

VII. Conclusion

I have argued, on a variety of grounds, that the dynamism of Catholic social thought is moving toward an expanded understanding of the common good that includes nonhuman creatures and the Earth itself. Like the principle of the common good in human social ethics, this broader common good affirms the reciprocal relationship between individuals and the whole of which they are a part. The common good is not just the set of conditions under which individuals may flourish, but it also affirms the intrinsically relational character of creatures. It points to the good of individual creatures as well as the good of the whole. Just as human beings are meant to live in society with other humans, so too should they perceive themselves as participants in a cosmic evolutionary development, as embedded in webs of ecological dependencies, as members of the ecosystems in which they live, as citizens of a greater Earthly and cosmic commons, as siblings in a "universal family." The cosmic common good is an essential component of our human identity. We are incomplete without the cosmos, without Earth, just as the cosmos is incomplete without our full participation.

Further chapters will broaden this vision of a Catholic cosmic common good. In the next chapter, I expand on the roots for the cosmic common good in a theocentric Catholic theology of creation by looking to Augustine and Thomas Aquinas. Next, I explore an alternative and cosmocentric theology of creation, one that is deeply informed by an evolutionary and ecological worldview, via the work of Thomas Berry. Together, these two chapters show how the theology of creation helps fill out and offer alternative ways of understanding the various facets of a Catholic cosmic common good that I have outlined here.

The concepts of a cosmic common good and creaturely dignity, and associated principles of cosmic subsidiarity and cosmic participation, offer a moral vision of the whole, but Catholic social thought contains further principles that help to explain how this vision can be lived out in everyday life, how it guides action, and how a moral vision becomes a pattern for moral decision-making. Following the chapters on Augustine, Aquinas, and Berry, I next expand on the ramifications of the cosmic common good in other principles of Catholic social thought, namely solidarity (and the preferential option for the poor) for the ways in which the cosmic common good touches our affections and can become ingrained in our behavior. I then look at rights discourse, for how it impacts our conceptions of legal justice. Together, this will create a platform, a grounding for a Catholic common good, that can be brought onto common ground with other traditions.

3

Classical Sources for a Catholic Cosmic Common Good

AUGUSTINE AND THOMAS AQUINAS

I. Introduction

A Catholic cosmic common good is intimately related to the theology of creation. To demonstrate this, I turn now to St. Augustine of Hippo and St. Thomas Aquinas, two foremost theologians in the history of Christian theology.[1] Augustine of Hippo is a multifaceted and prolific author who rightly deserves to remain a pillar upon which the Church builds its theological tradition.[2] Similarly, Thomas Aquinas ranks as the most prominent theologian in the Catholic Church, and his philosophy and theology remain the touchstone for Catholic ethical reflection in the modern era.[3] Moreover, both Augustine[4] and Aquinas[5] have been influential in the development of Christian and Catholic eco-theology and ecological ethics.

Writing in their patristic and medieval contexts, neither theologian offers ready-made concepts for ecological ethics,[6] nor would they easily affirm my formulation of the cosmic common good and creaturely dignity. Their premodern worldviews diverge sharply from what modern science describes of our universe, notably the 14-billion-year history of the cosmos, in which the story of the Earth occupies a minimal part; and the evolutionary development of life, in which humanity emerges from a common stream of life forms.[7] They exhibit and indeed helped establish the anthropocentric orientation of most Catholic theology, so their basic worldview clearly limited the common good to the human community. Thus my appeal to them here to outline a theocentric non-anthropocentrism does not represent a strictly historical representation of their positions.

Yet their nuanced and thoroughly theocentric understandings of creation offer a rich model of humanity's relationship to the cosmos and to the Earth that emphasizes the creatureliness and interconnectedness of all beings. Their descriptions of the universe are scriptural, philosophical, and theological, so one can still elicit a vivid depiction of a cosmic common good that they themselves did not articulate. At the same time, my exposition of Augustine and Aquinas here does not represent a fully constructive and creative retrieval, a project that would require much more space. Rather, I turn to them both in order to demonstrate how a Catholic cosmic common good has roots in the tradition's understanding of creation, and also to offer an alternative account for the facets of the cosmic common good I discussed earlier. These two figures are not the only or most important theological sources, but they represent how a deeply theocentric theology of creation has ample space for conceiving and articulating a cosmic common good.

II. A Fivefold Cosmic Common Good

The theologies of creation in Augustine and Aquinas suggest a fivefold dimension to a Catholic cosmic common good: (1) the ultimate good of creation to glorify God; (2) the good of individual creatures pursuing their own perfections; (3) the good of creatures for other creatures; (4) the good of a diversity of creatures; and (5) the good of the order of creatures.[8]

II.1. The Ultimate Good of Creation Is to Glorify God

II.1.1. Augustine

First, Augustine and Aquinas affirm that creation exists to glorify and serve God, and this in fact is its ultimate good. Augustine highlights two facets of creation's relationship to God. First, he confirms creation's utter dependence on God the Creator, an ontological dependence that underscores the priority of the distinction between God and creation before any distinctions between humanity and other creatures. A theocentric construal of the cosmos establishes a common ground that unifies humans and all other creatures. In a discussion Augustine has with his mother Monica, shortly before she dies, they wonder how they might encounter God through finite creatures: What if a person's body and mind were to be stilled, so that dreams, visions, and thoughts were silent, and all that the mind can know, such as Earth, water, and stars, were to speak no more, what would we hear? They reason that all transient creatures owe their existence to the Creator, and if we listened properly, we would hear all speak the common truth of this divine origin: "We did not make ourselves, but he who abides forever made us."[9] The belief in a Creator establishes a sense of sameness between humanity and all other creatures. God is in all things, and beyond all things, and the life of all creatures is moved by God, toward God, through the overflow of divine love.[10]

The second key theocentric theme in Augustine is that all creation exists to glorify God. In his autobiography *Confessions*, Augustine relates how at one point in his life he judged lesser creatures to be unnecessary in the scheme of the universe. He later realizes that all creatures have the capacity to reveal God to human beings, whether we recognize their goodness and beauty or not. Even more so, these creatures themselves exist to proclaim God's goodness. Drawing on Psalm 148, Augustine asserts that every kind of creature, from inanimate fire, snow, and storms to monsters and wild animals, from creeping insects and flying birds to mountains and trees, from kings and rulers to boys and girls, "... all give praise to the Lord's name."[11] All exist to praise God and find their ultimate good therein.

II.1.2. Aquinas

Aquinas distinguishes two kinds of common good that apply to the entire cosmos: an eternal and absolute common good, and a finite and temporal common good.[12] The former refers to God, while the latter indicates the order of the universe.[13] If the temporal cosmic common good is the order and relationship of the various parts, the absolute common good is God and the glory of God. Whatever good creatures may share in common, God remains the eternal and "universal good" of all creatures and of creation as a whole "because every creature according to its being naturally belongs to God."[14] For this reason, God is the "common good of all (*bonum commune omnium*)."[15] All creatures belong to God, and God is the primary end for all creatures and their creaturely inclinations. Only in this context does the temporal cosmic common good, the good of the order of creation, have its validity. In this way, Aquinas underscores the theocentric nature of the universe. The ultimate cosmic common good, for Christians, is the ability of each creature, and the universe as a whole, to contribute to the glory of God.[16]

For Augustine and Aquinas, a proper theology of creation begins in the orientation of all beings to God. A Catholic cosmic common good will be emphatically theocentric, focused on God as the primary good of all creatures. The next four goods, however, offer a theocentric appreciation of the goodness of creation and creatures in ways that may also be observable to those who do not share the same theological convictions. They reveal how Augustine's and Aquinas's theology of creation can include the cosmos and affirm the cosmic common good within their overriding theocentrism.

II.2. The Good of Individual Creatures Pursuing Their Own Perfections

Second, Augustine and Aquinas describe a good of individual creatures who possess a limited perfection through their existence that derives from God. Both theologians believed that creatures exist because they participate in God, and they have certain perfections that are natural to them because they participate in God's immutable perfection. All creatures have their own goodness, excellence, and beauty within the scheme of creation.[17] Different creatures exhibit varying degrees of perfections, and both Augustine and Aquinas place humanity's perfections above any other embodied creature's. Still, these perfections contribute to the goodness of any creature and belong to these creatures regardless of their benefit to others. Augustine and Aquinas thus provide a theological grounding for the intrinsic value of nonhuman creatures.

II.2.1. Augustine

Drawing on Wisdom 11:20,[18] Augustine describes how God ordains every creature to its place in the universe through measure, number, and weight. These three correspond to each of the Persons of the Trinity, and hence reflect Augustine's thoroughly Trinitarian understanding of creation. Of course, God is not identical with these three qualities as we experience them in creatures, but in the way that measure sets limits, number provides form, and weight draws all things "to a state of repose and stability," God is the true source of these because God limits, forms, and orders all things.[19]

Measure (associated with the Father) points to each creature's finitude and limits in the scope of the universe. All creatures are good within a hierarchy of goods, and all are equally dependent on God. God enjoys the limited perfections of creatures according to the limits that God establishes. Number (the role of the Son) gives form to creatures, and it describes how each creature fits harmoniously with the whole. All things are made through the Word, and this is evidenced in creation's splendor, abundance, variation, and power.[20] Weight (the work of the Spirit) signifies how creatures are drawn to dwell in a certain place or to fulfill a distinct role within cosmic order. In particular, the Spirit maintains creatures in existence by keeping them in motion and fostering a love that draws out their goodness.

Measure, number, and weight are the source of creaturely unity and signify another point of connection between humanity and nonhumans. Measure, number, and weight here refer not only to physical limits, but apply also to the realm of spirit or soul. Hence measure can indicate the ways in which human activity may be kept in control, or number gives order to the soul's affections, or weight signifies the weight of will and of love that discloses everything that one ought to seek and esteem.[21] Dunham comments, "When created beings participate in measure, number, and weight according to the divine intention, they reveal the goodness of God's work."[22]

Augustine exalts the figure of Wisdom, who "arranges all things sweetly" (Wisdom 8:1) through her endless motions that are "swifter and more active than all motions."[23] The Spirit's activity draws everything to stable quietude,[24] to rest in the place ordained for it by God. Rest bears a major significance for Augustine, made famous by his declaration in *Confessions* that "our hearts find no peace until they rest in you [God]."[25] God draws spiritual beings to rest in certain spiritual states,[26] and lures physical things to their appropriate space, so that water rests upon the earth, and oil rests on the water.[27] A creature's weight is its love, and every creature is meant to find its repose or its happiness by resting in God, and in particular, in the work that God has given it to perform. Thus there is a good of each creature to rest in God, and to do so by resting in its proper place or activity in the universe.

II.2.2. Aquinas

Aquinas likewise posits that creatures exist via participation in God, and that each creature possesses an internal harmony due to the form that God gives them. What Augustine describes in using the term "weight," Aquinas portrays through the idea of a "natural appetite" or inclination that provides the internal drive for each creature to seek its appointed purposes in creation. All creatures participate in God and therefore in the Eternal Law, which is God's ordering of the universe. Through this participation, creatures receive their natural inclinations for the activities God ordains for them.[28] The ultimate aim of every creature's natural appetite is God, and Aquinas describes this as a form of natural love that every creature bears for God. From their participation in Eternal Law, every creature derives a love that directs it back to God.

Yet Aquinas also discerns that creatures attain to God through distinct and assorted loves. Aquinas calls this "the fellowship of natural goods": insentient creatures are moved directly by God through their natural properties, such as a rock that falls to the earth; living creatures through their active propensities, such as that to grow; sentient creatures like animals via their inclinations to protect their own life or to reproduce; and human beings through their powers of reason and free will. Hence in human beings this natural appetite is also a rational appetite, while for all other creatures it remains an innate impulse that they do not knowingly direct. By nature, each creature "loves God above all things and more than himself," and each creature in its own way "naturally loves the common good of the whole more than its own particular good."[29] The pursuit of these various natural goods is part of the cosmic common good because they culminate in glorifying God. Aquinas thus extends Augustine and moves beyond his interchange of goodness and being by depicting each creature as perfect because of innate capacities instilled by God, which each creature is meant to realize.[30] Not only is the Spirit in effortless motion drawing creatures to their ends, as Augustine describes, but all creatures actively cooperate in pursuing and fulfilling their natural inclinations. Each creature is good not only through its internal harmony and by resting in its proper place in creation, but also in its activity as it pursues the natural appetites imprinted on it by God.[31] In doing so, each creature naturally loves God, the absolute cosmic common good, or the order of the universe, the temporal cosmic common good, "more than its own particular good."

Aquinas also describes these natural appetites in terms of each creature's likeness to God. All creatures exist because they participate in God, and so they also possess a kind of likeness to their creator, since "every agent intends to induce its likeness into its effect, as far as the effect can admit of it."[32] The final end of all things is to become like God, insofar as they are capable. The intrinsic ends and natural inclinations of creatures, instilled in them by God, enable them to obtain a particular degree of perfection. When a creature acts on and fulfills those impulses oriented to its proper end, it grows in its limited perfections, which constitute the creature's own likeness to divine goodness and perfection.[33] While human beings reach a likeness to God that other embodied creatures cannot, still there remain varying likenesses to God, various perfections, that can be attained by creatures. Moreover, as creatures return to God by fulfilling their limited perfections and manifesting their likeness to God, the universe realizes its ultimate perfection. The universe requires these multiform pursuits of perfection in order that the whole may reach its intended end.[34] This process, oriented to the glory of God, ought to be respected as part of our shared common good.[35]

II.3. The Good of Creatures for Other Creatures

Third, both authors recognize a common good that creatures are useful to other creatures, which corresponds to the instrumental value of creatures for each other. In this, they accept the dynamics of predation.

II.3.1. Augustine

Augustine certainly prizes the service that "lower" creatures provide to human beings, for whom they were made. But interestingly, Augustine uses this same point to stress that human beings should not question a wise creator who makes animals for purposes that humans do not understand. While human beings are allowed to suffer, as a punishment for original sin and as a test to help them increase in virtue, Augustine recognizes that animals deserve no punishment because they have no sins, and they cannot be perfected in virtue. Still, he states it is unreasonable to wish that animals not be nourishment for others, for there is a hidden plan that regulates the universe.[36] As we have seen, all things have their proper measure, number, and weight, and this order leads the creature to its appointed place in creation. To be a creature is to be nourishment for others. Augustine affirms that all creatures are praiseworthy in their own right, and that even when one creature transforms into another, they are all "governed by a hidden plan that rules the beauty of the world."[37] Augustine understands that this is difficult to perceive, but he insists that its truth is accessible to those who have grown in wisdom: "Although this truth may be hidden from the foolish, it is dimly grasped by the good and is as clear as day to the perfect."[38] A creature's capacity to provide nourishment to other creatures is a portion of its contribution to the beauty of the world, and as such is an element of the common good. Those who grow in their relationship to God will have an increasingly clearer understanding of this.

II.3.2. Aquinas

Aquinas describes an order of conservation, whereby creatures are ordained to be used by other creatures. Aquinas presumes human beings are the end for which nonhuman creatures are made, but he recognizes that intermediate creatures are also made for each other: "Consequently the elements are for the sake of the mixed body, the mixed body for the sake of living things: and these plants are for the sake of animals, and animals for the sake of man."[39] The utility of some creatures for others is not restricted to interactions between humans and nonhumans. Humans are meant to use creatures in two ways: first, to satisfy material needs; second, to understand God by contemplating nonhumans and their natural inclinations.[40] Aquinas also sanctions appropriate uses of human beings by other humans. Indeed, humans are the most useful of creatures for other humans, since they enable one to acquire the goods necessary to sustain this life and to know the truth about God.[41]

Similarly to Augustine, Aquinas associates the reality of evil with the fact of predation among animals. Aquinas affirms that nothing occurs in creation outside God's providential ordering, not only generally but even within individual beings, because all things participate in God.[42] By linking the goodness and order of the universe to God's providence, Aquinas raises the question of evil and disharmony among creatures. Aquinas acknowledges that God does not prevent all natural evil from occurring, and it would not be preferable if God did so. Unlike humans, who may have responsibility for the good of some part of creation, God has responsibility for the whole. Thus, God allows evil to affect some creatures "lest the good of the whole should be hindered." Indeed, because God oversees and provides for all creation, "it belongs to His providence to permit certain defects in particular effects, that the perfect good of the universe may not be hindered, for if all evil were prevented, much good would be absent from the universe."[43] Aquinas offers two examples to defend this. One is drawn from human experience: there would be no patience of the martyrs without persecution. The other stems from nature: a lion would not be able to live if it could not hunt prey.[44] The defects of violence and pain that we experience, either as part of the natural world or as part of human history, need not be opposed to the universal good for which God aims, which is a good that encompasses more than the particular good of any single species of creatures. If God sought to eliminate all evils, either natural or moral, then "much good would be absent from the universe." Thus another feature of a Catholic cosmic common good is that creatures are beneficial to other creatures. Although this is rightly identified as a natural evil, it is one that is necessary for the overall goodness of creation.

II.4. The Good of a Diversity of Creatures

Fourth, both theologians identify a common good of a variety of creatures, that the universe is enhanced by the extravagance and profusion of nonhuman species.

II.4.1. Augustine

Augustine marvels at the many different kinds of creatures who inhabit Earth. For Augustine, a diversity of creatures aids in praising and glorifying God. Augustine celebrates the vast number of creatures who both serve human needs and inspire astonishment at their beauty:

> Shall I speak of the manifold and various loveliness of sky, and earth, and sea; of the plentiful supply and wonderful qualities of the light; of sun, moon, and stars; of the shade of trees; of the colors and perfume of flowers; of the multitude of birds, all differing in plumage and in song; of the variety of animals, of which the smallest in size are often the most wonderful—the works of ants and bees astonishing us more than the huge bodies of whales? Shall I speak of the sea, which itself is so grand a spectacle, when it arrays itself as it were in vestures of various colours, now running through every shade of green, and again becoming purple or blue? Is it not delightful to look at it in storm, and experience the soothing complacency which it inspires, by suggesting that we ourselves are not tossed and shipwrecked? . . . Who can enumerate all the blessings we enjoy?[45]

Augustine remarks that these manifold blessings, resulting from the diversity of creatures, belong not just to the blessed who have been saved in faith, but to all human beings. While he also uses these experiences to demonstrate the surpassing excellence that God promises for eternal life, Augustine clearly appreciates and celebrates the beauty of so many species of creatures on Earth, who contribute endless praise to God.

Augustine concludes that all kinds of creatures are good and for a variety of reasons: "All natures, then, inasmuch as they are, and have therefore a rank and species of their own, and a kind of internal harmony, are certainly good."[46] We see here how Augustine detects the goodness of creatures (1) from the sheer fact of their existence, which corresponds to the fact that all creatures glorify God by the fact of their total dependence on God; (2) from their internal harmony, which expresses in alternative terms the common good of creatures resting in their limited perfections; and (3) from their appointed place in creation that belongs to them alone, and which differentiates them from other creatures.

II.4.2. Aquinas

For Aquinas, the diversity of species is a critical component of creation. In contrast to Augustine's rhapsodic celebration of the variety of creatures he encountered, Aquinas marvels more at the metaphysical fact that a diversity of creatures is necessary to reflect the goodness of God.[47] Aquinas states that because God is infinite and yet simple goodness, the universe requires many different kinds of creatures to best imitate the divine goodness: "For goodness, which in God is simple and uniform, in creatures is manifold and divided; and hence the whole universe together participates the divine goodness more perfectly, and represents it better than any single creature whatever."[48] Any single species of creature, however resplendent its natural perfections, is inadequate to represent the infinite perfection of God. The diversity of creatures is another justification for natural evil as well. Just as Aquinas allows for the existence of natural evil, in order that some animals may provide nourishment to others, so too does he allow for the corruption and death of individual creatures. While corruption is not good for the individual, it is necessary for the species to survive in perpetuity, and "it is in this that the perfection of the universe essentially consists."[49] Thus the common good of the universe requires a variety of creatures both for its own perfection and for its capacity to represent an infinite God.

As we shall see, both Augustine and Aquinas presume the superiority of the human being among Earthly creatures. Yet Aquinas never suggests that the universe would be enhanced if the Earth consisted primarily of humans. On the contrary, he perceives the presence of multiple species as a vital common good. Aquinas entertains an unusual and provocative hypothetical that compares the most extreme opposites: whether a universe in which there are only angels is superior to one containing angels and rocks. Even though angels surpass all other creatures in excellence (even surpassing humanity's intellectual and volitional capacities), Aquinas affirms the superiority of the latter:

> Although an angel taken absolutely may be better than a rock, still both natures taken together (*utraque natura*) are better than either one alone: and hence a universe in which there are angels and other things is better than where there would be angels only, because the perfection of the universe is seen essentially according to the diversity of natures, by which diverse

degrees of goodness are filled, and not according to the multiplicity of individuals in one nature.[50]

Though one species of creature may surpass another in excellence, no creature surpasses the entirety of creation as a whole. A sheer multiplication of creatures, even those most advanced in their likeness to God, would deprive the universe of degrees of goodness and thereby constrain its perfection.

II.5. The Good of the Order of Creatures

Fifth, Augustine and Aquinas affirm the common good of the order of creatures. Here they recognize not only that creatures can be valuable to each other, but that in fact the order and interconnections of creatures are a common good. There are two crucial dimensions to this order. First, both Augustine and Aquinas affirm a hierarchy of creatures, whereby not each creature is of equal value. Part of the goodness of creation, and an intrinsic element to its value, is the diversity and hierarchy of creatures, whereby some clearly exceed others in value and worth.

Second, and nevertheless, both assert the good of creation's ordering, not simply for humanity's use but for itself.

II.5.1. Augustine

Augustine confirms that human beings are made in the image of God and possess an incorruptible soul, and so "lower" creatures are ordained for human use.[51] Augustine clearly identifies differing goods corresponding to different creatures, and he in no way would equate the perfections of a human being with those of any other creature. God did not make all things equal,[52] and Augustine believes that human beings are "made to the image of God in that part of [their] nature wherein [they] surpass the brute beasts."[53] He adverts to a pedagogical purpose for natural evil when he admonishes humans to see the suffering of animals and strive for "that spiritual and everlasting life by which [they excel] all brute beasts."[54] Augustine acknowledges the disparate kinds of rest each creature can achieve. While irrational animals find peace in the "harmonious repose of the appetites," the human soul finds it in the "harmony of knowledge and action."[55] While the latter clearly exceeds the former, Augustine provides here another example of positing a superior human dignity amidst a more generalized creaturely dignity.

Alongside this hierarchy of creatures, Augustine maintains a focus on the good of the totality of creation. Augustine often speaks of a "tranquility of order," both to describe the proper arrangement of human society as well as the peaceful order of the universe.[56] In each case, order emerges when "unequal and equal" creatures are arranged in a suitable way. Inequality among creatures makes order possible, and order brings peace. "Because you did not make them all equal, each single thing is good and collectively they are very good, for our God made his whole creation *very good.*"[57] In this way, the peaceful order of creation is the universe's rest in God. While the Spirit leads all creatures individually to rest in God, the harmony of all things resting in their place in creation is also a way of creation's resting in God. The unity of the universe, found in the harmony of all things working together, represents the "tranquility of order," the peace of creation.

Augustine even detects the drive toward peace within the reality of death. All creatures pursue peace, between body and soul, between themselves and their inner circle, and with the entire universe. The most vital and intimate order, perhaps, is between the soul and the body. Augustine observes that the body seeks peace with the soul during its life, and after death it continues to seek peace, in one of two ways: if the body is embalmed, then a form of peace joins the parts of the body to each other; if not, in due course the body will begin to putrefy, which offends us "until it is assimilated to the elements of the world, and particle by particle enters into peace with them." In either case, the part seeks reunification back into a whole and fulfills the common good of the order of creation, as ordained by the Creator, who oversees the peace of the universe.[58] The overriding weight of any part, whether the parts of the body or an entire species, seeks its place in the order of the whole.

Though the reality that life feeds on death may not seem like a common good, Augustine acknowledges the importance of this cycle in creation, whereby some creatures perish at the appropriate time in order that other more powerful creatures may survive. This is "the appointed order of things transitory."[59] Augustine poignantly depicts the spiritual significance in accepting this when he recounts in his *Confessions* the profound sorrow provoked by the untimely death of his unnamed friend. This experience teaches him that "[i]f the soul loves [created things] and wishes to be with them and finds its rest in them, it is torn by desires that can destroy it. In these things there is no place to rest, because they do not last."[60] He compares the world's evanescing quality to language and speech, and to the passing of the seasons. If one part were to remain longer than its appointed time, its successor could not emerge, and the beauty and goodness of the whole could never emerge. Like in a song, things have their allotted time to arise, to live, and are then meant to die. Humans ought to love creatures, including our dearest friends, but not set our hearts on any one part of creation. Creatures are good for each other, and their passing away ensures that the symphonic splendor of the whole is possible.

Humans may criticize or inadequately appreciate creatures, either when their interests are challenged, or simply through ignorance. To the first, Augustine carefully distinguishes the order of creation from the order of utility. Utility measures instrumental value, and Augustine perceptively observes that human beings, in their ignorance, may conflate a creature's true value with human standards. Humans encounter creatures whose nature displeases us, such as the swarms that plagued the Egyptians, or the sun that can burn the skin.[61] In these situations, humans estimate these creatures based on their utility or the threat they pose to human desires, not on the goodness of their nature. Thus at times humans may prefer insentient objects over sentient creatures. Augustine recognizes that this human desire can be so strong that if we had the power, humans would "abolish [certain sentient beings] from nature altogether, whether in ignorance of the place they hold in nature, or, though we know it, sacrificing them to our own convenience. Who, e.g., would not rather have bread in his house than mice, gold than fleas?"[62] Augustine understands the temptation to judge creation according to our own standards of satisfaction, and he challenges us to view the cosmos from God's perspective. These creatures glorify God through being what they are, regardless of the benefits they provide or the discomfort they inflict for humans. Mosquitoes glorify their Creator, even if we find it necessary to kill them in order to protect ourselves from malaria.

Humans also misjudge the goodness of the order of creation through ignorance. Augustine complains that heretics "do not consider how admirable these things are in their own places, how excellent in their own natures, how beautifully adjusted to the rest of creation, and how much grace they contribute to the universe by their own contributions as to a commonwealth."[63] Here Augustine connects the beauty of a creature's own excellences and its place in the universe to the grace it contributes to the whole. Echoing a Catholic cosmic common good, Augustine recognizes a link between individual creaturely dignity and a common good of diverse subjects. Augustine wisely points out that the defects or faults we perceive in creation are a sign of the excellences they have received from God. If we recoil from pain, death, and decay, then obviously some aspect of the creature pleases us, for we are displeased when it is removed. Physical pain itself is a reminder of the body's goodness. Pain has a powerful effect on the soul, stimulating it to strive "to hold the unity that belongs to its nature when it feels, not with indifference but almost with indignation, that unity wasting away and disintegrating."[64] If human beings do not perceive the beauty of the order of creation, it is because we are mortal and enmeshed in its transience and cannot see the whole, "in which these fragments that offend us are harmonized with the most accurate fitness and beauty."[65] In these moments it is imperative to believe and trust in God's wisdom, lest we manifest our ignorance by finding fault in the work of a perfect Creator. Augustine does not deny the validity of the order of utility or of perceiving creatures as valuable instrumentally, but he rightly refocuses on creaturely dignity within the order of creation, which human beings so easily misunderstand.

II.5.2. Aquinas

Aquinas similarly integrates a gradation of value among creatures into an appreciation for the order of creation. As we have seen, all creatures exist because they participate in God, and every creature possesses a likeness to God. As it seeks God's goodness as its final end and fulfills its inclinations, it attains to a greater likeness of God. Though all natural inclinations emerge because of a creature's participation in God, some inclinations are more precious and inclusive than others, and so some creatures are capable of a superior and more perfect likeness to God. Aquinas depicts a nuanced scale of value that ranges by degrees. Thus the rock may fall to Earth by a natural love, but the plant adds to this simple tendency the inclination to grow and multiply; the animal adds the inclination to reproduce and raise offspring. Mixed elements are more perfect than primary elements; plants than mixed elements; animals than plants; and this finally culminates in human beings who stand above all other Earthly creatures, who possess all the perfections of these lower creatures in addition to the powers of rationality, the capacities to know the truth and to act freely.[66]

Lacking an evolutionary worldview, Aquinas confirms that the form of the universe, including the diversity of creatures and its intricate order, is directly intended by God and is not the result of chance. Differentiation and order are due to God's providential wisdom.[67] Furthermore, the distinction of things in nature is not as a result of sin, as Origen theorized, nor does a variety of creatures diminish in any way the superior goodness of the human person. Only humans are made in the image and likeness of God, and only humans have the power of reason to know or understand[68] and a "capacity for the highest good."[69] Thus other Earthly creatures are considered "less noble" than human beings and exist for humanity's sake.[70] Still, as we have seen, differences among creatures are integral to the universe's form and are necessary for the universe's goodness: "As the divine wisdom is the cause of the distinction of things for the sake of the perfection of the universe, so is it the cause of inequality. For the universe would not be perfect if only one grade of goodness were found in things."[71]

Due to the "distinction of things," Aquinas identifies the ordered interconnections among creatures as creation's preeminent good. Though higher creatures may possess a greater likeness to God than lower ones, the order of the universe is its "highest good,"[72] its "perfection,"[73] and its "chief beauty."[74] There is a parallel, therefore, between cosmic goodness and cosmic order. As we have seen, only a universe composed of a diversity of creatures can best imitate the divine goodness. Similarly, the ordering of creatures, ranked according to a hierarchy of values, represents the most important aspect of the universe. Not simply a diversity of creatures, but their mutual ordering to one another and their proper functioning, best glorifies God: "That which is good and best in the effect is the end of its production. But the good and the best in the universe consists in the mutual order of its parts, which is impossible without distinction: since by this order the universe is established as one whole, and this is its best. Therefore the order of the parts of the universe and their distinction is the end of the production of the universe."[75] Distinction makes order possible, and order is the highest good. God is the true final end, but in a finite and temporal way, the order of the universe characterized by the interconnectedness of creatures is the purpose, the telos, of creation.

The universe can be considered a common whole in two ways. First, all creatures are unified by the fact that they all necessarily and utterly depend on God for their existence. Only God exists by necessity, while all other creatures exist through participation in God.[76] Thus the universe of creatures is unified in its distinction from the Creator, who is the ground of creaturely diversity. Second, all creatures have relation of order not only to God but also to each other, and this order expresses the unity of the cosmos.[77] It is not just ontological dependence on God that bonds creatures together. Rather, the order that God has established in creation signifies a second way in which creatures are related and linked to each other.

Aquinas affirms that this order exceeds in goodness and value any other facet of the universe. "Now the best among all things caused is the order of the universe, wherein the good of the universe consists, even as in human affairs the good of *the nation is more God-like than the good of the individual.*"[78] Just as the nation's good exceeds that of the individual's, the integrity of the universe consisting in its order outweighs the well-being of any subset of creatures. Aquinas indicates that there is a realm of ontological and thus moral value distinct from that of human affairs, namely the good of the universe. One might conjecture therefore that the cosmic common good "is more God-like" than the merely human common good because "in all things the perfection of the whole takes precedence of the perfection of each part,"[79] and this is supremely true for the cosmos.

Aquinas employs various analogies to make sense of this order. He compares God to a master craftsman who created various kinds of creatures in order to bring about the best possible creation:

> Since the good of the whole is better than the good of each part, it does not befit the best maker to lessen the good of the whole in order to increase the good of some of the parts: thus a builder does not give to the foundation the goodness which he gives to the roof, lest he should make a crazy house. Therefore God the maker of all would not make the whole universe the best of its kind, if He made all the parts equal, because many degrees of goodness would be wanting to the universe, and thus it would be imperfect.[80]

Here Aquinas combines a theocentric sense of dependence on God, the superior value of the human person, and yet the overriding primacy of the cosmos. Human actions that structure and transform the Earth solely according to human valuation thus "lessen the good of the whole" in order to increase the good for humans. Ecological degradation, in a Thomistic lens, means that humans have taken God's ordered creation and made it into a "crazy house."

Similarly, Aquinas likens creation to a harp to describe the beauty of cosmic ordering: "The universe, the things that exist now being supposed, cannot be better, on account of the most noble order given to these things by God, in which the good of the universe consists. For if any one thing were bettered, the proportion of order would be destroyed, just as if one string were stretched more than it ought to be, the melody of the harp would be destroyed."[81] Thus altering any part of the universe's intrinsic ordering would vitiate the sublime harmony that God seeks for creation. Aquinas continually contextualizes a theological vision of humanity's superiority within a broader scheme of the superior good of cosmic order, and he continually thinks in terms of species before individuals, and the entirety of the whole before any one group of parts. Aquinas recognizes differing grades of goodness, and yet he consistently upholds the superiority of the entire universe as a whole and its order of diverse creatures. The following demonstrates again the way in which a theocentric view of creation can affirm the intrinsic goodness of every creature and its inclinations, the superior value of the human person, the cosmic harmony of ordered and interconnected parts geared toward the common good, and the purpose of creation, culminating in the praise of God:

> So, therefore, in the parts of the universe also every creature exists for its own proper act and perfection, and the less noble for the nobler, as those creatures that are less noble than man exist for the sake of man, whilst each and every creature exists for the perfection of the entire universe. Furthermore, the entire universe, with all its parts, is ordained towards God as its end, inasmuch as it imitates, as it were, and shows forth the Divine goodness, to the glory of God. Reasonable creatures, however, have in some special and higher manner God as their end, since they can attain to Him by their own operations, by knowing and loving Him. Thus it is plain that the Divine goodness is the end of all corporeal things.[82]

Aquinas perceives a good within individual creatures, but even more so in the totality of creatures, as a universe ordained as a whole toward God, and all to the glory of God. While God in Godself as the source of all good is the absolute cosmic common good, the order of interconnected parts represents the temporal cosmic common good to which all creatures ought to contribute. The cosmic common good reflects the interrelatedness of creatures to each other and to the whole, whereby the universe achieves its greatest perfection and creation reflects the goodness and wisdom of God. Aquinas finds scriptural roots for cosmic order in Genesis 1:31, in which God declares all created things "very good": "Hence it is said: *God saw all the things that He had made, and they were very good*, after it had been said of each that they are *good*. For each one in its nature is good, but all together are *very good*, on account of the order of the universe, which is the ultimate and noblest perfection in things."[83]

III. *Implications for a Catholic Cosmic Common Good*

Augustine and Aquinas demonstrate the roots in classical theology for an expansive vision of a Catholic cosmic common good. As it emerges from a Christian ground, the cosmic common good is both theocentric and cosmocentric, emphasizing the inherent and inalienable goodness of creatures for their own sake; the instrumental goodness of creatures to each other; the intrinsic and instrumental good of the cosmos as a whole; and the dynamic and interconnected whole of the universe, as it exists to glorify God.[84]

Both Augustine and Aquinas depict creation's goodness in terms of its unity and harmony, and they offer compelling theocentric grounds for discussing cosmic unity and the cosmic common good in a variety of ways. First, each creature individually depends utterly on God for its existence and is oriented to glorify God as its greatest purpose. Far from a renewed pantheism or eclipse of the transcendence of God, this grounding for the cosmic common good places God and the divine goodness at the center. Augustine and Aquinas exemplify how a non-anthropocentric cosmic common good is the most adequate ethical formulation for understanding God's relationship to creation. Their theocentrism is evident not only in the fact that the entire universe exists for God and to glorify God, but also in the intrinsic goodness of creatures, derived from their participation in God; the intrinsic goodness of diversity, which emphasizes that the only true fullness of perfection exists in God; and the instrumental goodness of the entire cosmos, which points to the fact that all creatureliness must be oriented to something beyond itself, to something non-creaturely.

Second, by grounding the existence of every creature through its participation in God, they lend a broad metaphysical dimension to the principle of participation in Catholic social thought. Participation cannot refer solely to human social life because it is the foundation of existence for all that is. By linking the ontological dependence of creatures on God and their participation in God to the possession of creaturely inclinations or to their "weight," they also give participation a moral quality beyond its metaphysical or biophysical reality. Fostering participation for all creatures means allowing creatures to participate in cosmic, planetary, and biophysical processes, and it calls humans to cultivate the conditions in which creatures can enact and engage those inclinations. In light of the three scientific grounds discussed in Chapter 2, the ethical component of participation highlights the ways in which those cosmic dynamics are currently being frustrated in fundamental ways.

Third, each creature possesses inviolable dignity due to the perfections that stem from its participation in God. This provides a sound theological basis to the claim that inherent dignity must be understood to be creaturely rather than just human, even while the "grades of goodness" in creation indicate differentiated dignity and the supreme value of the human person. Creaturely perfections are true goods, and inasmuch as any good is oriented to the service of God, then it behooves humans to allow other creatures an opportunity to fulfill these works and to offer God the delight God has in these limited perfections. The ends of creatures are to conform to the nature of God's goodness and love, not simply the utility that one creature may have for humans. Every creature possesses a kind of perfection and a way of excellence simply by dint of being God's creature. While for both of them this is a thoroughly theocentric principle, it may still bear meaning outside a theocentric context. Augustine and Aquinas call our attention to the myriad ways in which creatures other than humans demonstrate a perfection that should draw our admiration and wonder. The speed of the cheetah, the sinewy strength of a python, the canny survival instinct of the cockroach—these all manifest kinds of perfections that add another layer to a Catholic cosmic common good. With or without human perception or acknowledgment of these creatures, their very activity contributes to the cosmic common good.

Fourth, the good of a diversity of creatures offers a theological defense for the intrinsic good of biodiversity. God does not will a multiplicity of individuals of any creature, even the human species. Only a diversity of creatures can adequately represent the divine goodness. A Catholic cosmic common good therefore demands the good of many species, rather than a mere multiplication of individuals within one species. Biodiversity can be considered both an intrinsic and instrumental kind of good. For example, those ecosystems composed of many differing types of creatures are more resilient at withstanding climactic fluctuations and other shocks and thus are more capable of continuing to support diverse forms of life; species that incorporate greater genetic diversity are also more capable of handling challenges such as environmental changes or diseases. Thus biodiversity can be useful for the survival and flourishing of other creatures. At the same time, however, Augustine and Aquinas also point to its intrinsic goodness in light of the Creator's intentions for the universe. Again, a theocentric theology of creation underscores the common good of biodiversity for its own sake.

Fifth, the order and interconnections of creatures, as well as the good of creatures relying on others for their survival, is best represented by the modern term "sustainability." This term is admittedly vague and is employed in various, sometimes competing ways. Yet it points to what is most desperately needed: a pattern of human culture that contributes to the common good of all creatures by ensuring that human activity does not endanger the capacity for creatures to survive and thrive into the future. Of course, an evolutionary understanding negates any "tranquility of order" as Augustine and Aquinas envisioned. Order emerges over time and at a tremendous cost to creatures, both individuals and entire species. Still, God wills the good of the whole, and that good is marked not only by perfections within individuals and certain species, but also the perfection of an overall diversity of creatures who live embedded in a web of relationships. If the order of the universe is its greatest good, then humanity must work to allow creatures to fulfill their natural inclinations, in the contexts and according to the order in which those inclinations evolved.

Sixth, the primacy of the cosmos underscores the importance of contributing to the cosmic common good, not only as a moral responsibility but as a vocation. Augustine and Aquinas both assume that all creatures are made for and inclined to God and will not find rest or happiness until they fulfill God's purposes for them. For this reason, each describes a natural inclination among all creatures to seek the common good, based on its created nature, because every part flourishes when it contributes to the whole. True goodness is found in contributing to the common good, not taking from the commons for one's own private good. Augustine comments, "So whenever you show greater concern for the common good than for your own, you may know that you are growing in charity."[85] Similarly, Aquinas states that "the part does indeed love the good of the whole, as it becomes a part, not however so as to refer the good of the whole to itself, but rather itself to the good of the whole."[86] Even more so, for Aquinas, creatures that have a larger share of God's goodness and represent a greater likeness will have a keen appetite for seeking the common good and are called to contribute more to it. Every part naturally is willing to sacrifice on behalf of the good of which it is a part, suggesting a new pattern of human involvement in the cosmic common good. For a human being to grow in her likeness to God, she must not safeguard merely the human common good but the common good of all, and of all creatures, even beyond her own species.[87] Unless she chooses on behalf of the common good, she is not properly conforming her will to the divine will.[88] Promoting the Earth's flourishing is not only integral to the human common good, but it is humanity's participation in the cosmic common good.[89] Thus Augustine and Aquinas offer not only content for a Catholic cosmic common good but a cautionary reminder as well: the more we as individuals, or species, prefer our own good to the good of the whole, the more we deviate from God's purposes for creation. We hinder creation's capacity to give us a proper understanding of God, and we sully the most beautiful and perfect aspect of the Creator's work.

Thus Augustine and Aquinas provide a solid theological bedrock for a Catholic cosmic common good and illustrate the fullness of what it should entail. These two patristic and medieval theologians remind us not only of the good of individual creatures or the need for a diversity of species, but also that the whole universe possesses its own intrinsic goodness and worth that surpasses in excellence any individual creature, and its most valuable feature is the order among its various parts. God desires harmonious relationships between creatures, which may include predation and death, but always for the greater good of the order and diversity of the universe. They indicate that the Earth's flourishing is integral to the human common good because it is part of a cosmic common good that includes but also transcends and surpasses human well-being. They offer a theocentric and doxological ecological ethic that stresses the interdependence of humans and nonhuman creatures and their common destiny of glorifying and serving God. Humanity's participation in and contribution to the cosmic common good acknowledges God's goodness and wisdom by upholding the order that God has instituted.

Neither Augustine nor Aquinas offers a true ecological ethic, though there is reason to conjecture that were they alive and writing today, in light of advances in scientific understanding of the cosmos, each would likely move in similar directions.[90] There remains a fundamental anthropocentrism that permeates their cosmic vision: humans are clearly superior to the "brute beasts," and in their conception of the end of the world, both exclude the possibility of nonhuman creatures from entering it.[91] While they acknowledge the instrumental good of creatures for each other and chastened human presumptions regarding the value of nonhumans, they also presumed that humanity occupied a privileged rung in the hierarchy of creation that justified the instrumental use of other creatures. There is a sense of commonality between humanity and nonhumans, but we have not yet entered the realm of the cosmic commons, marked by a shared sense of mutual belonging. Thus we turn now to Thomas Berry, who incorporates the story of an evolutionary universe into his theology of creation and balances theocentrism with a radical and pervasive cosmocentrism.

4

Thomas Berry and an Evolutionary Catholic Cosmic Common Good

I. Introduction

Contemporary Catholics have built upon the tradition's theologies of creation most notably by incorporating the insights of the evolutionary and ecological sciences. Whereas Augustine and Aquinas presumed the universe to be static, and species to be created directly by God, science discloses a universe in a state of continual change, developing over billions of years. This enriches our conception of the cosmic common good and its themes of the intrinsic goodness of creatures and the overriding good of the whole.

While many could be drawn upon to demonstrate this trajectory, I focus here on one exemplary thinker: Passionist priest, Thomas Berry, C.P. (1914–2009). Technically not a theologian, Berry's academic expertise was in cultural history, and due to his reverence for Earth he considered himself a "geologian." Yet Berry was heavily influenced by and indebted to the theological vision of the Jesuit paleontologist Pierre Teilhard de Chardin, and was president of the American Teilhard Association for many years. From Teilhard, Berry learned the centrality of evolutionary theory and developmental time and that the universe is simultaneously a physical and a psychic reality.[1] Following Teilhard, Berry's work is suffused with a sense of awe for nature and its ability to mediate the divine. His "theology" of creation has been formative for countless eco-theologians and as such introduces key insights into a Catholic cosmic common good. Similar to Augustine and Aquinas, the "cosmic common good" is not a term that Berry employs, but it does fit well with his overall worldview. And also similarly to Augustine and Aquinas, there are myriad aspects of Berry's work that can contribute to ecological ethics,[2] but I limit myself here to two themes that invest something new into the principle of the cosmic common good that we have explored with Augustine and Aquinas: first, the conception of a cosmic story; and second, Berry's description of a threefold nature shared by all creatures.

I.1. Theocentrism in Berry's Cosmic Common Good

Berry's theocentrism is admittedly not as explicit as Augustine's and Aquinas's, yet he preserves a critical role for the divine and sacred source of the universe.[3] For Berry, the universe is not only the "primary revelation of the divine,"[4] but it is also in many ways the foundational sacrament and the "primary sacred reality" that can help humanity recover a sense of the sacred and our capacity for wonder.[5] Rather than a robust and firm declaration of faith in the Christian God, Berry prefers instead to speak of "the numinous presence" or "the divine."[6] In comparison with the compelling ecological ethics that many others today root in traditional orthodox Catholic faith, Berry's references to the numinous[7] may appear inadequately theocentric. Indeed, Berry comments that the word "God" is overused and refers to a mystery that exceeds human understanding.[8] On the other hand, his modesty in naming the divine as definitively Christian has an advantage, namely that Berry is able to describe the cosmos's intrinsic goodness in a way that can find affirmation and approval both in non-Christian religious traditions and among environmentalists. Berry's engagement with and respect for non-Christian traditions is likely the impetus that led him to adopt a general and vague term like "numinous" that might make some sense of both Christian religious experience and that of other traditions. Furthermore, non-religious environmentalists could bracket out his references to the numinous and find much to inspire their work, while people of every religious and cultural background might find in Berry's account of the universe's goodness an inducement to reshape their own traditions.

Moreover, when Berry began piecing together his vision of the New Story of the cosmos,[9] the overwhelming thrust of Western society and of his own Catholic faith was to envision the Earth as a repository of resources that exist for humanity's use. His scholarly efforts were fueled by a desire to counteract this myopic anthropocentrism. He longed to return our gaze to the stunning beauty of the Earth and the cosmos and to return us to our creaturely existence and our cosmic identity. In this light, I think Berry may have feared that any rigorous discussion of the Christian God would allow his audience to bypass nature's glorious dynamism and, more importantly, its increasing vulnerability and endangerment. A call to perceive the beauty and goodness of creation could become an excuse by some Christians to circumvent the endangered goodness of Earth and to use the universe's beauty to return to a God who cares for humanity alone. As a result, veiled references to the numinous serve to return the reader to the glory of the cosmos.

At times, Berry's cosmocentrism may seem to threaten sacralizing nature in exactly the ways that some Catholics fear. Yet it is also due to his faith in the "numinous presence" that undergirds the cosmos, and the need for humanity to encounter this presence in its cosmic manifestations, that he continually directs us to the universe as the primary sacred reality. With this understated yet firm theocentrism in mind, I now turn to two dimensions of Berry's work that demonstrate how the sciences can enrich a classical theology of creation.

II. The Cosmic Story

The first and most prominent contribution that Berry makes to a Catholic cosmic common good is his articulation of the new story of the universe, the cosmic story. Berry remains the most influential source for eco-theologians to take the account of cosmic development and human origins as described by the sciences and insist that these facts and processes are best understood in terms of a coherent narrative. Along with his collaborator, physicist Brian Swimme, Berry weaves the scientific data into a mythic and revelatory story with the power to transform humanity and our relationship to the Earth.[10]

I would like to draw out three aspects of the cosmic story that enrich the cosmic common good: the human need to situate oneself within a story; the cosmic story as described by science; and the cosmic story as a personal story.

II.1. Humanity's Need for Story

First, for Berry, all human societies need a functional cosmology embedded in stories that furnish them with a sense of the human person's place in the cosmos. Rather than philosophical or theoretical reflections on what it means to be human, or historical or scientific accounts that aim for objectivity, stories of origins are mythic and poetic narratives that express a people's understanding of themselves in the broader universe and enable people to be members of a particular community. They shape a community's perception of the world and convey a sense of purpose to its members. A people's story of the universe and the human role in it "is their primary source of intelligibility and value."[11] Cosmologies communicate a sense of belonging and provide a rationale for the meaning of suffering and death. A cosmology supplies the energy that people need to transcend themselves, to embark on arduous tasks, and to weather the struggles of life, because a narrative of the universe and humanity's role in it can place everything in a larger context and give those struggles direction and purpose.

Berry identifies a link between the story a people tell and the "great work" in which they are engaged. The ancient Greeks told a story about the importance of ideas and the spirit that shaped the development of Hellenistic thought and the direction of the Western world; the medieval Europeans retold that story through a Christian lens that made possible the construction of vast cathedrals and places of religious worship. Each age has a great work, and each great work finds its source in the narrative that the people tell.[12] Today, Berry identifies our common planetary great work as the call to recast the human-Earth relationship and direct our efforts toward a sustainable Earth: "The Great Work now ... is to carry out the transition from a period of human devastation of the Earth to a period when humans would be present to the planet in a mutually beneficial manner."[13] The story we tell will empower this work, or detract us from it.

The category of narrative clarifies the religious sources of the ecological crisis and outlines the kind of necessary response. Key to addressing ecological crises is rediscovering the religious power of cosmological narratives that shape our cultural worldviews. For Berry, our conventional origin stories have begun to unravel, and the various myths we have subscribed to—endless progress through industrial technology, or humanity's superiority over the natural world—have led to a planetary emergency. Humanity, Berry informs us, has brought about an end to the Cenezoic Era, a period of time on Earth since the demise of the dinosaurs 65 million years ago.[14] Many perceive the defects of these myths, but no other narrative has emerged to replace them. A central task for theological ecological ethics, then, is to uncover and dismantle the cosmological narrative that undergirds and drives the search for "progress" in the form of unbridled production and consumption of economic goods. This generation has entered a crisis moment, not simply because of ecological degradation, but because "we are in between stories."[15] The Bible, Berry believes, is unfortunately no longer a functional story of humanity's place in the universe, even for Christians.[16] The new story of the cosmos can provide the transcultural foundation for a renewed religious orientation that can sustain the energy required to adapt to the reality of ecological breakdown and to undertake the Great Work of our times of ushering in the Ecozoic era.[17]

II.2. The Epic of Evolution

The journey of the universe, as described by all the major contemporary sciences—which Berry calls the most important discovery of the twentieth century[18]—becomes a sacred narrative that discloses something of the mystery of the Creator and provides the basis for responding to an imperiled Earth. The "epic of evolution," he says, is "our sacred story."[19] Following Teilhard de Chardin, Berry views the evolutionary theory of developmental time not simply as scientific fact but as a new condition for humanity's self-understanding.[20] Just as Copernicus altered humanity's sense of spatiality, so too does evolution alter our conceptions of time and our relationships to all we perceive. Mary Evelyn Tucker explains, "For Teilhard and for Berry, then, the perspective of evolution provides the most comprehensive context for understanding the human phenomenon in relation to other life-forms."[21] While the new story may not mandate or proscribe choices on specific ecological questions, it is vital because it provides the context and proper moral perspective "for implementing the specific kinds of social, political, and economic changes that will be needed to sustain and foster life on the planet."[22] The story that humanity tells about itself, including its relationship to God, must be understood within this longer and more encompassing narrative, and this story can then become the basis for social and cultural change.

Three aspects of this story deserve particular focus: its emergence, its creativity, and its celebration.

II.2.1. Cosmogenesis

First, Berry highlights that the universe is emergent and multiform rather than static and unitary. Berry uses the term "cosmogenesis" to interpret the insights of the contemporary sciences cosmologically, and this term reveals important implications that the term "cosmos" may conceal. Cosmogenesis denotes that the universe changes, develops, and emerges only over unfathomable stretches of time, even as it appears to our limited human gaze and powers of comprehension as stable, solid, and indeed even eternal, as it was for the ancient Greeks. Yet at every level of existence, the universe is marked by change. From the quivering strings that make up subatomic quantum existence to the lingering evanescence of a young star that will reach its life span only over billions of years, the cosmos is active and in motion. Thus cosmogenesis stresses that the universe is constantly in flux and is shifting in discrete yet unpredictable directions.

Similarly, cosmogenesis bears theological significance by crediting the universe for being its own source. Berry's formulation here need not undermine the classical Christian doctrine of God the creator, who undergirds creation as its constant source, support, and ultimate goal. In terming the universe a cosmogenesis, Berry highlights the power inherent in the universe that the sciences describe, and rather than underscore the divine presence that makes the cosmos possible, Berry directs our attention back to these powers themselves. The ability of the cosmos to develop into its current state, Berry suggests, is a feat worthy of contemplation and awe. Thus he argues that through the process of evolution, the universe transforms itself by self-governing mechanisms over immense spans of time. The universe, Berry claims, "is self-emergent, self-sustaining, and self-fulfilling."[23] Berry points to the "primordial flaring forth," the beginning of the cosmic journey,[24] and the process of cosmogenesis that continues even now. The story of the emergent universe ought to heighten our appreciation of not only "that numinous mystery that pervades all the world"[25] but also the mysterious cosmos, which is its own temporal source. At every level of existence there is a tendency toward self-organization, which is always in process, and it is a power that belongs to the cosmos itself. As we shall see, the tripartite structure of each creature intensifies the autonomy of the universe in its own emergent becoming.

Some scientists caution that we must not read into the story of the cosmos a kind of determinacy or inevitability in the process of evolutionary development. The cosmos is riddled with untested possibilities that, had they been actualized, would have led to drastically different results. At the origin of the universe, for example, the initial laws of physics had not yet formed into existence. If matter had exploded outward too quickly, the speed would have been too great for atoms to bond and for heavenly bodies to emerge; if the initial speed had been too slow, the force of gravity would have drawn all matter inward and collapsed upon itself again. No cosmic law demands the existence of stars and planets, let alone sentient and self-conscious creatures. Still, Berry rightly asserts that, given the universe and the emergence of life as we experience it, a latent power in matter has allowed the cosmos to have developed to this point, which bears theological depth. The power of the cosmos to become much more and to unfold over time orients our wonder and is a testament to the enduring legacy of cosmogenesis.

II.2.2. *Creativity*

Second, Berry emphasizes creativity in the emergent cosmogenesis. Creativity lies in the balance between discipline and wildness, the two guiding forces of the universe.[26] Some might see in the "Big Bang" and the ensuing process of evolutionary development a wild and senseless chaos, but Berry perceives a sense of order. For example, in the curvature of space and the force of gravitational attraction, there is a constant interplay of law and chance and the possibility of a creative disequilibrium. The planet Earth represents how an ideal balance between the forces of discipline and wildness allows the possibility of creativity. An excess of discipline results in the hard rock form of Mercury, with no possibility of fluidity or change, while Jupiter represents too much gaseous wildness, without the chance for stability.[27] The evolutionary history of the cosmos reveals a general process from lesser to greater complexity, and from lesser to greater consciousness, which are the marks of its vigorous creativity.

Again, scientists caution us not to read intentional creativity into this process. The theory of natural selection demands that changes happen unpredictably, and at least until recently no creature could self-consciously direct the pattern of evolution or of life's development. Still, in Berry's telling of the cosmic story, the flowering of life on Earth manifests how this self-organizing process of cosmogenesis has clearly been fantastically fecund, bringing forth manifold instances of novelty and innovation, and most intensely on planet Earth. Creatures of unimaginable color, size, and inclination point to powers of creativity that can only be described as awesome.

In a theological and theocentric framework, it is difficult not to see in the emergence of complex life forms the trace of divine intentionality and thus determinacy for the universe as it is. Given who God is, self-conscious creatures who dwell amidst a teeming variety of life seem inevitable. While scientists may rightly argue that nothing in the universe itself logically demands this kind of creativity, a theological framework can still credit the presence of a loving and living God who makes it possible. More importantly, Berry insists that we see in this creative process not only the infinite creativity of God but also the inherent and vehement creativity of the universe to forge something new.

II.2.3. Celebration

Third, the story of the emergent and creative cosmogenesis is fundamentally a story of celebration.[28] Berry calls us to see the universe in its vastness and through its many transformations as a "single, multiform, celebratory expression." Every creature and event in nature is "a poem, a painting, a drama, a celebration."[29] By appealing to artistic images such as a poem or a drama, Berry links the universe's creativity to the wonder and joy that we experience in significant artistic events. The universe (and more locally the Earth) allures, entrances, and enwraps us in its own celebratory movement of existence. To be human is not to discover and celebrate the wonder of creation as it presents itself to us; more properly, the human celebration of planetary and cosmic beauty is the human participation in the universe's own preexistent and ongoing celebration. Celebration is multiform, encompassing a variety of expressions, yet it is also singular, stemming from the universe's origins even unto now. Berry draws on artistic metaphors to express celebration, not only due to the connotations of creativity or to our corresponding emotions of joy when we encounter inspiring works of art, but also because art demands an interpretation that appreciates the wider context in which it appears. Berry calls human beings to approach nonhuman creatures as reverently as we might a work of art, and to perceive our own participation in life as one element of the universe's drama. Berry likens cosmogenesis to a symphony, urging us to view the Earth and its transformations over time as symphonic movements. Later musical notes and themes, such as humanity itself, make sense only in the context of what precedes them.[30] Berry calls human beings to understand themselves as part of the drama of life, rather than the sole act. All the world's a stage, but all cosmic creatures are the players.

II.3. The Cosmic Story as Our Personal Story

Drawing together Berry's understanding of the human need for a worldview grounded in a functional narrative, with his call to respect the story of the emergent universe as a new sacred story, we come to the third important dimension of the cosmic story: the story of the universe is a personal story, the story of each individual creature.[31] The epic of the creative and celebratory cosmogenesis is our own story. This is not simply the past, or a mere prologue to the present. In a mystical way, we need to understand that we and every other creature were present at the origin of the universe, even if just in seed form. Peter Ellard explains: "We were the fireball, the initial forces, the first hydrogen atom. ... Everything about us was there and we have been evolving ever since."[32] Seeing the cosmic story as our personal story is analogous to other ways in which our identity is forged through narratives. For example, it is expected that Americans should know something of their national history in order to understand themselves as Americans, or that Catholics should know and celebrate salvation history so as to understand themselves as children of God. Berry reminds us that all human beings should know and celebrate our cosmic history in order to know and understand ourselves truly. Only by appropriating this story as a personal story do we appreciate life's meaning or derive the moral strength to heal an imperiled Earth.

Viewing the cosmic story as a personal story also calls us to know ourselves as members of the particular bioregions and places on Earth that we inhabit. For example, in Berry's book *The Great Work* is a chapter entitled "The North American Continent." Berry claims that Americans cannot live on the continent of North America in a fitting way without knowing something about its unique attributes.[33] This is not just an intellectual exercise: knowing the story of the cosmos, and one's place in it, has important consequences for the ways in which we relate to ourselves, to our fellow creatures, and to God. We are cosmic creatures who belong to the whole, but we embody this in and through concrete, particular places.

II.4. The Cosmic Story and a Catholic Cosmic Common Good

Berry's analysis of the contemporary need for the cosmic story, detailed by contemporary science, as our own story marks a significant contribution to the cosmic common good. Many theologians root a concern for Earth in compelling reinterpretations of key theological doctrines including renewed understandings of creation, yet Berry points to the central importance of a *functional story* that puts these various images and ideas into a coherent and narrative whole. The journey of the universe offers a comprehensive worldview for the cosmic common good, which in turn can provide us with the psychic energy to undertake the massive lifestyle shifts we need and a meaningful way to discuss the intrinsic value of creatures and of the cosmos as a whole. Creatures represent an integral part of the cosmic common good, not only through their inherent goodness or their role in creation, as Augustine and Aquinas might insist. In addition to this, they are part of an ongoing narrative—the cosmic story. Augustine himself hints at this when he discusses the universe as a symphony that only finds its coherence when individual creatures arise, play their part, and exit. Berry intensifies this awareness by wedding it to contemporary science and its story of a 14-billion-year-old cosmos and a 4-billion-year-old Earth.

Thus when human beings encounter a waterfall, animal, or mountaintop, they might remember that it *has* a story, a story that is both its *own* story and a contributor, along with ours, to a great cosmic story. We share a common history related to a common Creator, and in perceiving this shared narrative, Christians may better appreciate the theocentric nature of the cosmic common good. The story of the emergent and creative cosmogenesis thus leads us back to the creative source from which it came. The cosmic story is not "really" about humanity or merely a background to the human story. Humans are part of this story which has a cosmic scope, and the human chapter is a prominent but late component of an immense narrative. Peter Ellard proposes that to answer the question, "How old are you?" one must answer, "14 billion years old."[34] Similarly, this waterfall, this animal, this mountaintop are 14 billion years old—creative and emergent entities whose roots stretch back to the origins of the universe, a participant in cosmogenesis no less than we.

Yet Berry's telling of the cosmic story also short-circuits any attempt to leap too quickly from the cosmic story back to the Divine Author. Berry's interpretation of the story of cosmic evolution infuses our perception of the universe's power, goodness, creativity, and celebration, and it returns our gaze to the cosmos as our primary contact with the divine. While an Augustinian and Thomistic theology of creation reinforces an appreciation for the goodness of creatures and for the order of the cosmos as a whole, Berry senses that in an age of ecological devastation, more is required. He emphasizes similar aspects of creaturely dignity as Aquinas and Augustine do, but always to prompt our wonder and awe at the universe itself and not merely for the numinous source from which they emerge.

The cosmic story adds a further dimension to the ontological foundation and expansion of cosmic participation that Augustine and Aquinas provide by indicating the significance of creaturely participation in the story of universe. Nonhuman nature is intrinsically good and valuable, not just because it exists, performs certain kinds of activities, or pursues distinct inclinations. A creature's goodness and value include its place within the overall arc of the universe's history. The history of the cosmos is part of its cosmic common good, and in turn the cosmic good is integral to the good of each individual creature. The cosmic common good is found not only in how the myriad parts of creation interact, but in their shared history, a narrative that bears theocentric promise and can point us back to the Author and prompt us to celebrate, but only if we first see this story as one that belongs to the cosmos itself. The cosmic story is a sacred story, and each participant in it a graced character. Knowing this story and understanding nonhuman nature's past and continuing role enable Christians to discern God's presence in nature and to encounter God in those places more deeply; moreover, it enhances our human capacity to see other creatures as products and participants in cosmogenesis, just as we are; and it encourages all humanity to see these creatures as celebratory works of art.

The category of narrative also broadens a sense of cosmic subsidiarity. Berry reminds us to know the story of our bioregion as the history of our local cosmic commons. Part of the effort in moving toward bioregional rather than political subsidiarity will be to connect inhabitants to their local area by means of a shared story. This story helps to make the Earth and our particular place on it a home, and it reinforces our participation in a cosmic and planetary common good. When humans celebrate this story, they are better able to cherish the universe as a proper home and their nearby fellow creatures as neighbors.

III. *The Threefold Nature of the Universe*

A second theme of Berry's work intensifies our understanding of the multiform and emergent universe and our appreciation of the cosmic common good: a three-fold nature shared by all creatures: differentiation, subjectivity, and communion.[35] These three forces are the basic principles of the universe,[36] and they guide the cosmos in its process of cosmogenesis. There is a parallel in each to the themes discussed in the previous chapter. Again, Berry echoes these classical contributions with the distinctive addition of rooting them in the story of evolution and by emphasizing the power and goodness that belong to the universe qua universe. These three common characteristics deepen a Catholic appreciation of creation's goodness by welding the identity of the human to all other creatures and to the universe as a single entity.[37]

III.1. Differentiation

While the universe as a whole could be considered a single major energy event, from the "primordial flaring forth" to now, differentiation speaks to the way in which the universe articulates itself in infinite variety and form, granting a particular identity to every living thing. "Reality is not some infinitely extended homogeneous smudge. Each articulation is unrepeatable and irreplaceable at whatever level, from the subatomic to the galactic."[38] Berry often refers to Aquinas's remark that God's goodness could not be represented adequately by one or two beings, and so the entire universe represents the divine goodness better and more completely than any individual creature.[39] Thus differentiation is an alternative way of speaking about the diversity of creatures in creation, which for Aquinas and many others is integral to the harmony and perfection of the universe. Other terms that Berry and Swimme use to describe differentiation include "diversity, complexity, variation, disparity, multiform nature, heterogeneity, articulation."[40]

Berry's depiction of differentiation mirrors Augustine's and Aquinas's concern for biodiversity in that it emphasizes the radical otherness of creatures from one another and the importance of such diversity. Differentiation highlights the distinctiveness of every species and indeed of every individual creature. Berry extends this traditional teaching by linking it to the cosmic story and the emergent cosmogenesis. Differentiation grants a uniqueness to every being, asserting that its individual contribution to the wondrous cosmic story must be respected.

III.2. Subjectivity

Second, every being in the universe possesses its own real degree of subjectivity, which Berry also describes as its interiority, inner spontaneity, and unique articulation.[41] Again following in the wake of Teilhard de Chardin, Berry sees cosmogenesis as both a physical and psychic process. The potentiality of consciousness is inherent to the universe itself. By arguing for subjectivity, Berry locates a sacred dimension of autonomy and individual identity within every creature, which may remain inaccessible to human reason.[42] If differentiation focuses our attention on the multiform nature of the universe and the uniqueness of creatures, subjectivity urges us to respect each creature, and each habitat as it is composed by various creatures, as its own individually existing entity. Each has its own relation to and resonates with the mystery of the divine.[43] Berry even elevates this to an ethical norm, commenting that the "interior articulation of its own reality is the immediate responsibility of every being."[44]

A helpful way of envisioning the depth of the individual is through the term "autopoiesis": self-creation, or the ability of each entity to organize itself and to "participate directly in the cosmos-creating endeavor."[45] Berry and Swimme describe how this can pertain even to non-sentient beings such as a star: "The star organizes hydrogen and helium and produces elements and light. This ordering is the central activity of the star itself. That is, the star has a functioning self, a dynamic of organization centered within itself."[46] Berry thus balances the Augustinian and Thomistic theme of the goodness of every creature's natural inclination, and its innate tendency to rest in its place in creation, by again attributing this activity not just to a divine source but to the creature's ability to create itself. The goodness of each creature's natural inclinations is a cosmocentric, not only theocentric, reality.

The unique self-conscious subjectivity of the human being, is therefore only an instantiation of a broader and more fundamental cosmic subjectivity that gives all matter, from the very beginning, its own living interiority. For Berry, the human being retains a privileged position in the universe—not as a creature set apart or above, but as a mode of the universe itself. He defines the human person as "that being in whom the universe celebrates itself and its numinous origins in a special mode of conscious self-awareness."[47] Self-consciousness therefore properly belongs to the universe, in its human expression. This quote ties together a number of Berrian themes: the origin of the universe in the "numinous," the divine; the universe as an extensive and extended celebration; and, in that context, the elevated character and vocation of the human person, who is a mode of the universe itself. Human consciousness represents the intensification of cosmic subjectivity. Berry comments that as we have become accustomed to think of the human being as a microcosm, containing the various levels of existence present in the universe, we must also perceive the cosmos as a macroanthropos.[48]

III.3. Communion

Third, every creature exists for communion, mutuality, and reciprocity.[49] Though each entity in the universe enjoys subjectivity and independence, it is also simultaneously and intrinsically connected to everything else. Mutual presence is both a statement of reality for creatures but also their goal and fulfillment. Berry thus argues that a sense of alienation—from others and from the Earth—is a modern invention. The universe is constructed as a differentiated whole, and no creature can truly extricate itself from the interlocking web of creation: "Alienation is an impossibility, a cosmological impossibility. We can *feel* alienated, but we can never *be* alienated."[50] In fact, humans are always related to the Earth because we *are* Earth, we are the expression of the universe's self-awareness. Distinctively human capacities are not elevated above Earth and other Earth creatures, but instead are an elevation of Earth itself. Modern science, Berry avers, attests to the universe's coordinated unity: to exist is to exist in communion. Differentiation and subjectivity are therefore the conditions of possibility for communion. Difference and depth allow relationship. As Berry famously stressed, "The universe is a communion of subjects, not a collection of objects."[51]

Communion inheres into the makeup of the universe itself. It springs from and reinforces the intrinsic goodness of every individual species and creature. Every creature has its own role to fill in the universe and declares itself in its own voice to every other creature. "This capacity for relatedness, for presence to other beings, for spontaneity in action, is a capacity possessed by every mode of being throughout the entire universe."[52] The mutual order of creation that Augustine and Aquinas emphasize has in Berry achieved greater prominence. In this community, each being declares itself not just to God but to the entire universe, and in its own authentic voice. More than a mutual order of parts, each creature in the emergent universe is intrinsically designed for relationship, for communion in the community of life to which it belongs. Once again, Berry intensifies the import of the common good by positing it as a good that belongs to the community of creatures, for themselves and apart from whatever divine purposes they may also fulfill. In Berry the ethical vision of a cosmic common good seems epistemologically more accessible, since the integral relationship of each part to the whole and of the whole to each part, which the principle of the common good expresses, is a natural description of the "capacity for relatedness" that belongs to every creature.

These three basic cosmic principles exist in dynamic relationship to each other. Thus differentiation allows the other to be truly other, and it challenges and resists all forms of or attempts at absorption into the self. Subjectivity allows the other to be for itself, just as I am for myself. It posits a depth, a mysterious ground to the other, just as I perceive in myself and as we currently limit only to other human beings. Subjectivity speaks to the spontaneities of other creatures, the power of the emergent cosmos alive and active in this particular creature and in this particular habitat. Finally, only when the above two have been articulated—the other is other, and the other is for itself—can the other and I be for each other. Here communion, being a community of beings in relationship to each other, is the telos, but not without the indispensable principles of differentiation and subjectivity. Moreover, each can foster the other. The drive to communion, for example, can lead to greater differentiation and autopoiesis. Through the combination of elements, molecules arise. Hydrogen and oxygen combine to become water, which is neither hydrogen nor oxygen but instead something new, something with profound depth and character.

This tripartite schemata also offers an alternative critique of the planetary forces that imperil Earth. While Augustine and Aquinas offer a robust theological defense of biodiversity and sustainability, Berry links these to the goodness of the emergent universe and its creatures. The cosmic process of differentiation, and the irreplaceable articulation of energy that is each creature, therefore represents a kind of divine rebuke of the modern industrial paradigm that prefers monocultures and homogeneity.[53] Subjectivity deepens the sense of rest that each creature may find, knowing that the rest in God is truly the creature's own, in the context of its cosmic home. And communion constitutes a stronger defense of the order of creation because communion is not simply designed by God (though that is not ruled out) but is an impulse that lies at the heart of every creature.

III.4. Wildness

An important and noteworthy component of these three features is wildness, which as we have seen is integral to the evolutionary process. Berry approvingly cites Henry David Thoreau's essay in which Thoreau claims, "In wildness is the preservation of the world." For Berry, this represents one of the most trenchant critiques of modern civilization. Wildness—or "that which is uncontrolled by human dominance"[54]—belongs essentially to every creature.

Wildness belongs to each of the three basic principles of the universe. As part of differentiation, wildness signifies the cosmos's drive toward greater complexity. Wildness finds its strongest expression in the creature's inner spontaneities, and so we might think of it as the power that lies behind subjectivity and autopoiesis; wildness indicates that every creature in the cosmos, as well as the cosmos itself, is meant to lie outside the control of human dominance. In its interiority, each creature belongs to itself, and wildness is the ability of the creature to participate in autopoiesis, or self-creation. Finally, wildness is also related to communion. Berry remarks that violence in nature even satisfies some taste for wildness deep in the human soul.[55] Berry calls on human beings to learn to participate in wildness, as an avenue to communion. The key here, I believe, is the ability to allow Earth (including the human person) to be itself outside human (or simply rational) control.[56] The Earth and all its creatures need to allow wildness to exist and to emerge because it is essential for creativity and the possibility of greater cosmic development.

III.5. Berry's Meadow

Berry relates an experience from his childhood that helps us understand how these three features can exemplify a cosmic common good and can deepen our sense of belonging to an intrinsically good cosmos. Berry recalls one particular day when, at age eleven, he walked into the meadow near the home where he grew up in North Carolina, and he became poignantly aware of the effulgence of life and the beauty of wild Earth encompassing him. In this passage we detect a number of Berrian themes: the power of differentiation and the diversity of creatures; the mysterious depth of each creature declaring itself to the universe; and the profound sense of oneself as connected to nonhuman creatures, as a mode of the Earth itself, rooted in an immense planetary community.[57] Berry's reminiscence of this meadow illustrates how a particular location and particular moment can become revelatory and can draw us in to the cosmic story as a personal story. This is Berry's own mountaintop, where he perceived the sacred so profoundly and met the Creator.[58]

> Down below was a small creek and there across the creek was a meadow. It was an early afternoon in late May when I first wandered down the incline, crossed the creek, and looked out over the scene. The field was covered with white lilies rising above the thick grass. A magic moment, this experience gave to my life something that seems to explain my thinking at a

more profound level than almost any other experience I can remember. It was not only the lilies. It was the singing of the crickets and the woodlands in the distance and the clouds in a clear sky.[59]

Thus it was not really any particular aspect of the meadow that captivated him. What entrances Berry most is the dynamic combination of all these creatures and their innumerable, interrelated activities. The magnificence of the universe crystallized for Berry in that meadow.

The meadow, with its differentiated articulations of life, its creatures who possess an inner spontaneity and wildness, offers Berry an opportunity for communion, and therefore access to the numinous and mysterious source from which it comes. For years Berry returned to this meadow epiphany as the quintessence of his Weltanschauung, personal vocation, and ethical framework: "Whatever preserves and enhances this meadow in the natural cycles of its transformation is good; whatever opposes this meadow or negates it is not good."[60]

This incident epitomizes the importance of personal experiences and of one's connection to her local bioregion in the cosmic common good. Theory devoid of tangible and embodied encounters with the living Earth cannot motivate true change. Berry conjectures that a viable future for the planet will result not from scientific or philosophical insights or from innovative socioeconomic proposals, but rather because of a "renewed presence to some numinous presence manifested in the wonderworld about us."[61] In viewing the May lilies blooming in this meadow, Berry experienced an intensely personal encounter with the local cosmos. This entry into life-changing and life-affirming mystery, embodied in and pulsating through nonhuman nature, is at the heart of the cosmic common good because it underscores our vital participation in the "wonderworld" of the cosmos as integral to our own fulfillment. The cure for alienation is to return to the Earth and to the cosmos and to read the cosmic story as one's own.

III.6. The Threefold Nature of Creatures and a Catholic Cosmic Common Good

Berry's description of a threefold nature shared by all creatures points to a cosmocentric cosmic common good, pervaded by the mystery of God and yet radically oriented to the mystery that is the universe itself. Each creature has its own uniqueness, depth, and place in the cosmos. The threefold dimension to creatures alerts us to see them as independent from us, with their own individuation and self-motivated goals. In addition, each creature is meant for communion with the others. In communion with them, humans understand their true cosmocentric identity. Knowing this threefold structure, Catholics may be drawn into greater relationship with the cosmos and the numinous source that pervades it.

Christians may perceive nonhumans as diverse articulations of the Creator; in recognizing their wildness, Christians appreciate their independent existence and their belonging to God; and in communing with them, Christians thus better encounter the Creator. In a non-theistic framework, these three principles continue to stress humanity's cosmic identity and the intrinsic and cosmocentric value of all creatures. When humans are open to nature's inherent differentiation and subjectivity, they can recognize these dimensions within themselves as well.

IV. Implications for a Catholic Cosmic Common Good

Berry's theology of creation contributes to a Catholic cosmic common good by stressing a cosmocentric valuation of creation and creatures, and by highlighting the autonomy and goodness of creation for itself. While Augustine and Aquinas demonstrate the possibility of a cosmic common good in classical theologies of creation, it must be acknowledged that their cosmic vision is undoubtedly eclipsed by their overwhelming theocentrism. Their theological ethic would be close to a Creator-centrism, rather than a creatio-centrism,[62] or even an anthropic Creatorcentrism, where the goodness of creation exists to support humans in their journey to God. Truly, anthropocentrism never really departs from Augustine or Aquinas.

By contrast, Berry balances a patristic theology of creation by directing us repeatedly to the cosmos on its own terms. Though I maintain that it is thoroughly rooted in an understated theocentrism, the thrust of his vision is to return our gaze to the cosmos itself. While Berry does not employ the category of a cosmic common good, he clearly emphasizes an appreciation of humanity's "cosmocentric identity."[63] In the meadow, he discerns a maxim that whatever supports the common good of this meadow is good, and he expresses well the holism of the cosmic common good: "The basic ethical norm is the well-being of the comprehensive community and the attainment of human well-being within that community."[64] In Berry's prose, one senses a pulsating energy, the wild yet disciplined creativity that courses through the universe. Though the "motionless motion" of the Spirit that Augustine describes is not denied, in Berry the real and independent motion of the universe comes to the fore. He demonstrates the religious power of a worldview focused on the cosmic common good, as evinced in his own mystical experience of the meadow.

The themes of the cosmic story and of the threefold nature of the cosmos provide further grounding for and expand the features of a Catholic cosmic common good such as creaturely dignity, cosmic participation, and bioregional subsidiarity. The story of an emergent, creative, and self-celebratory cosmos, stemming from discoveries by modern science, discloses the pressing need for a cosmocentric story that contextualizes human endeavors. Berry thus highlights the narrative dimension of the cosmic common good. Additionally, the tripartite structure of each creature and of the cosmos as a whole offers a variant to concepts articulated in a classical theology of creation and helps to return focus to the intrinsic goodness, beauty, and activity of creatures.

The cosmic story, the universe's three basic organizing principles, and in particular wildness also shed light on the five variegated dimensions of creation:

1. The goodness of the cosmos as a whole derives clearly from the fact that it has one evolving and developing cosmic story, and the drive to communion creates one cosmic community. Berry's conception of the universe as a "communion of beings" echoes Pope Francis's understanding of creation as "a reality illuminated by the love which calls us together into universal communion."[65]

2. Wildness speaks to the importance of wild and undomesticated nature, and the ability of those creatures and those habitats to pursue their inner spontaneities.

3. Wildness also provides a context for understanding the power for destruction that we encounter. Berry has been criticized for being too sanguine about the suffering that creatures endure, yet Berry clearly acknowledges the violence that a cosmogenesis entails. He warns against a romantic and rosy view of the natural world, recognizing dangerous forces that can frighten and threaten, but whose overall purpose is to strengthen life.[66] The violence of destructive nature may call for some kind of redemption in the future, but it should never mask the undeniable beauty of the universe that we are called to celebrate.

4. Even domesticated nature and tamed creatures possess wildness and subjective depths that exceed us, even as we control their destiny. This tree, this park, this pigeon: they are all part of the cosmic story that is our own story; they are witnesses to the universe's drive to differentiation; they possess their own subjectivity; and they are made for communion. We must continue to reverence and allow the component of wildness, even in domesticated nature, lest we forget that these creatures possess their own inner spontaneities.

5. Degraded nature reveals that humans are interrupting and even counteracting the cosmic story of cosmogenesis; we are hindering each creature's internal drive for self-expression; we are limiting the universe's drive toward creative differentiation; and we are thus obscuring the potential for communion, for ourselves and for other creatures. By the same token, those who exert effort to rehabilitate the natural world by cleaning up a mountaintop or removing debris from a river are entering a new chapter into the cosmic story and are furthering the possibilities of an Ecozoic era. They enact their communion with other creatures by attending to their needs and by striving to enable their unique spontaneities to reemerge, even when such efforts fail. The

cosmic story and the threefold principles provide a cosmocentric ground for liberating and restoring nature to its own interior wholeness, as parts of an emergent and creative cosmic drive to differentiation, and as opportunities calling us to deeper communion.

The classical and contemporary Catholic understandings of creation as I have presented them here form bookends: Augustine and Aquinas emphasize the thoroughly theocentric aspect of the cosmic common good while upholding the goodness of creation. Berry interprets the evolutionary sciences to offer a thoroughly cosmocentric cosmic common good that acknowledges the numinous origin of all existence but does not allow this to overshadow and eclipse the goodness that inheres in creatures and creation directly. Together they further the cosmocentric orientation of the cosmic common good: a framework rooted in the divine that emphasizes the intrinsic and instrumental valuation of all creatures and the importance of relationship between the parts and the wholes they comprise, and that situates humanity as a privileged actor capable of furthering this common good.

5

Earth Solidarity

TWO RELATED TERMS of Catholic social thought are integral to a full understanding of a Catholic cosmic common good because they further and promote the moral vision of the common good: solidarity and rights. Expanding solidarity and rights to become Earth solidarity and Earth rights helps illuminate the questions: How might humans love the cosmos and feel and act like members of a cosmic community? What do humans owe to the cosmos, and in particular to Earth, as a matter of justice?

Earth solidarity deepens humanity's participation in the cosmic common good by drawing in other key ethical categories such as virtue, character, emotions, and actions. While the cosmic common good provides a template and context for understanding our role in creation and the good of nonhuman creatures, the virtue of Earth solidarity taps into the heart of what actually drives decision-making and filters our experience. When we encounter an instantiation of a flourishing Earth community, even if only in images, Earth solidarity arises as a positive sense of communion and relationship. It is the awe, wonder, and quietude that overwhelmed Berry in the meadow near his home. In this way, Earth solidarity celebrates the good of other creatures and our common cosmic belonging, and as the virtue intensifies it leads to concrete and long-term actions, both personal and structural, that embody the cosmic common good. Earth solidarity also arises as the feelings of anger or disgust at the revelation of an imperiled Earth and the unnecessary degradation of life. Here Earth solidarity points to the lost possibilities of communion, to the injustice of both nonhuman and human suffering because of negligence and avoidable choices, and the determination to address that injustice to whatever extent possible.

This chapter will begin with a brief overview of the theological and ethical significance of solidarity and its relationship to the common good as it is found in Catholic social thought, focusing in particular on four features of solidarity as a virtue in St. John Paul II. Then, I outline some of the levels and dimensions of Earth solidarity.

I. *Solidarity in Catholic Social Thought*

Like Catholic social thought in general, the earliest usages of solidarity were meant to encourage people to see themselves as members of a larger community and to attend to their neighbors in need. Solidarity highlights the moral requirement to commit oneself to the dignity of human persons and to the one human family, and in its earliest forms is "close in meaning to friendship and social charity."[1] Solidarity stands in opposition to conceptions of the human person that deny her essentially social nature or that privilege individual happiness over the common good: "The ever-present temptation to individualism and greed must be countered by a determined movement toward solidarity."[2] At the same time, solidarity opposes all forms of collectivism in which the individual part is sacrificed for the good of the whole because solidarity represents a commitment to both the inherent dignity of each human person and the value of our global human interdependence. Solidarity, therefore, becomes a vital corollary to the common good because it actively supports and promotes people to work for the common good, while also affirming the essential dignity of each individual person. Solidarity emerges as a unique combination of justice and charity, binding people together into a single family in love, and attentive to the injustices that hinder that union.

I.1. The Preferential Option for the Poor

Another significant principle of Catholic social thought that enhances solidarity is the preferential option for the poor. While concern for the poor is a theme that pervades the scriptures, the ministry of Jesus, and countless theologians and spiritual writers, the exact phrase "preferential option for the poor" was used first by the Bishops' Conference of Latin America in 1979.[3] The bishops in these countries observed with distress the sharp and extreme gap between the rich and the poor that was hindering the Church's ministry to their people. Thus the "preferential option for the poor" argues that utmost concern must be shown to those in the greatest need. It certainly does not indicate that the rich are less loved by God or that their interests should be sacrificed in order to benefit the poor. Rather, the preferential option for the poor stands as an intensification of the principle of solidarity: economic and political systems, at every level of society reaching up to the entire international order, should be assessed based on their effects on the poor. As the US Bishops describe it, "we are challenged to make a fundamental 'option for the poor'—to speak for the voiceless, to defend the defenseless, to assess life styles, policies, and social institutions in terms of their impact on the poor.[4] Pope Francis affirms that "the principle of the common good immediately becomes, logically and inevitably, a summons to solidarity and a preferential option for the poorest of our brothers and sisters."[5] Thus the preferential option for the poor becomes a way of focusing the ethical impetus of solidarity, ensuring that commitment to the dignity of the human person is addressed in the lives of those for whom that dignity is most compromised. It names the Christian commitment to include in the common good those most marginalized and excluded. Moreover, it can represent the Church's hallmark contribution to discussions of economic and political decisions at every level.

The preferential option for the poor contends that, first, the poor should receive the priority of attention from society because they are the test case for determining how well a society is actually fulfilling the conditions of the common good. Second, the marginalized must not only be included in the common good, but their own moral agency must be respected, and their voices and perspectives must be heard. The option does not exclude other groups, but it privileges the marginalized in determining how well the common good is actually being realized. The option for the poor then is more than just concern for the poor; it strives to enable their full and equal participation in the common good. It recognizes them not as passive recipients of aid but as agents whose active contributions to the common good must be supported and enhanced.

I.2. Dynamics of Solidarity

Catholic social thought articulates solidarity in multifaceted ways: as a fact, an attitude, a duty, a principle, and finally culminating in the understanding of solidarity as a social virtue. First, solidarity can represent simply the law of human interdependence. This acknowledges the basic bondedness of the human family, and in a way recognizes what the common good affirms: the human person has a social nature, meaning that we are communally oriented and meant to live in interdependent relationships with other human beings. Two other factors make solidarity more acute. First is the fact that the interdependence of peoples and nations is growing. Second, in conjunction with the preferential option for the poor, solidarity recognizes the growing gap between the rich and poor. This initially arose as a concern about the gap between rich and poor within nations, and then more broadly as global divides between richer and poorer nations, the developed and developing worlds, the global North and South. Increasing connectedness between nations has both positive and negative aspects, and so Catholic leaders employed solidarity as a way of combatting ingrained cultural and human tendencies that militate against the recognition of our common humanity. Like the focus on the common good, solidarity responds to the new reality of global interdependence by expanding people's vision beyond one's nation-state to include the entire human family, predicated on our common and equal human dignity. Solidarity as reality expresses a metaphysical law of humanity's common origin in God, their social nature, their equality in being made in the image and likeness of God, and the need to honor this fact in a moment of increasing international interdependence and injustice. Solidarity was therefore meant to strengthen appeals to the common good and to awaken people to their responsibility to combat social injustices, focusing especially on the gap between rich and poor, first within developed nations and next between developed and developing nations.

The second dimension of solidarity is as an attitude, which arises as an awareness and positive appreciation of one's relationship to the whole and the well-being of other human beings. While the common good stresses the interdependent nature of part to whole and the essentially communal nature of flourishing, this basic fact of existence does not necessarily lead each part to actually choose actions that advance the good of the whole. Aquinas and Augustine presumed that each part, when acting appropriately, naturally seeks the common good above its own particular good, but of course this represents more the ideal than the reality. Solidarity as an attitude recognizes that someone could affirm and support increasing interconnections among peoples but do so purely out of self-interest and with no regard for the common good. Social interdependence does not "rule out domination or exploitation."[6] Thus John Paul II observes and approves the growing awareness of human dignity and "the conviction [that] is growing of a radical interdependence and consequently of the need for a solidarity which will take interdependence and transfer it to the moral plane."[7]

The attitude of solidarity names our feelings and emotional experiences as we recognize human interdependence and the good of others as a positive value to be pursued and maintained. Solidarity affirms the basic vision of the common good, namely that we do not realize our full human dignity unless we share our lives with others. Solidarity as attitude requires people to "cultivate a greater awareness that they are debtors of the society of which they have become part."[8] Solidarity emerges as the attitude that accompanies the planetary common good of the one human family. Thus solidarity points not only toward changes in economic and political structures, but more importantly to a transformation of people's attitudes. International programs may not persist over time, but a change in people's understanding can be enduring.[9]

Third, solidarity is configured as a moral duty and a set of required actions, or prescriptive commands, that are especially incumbent on the wealthy and powerful to extend themselves to those who lack resources and power, due to the basic dignity of all. Solidarity leads us to support projects and endeavors that enhance the common good of all but that do not necessarily benefit us directly. Paul VI, for example, points to the problems of underdevelopment, such as hunger and disease, as not merely problems of the poor but problems for all of humanity. For Paul VI, solidarity is a subset of justice and therefore is incumbent on all: "The duty of promoting human solidarity falls on the shoulders of all nations."[10] Paul VI defines mutual solidarity as "the aid that the richer nations must give to developing nations," which, together with social justice and universal charity, form part of the moral obligations of being a wealthy nation.[11]

Fourth, solidarity becomes a moral principle or general ethical criterion when we apply solidarity to existing national and international policies, assessing whether and to what extent they fulfill our duties to human beings. The US Bishops suggest that solidarity should be a mark of any authentic economic policy because "alleviating poverty will require fundamental changes in social and economic structures that perpetuate glaring inequalities and cut off millions of citizens from full participation in the economic and social life of the nation."[12] Solidarity strives to guide the moral response to increasing globalization and interdependence, and to the struggles of peoples and nations in search of development, an improved economic lifestyle, and peace.

Fifth and most important, solidarity is a virtue, which in many ways provides the entire context for understanding solidarity as an attitude, duty, and principle. To draw out various aspects of solidarity as a virtue, I focus especially on John Paul II's *Sollicitudo Rei Socialis*. Highlighting the connection between individual goods and the common good, John Paul II extrapolates this theme and offers his famous and now classic definition of the virtue of solidarity as a commitment to the common good of all:

> [I see] the positive and moral value of the growing awareness of interdependence among individuals and nations. . . . [M]en and women in various parts of the world feel personally affected by the injustices and violations of human rights committed in distant countries. . . . Our human interdependence is not a feeling of vague compassion or shallow distress at the misfortunes of so many people, both near and far. On the contrary, it is a firm and persevering determination to commit oneself to the common good; that is to say to the good of all and of each individual, because we are all really responsible for all.[13]

In this and other passages, John Paul II points to solidarity as a social, perceptual, and theological virtue.

II. The Virtue of Solidarity
II.1. Solidarity as a Virtue

First and most importantly, John Paul II establishes solidarity as a virtue and the comprehensive context for understanding solidarity as an attitude and a duty. John Paul II connects solidarity as attitude—the "growing awareness of interdependence" and concern for those who are ill effected by injustices—with solidarity as a virtue, the "firm and preserving determination to commit oneself." Virtues encompass, synthesize, and expand the meaning of attitudes, duties, and moral principles. In the Thomistic and therefore Aristotelian tradition upon which Catholic social thought is based, a virtue is a disposition or orientation that inclines one to do that which is good. Virtues become habituated through actions and in time become a second nature.[14] A virtue thus engages not only what we do and how we feel, but the character of who we are. Kevin Doran remarks that solidarity is meant to have a transformative role, sparking the individual's growth as a moral agent: "The first end of solidarity is the goodness of the person who acts."[15]

Virtues incline an agent in two ways: first, to engage in specific, concrete acts that are good; and second, to experience certain affective and emotional states that correspond to these actions. Solidarity as a virtue begins with our emotional responses to the concrete conditions of others; this helps form an interior disposition that leads to discrete actions. Emotions and actions together contribute to shape the kinds of people we become. This becomes prominent in the phrase "commit *oneself.*" What is primarily being offered here is oneself, the entirety of the person who enacts solidarity. For this reason, Meghan Clark acknowledges that not all acts of aid to others are necessarily acts of solidarity. To habituate an agent in the virtue of solidarity, an act must be done with the intention of promoting the other's participation in the common good. Acts of solidarity ought to be formed by the perspective of the one we aim to help, in the willingness to be equally present to the other in this act.[16]

By uniting action and affect, solidarity helps to channel and regulate people's feelings of sorrow at witnessing the suffering and injustice of people, even people whom one has never met. By itself the attitude of solidarity—the awareness of interdependence and the sorrow at injustice—is insufficient. Thus solidarity, which affirms our human interdependence, is not "a feeling of vague compassion or shallow distress." Instead, it directs an agent to commit herself to the common good. As a "firm and persevering determination," solidarity becomes a "second nature" that inclines people to act for the common good and to commit oneself to others, regardless of how feelings may wax and wane. It is one thing to feel overwhelming sorrow at others' misfortune and make a donation; it is another to sustain efforts for those persons and commit oneself to them as equals over many months and years, when that initial feeling has perhaps dwindled. In turn, by engaging in acts of solidarity, one's initial "vague feeling of distress" might become something profound and enduring, paired with a similarly capacious sense of joy when another's distress is relieved. Thomas Massaro, S.J., summarizes, "Solidarity begins as an inner attitude and, when it has fully taken root within a person, expresses itself through numerous external activities that demonstrate a person's commitment to the well-being of others."[17]

II.2. Solidarity as a Social Virtue

Second, John Paul II introduces solidarity as a specifically *social* virtue. All virtues aim at particular ends, and so the virtue of solidarity is aimed toward the common good and to the capacity of each person to participate in the common good.[18] Solidarity inculcates in agents a sense of social responsibility and develops one's personal connection to the common good and to other members of that community. It affirms one's membership in the global human family and reminds us that one's global citizenship connects her to every human being on Earth. In addition to our moral responsibilities toward God, self, and neighbor, solidarity adds our duties to the society and world of which one is a part. Like the common good, solidarity in Catholic social thought represents a challenge to Western notions of individualism, which at times threaten to extricate individuals from society and to diminish each person's duty to the common good.

Solidarity emphasizes an essentially personal component to the common good. It entails the feeling of being personally affected by the injustices suffered by others and the personal commitment to end that misery by contributing to the common good and fulfilling the innate bonds of relatedness between all human beings. Solidarity directs the individual to see how her role in social systems might bring about greater justice and flourishing for others, especially if she is in the position to bring about change. Solidarity is a call not only to offer financial support, but also to enact one's common belonging to a greater common good by offering oneself in relationship to others. Meghan Clark therefore perceptively distinguishes solidarity from the traditional virtue of justice, which seeks to render to each what she is owed.[19] By contrast, solidarity impels a person to seek the full participation of others in the common good in light of their shared belonging and the potential for mutual relationship. Solidarity recognizes not only that I am a part of a larger whole, or that my flourishing is bound up with others, but that the common good is composed of my relationships to others. Thus my own rights and self-identity are bound up with the capacity of others to fulfill their own fundamental right of participation. In this way solidarity becomes an integral aspect of the common good itself.[20]

Like any virtue, the virtue of solidarity would be positioned between two opposing vices, which represent either an excess or a deficiency of some kind. Since solidarity is the commitment to the interdependent and communal identity of the person and the common good of the whole human family, Meghan Clark positions the virtue of solidarity between the social vices of excessive individualism and collectivism. The extreme of deficiency is the vice of excessive individualism, or the notion that humans begin as atomized monads who may selectively choose to enter into social relationships. The extreme of excess is the vice of collectivism, which allows some individuals to be sacrificed for the greatest happiness of the most people.[21] Solidarity holds in tension the dignity of the person and the dignity of the common good.

Given the principle of subsidiarity, which focuses on the intermediate social associations that help to constitute the common good, solidarity may characterize not only individuals but also institutions and whole communities. Since human beings are essentially communal and participate in various kinds of communities and institutions, these communities in turn shape the personal inclinations of their participants. Daniel Daly contrasts "structures of virtue" and "structures of vice" to argue that people can be morally shaped by the groups to which they belong. Vices range in a continuum, from individuals with distorted worldviews and an insufficient view of the human person, building up to larger communities and structures that institutionalize that deficiency or excess in some way. Structures of vice are "the social structures that in some way consistently function to prevent the human good, the common good, and human happiness, and the socially rooted moral habits willingly internalized by moral agents that consistently prescribe sinful human acts, and produce human unhappiness."[22] Solidarity requires not only personal practices but structures of virtue, institutions that pursue solidarity and form persons and communities by reorienting them to the common good.[23] For Clark, the promotion of participation and human rights is the central way that a community can cultivate the virtue of solidarity.[24]

II.3. Solidarity as a Perceptual Virtue

In another section describing solidarity, John Paul II suggests two other aspects of solidarity. He writes,

> Solidarity helps to see the "other"—whether a person, people or nation—not just as some kind of instrument, with a work capacity and physical strength to be exploited at low cost and then discarded when no longer useful, but as our "neighbor," a "helper" (cf. Gen. 2:18–20), to be made a sharer, on a par with ourselves, in the banquet of life to which all are equally invited by God. Hence the importance of reawakening the religious awareness of individuals and peoples . . . [so that] the exploitation, oppression and annihilation of others are excluded.[25]

The third dimension of solidarity that arises in this passage is its *perceptual* quality. Virtues not only incline us to feel and to act, but they may also incline us to notice and observe, and to see reality more clearly. Virtues shape our vision of what is true and good. Thus John Paul II extols the "growing awareness" of interdependence and pairs this with the "feelings of distress" that many experience.

Solidarity shapes one's perception of global justice and orients someone to be ready to recognize certain indignities as injustices, rather than merely the ineluctable result of unalterable political and economic realities. It helps us to "see the other" more clearly, and this includes oneself, other human beings, and the common good to which all belong. By attending to these feelings of distress, and by valuing them as morally praiseworthy, solidarity continues to enhance one's growing awareness of her membership in the one human family. Then, one is empowered to witness to those personal and structural choices that would better advance the common good.

II.4. Solidarity as a Theological Virtue

Fourth, John Paul II hints at the ways in which solidarity can function as a distinctively *theological* virtue, leading persons to perceive the other with a religious awareness of her dignity and goodness, gifted by God. In addition to seeing the other as a fellow member of the global common good and not just as a mere instrument, solidarity can also reawaken our religious awareness of others and reveal them as "neighbors" and "helpers" and "sharers" in the banquet God intends for all. Thus solidarity is a theological virtue in the sense that it leads us back to God, the divine source of every person. In *Centesimus Annus*, John Paul II offers a parallel vision of how solidarity is linked both to the capacity to esteem the inherent value of others and to our relationship to God: "When man does not recognize in himself and in others the value and grandeur of the human person, he effectively deprives himself of the possibility of benefitting from his humanity and of entering into that relationship of solidarity and communion with others for which God created him."[26] The "other," he points out, is not merely a source of work capacity or a market for consumer goods. The other is a human being, a neighbor with whom one can be in relationship. Thus the virtue of solidarity affects and forms our affective experiences, our actions, our perceptions, and our religious awareness of the dignity of the other with whom we live in community, in a global human family. It might enlighten our intellect and enable us to see the neighbor—even a neighbor who lives halfway around the world and whom we will never encounter directly—in her fullest truth, as a child of God.

In a way, the virtue of solidarity must also be linked to the theological virtue of hope. In examining the role of the Solidarity movement in Poland, Gerald Beyer remarks that an ethic of solidarity is an ethic of hope that "recognizes the gravity of human evil" but enables individuals to persevere in the face of suffering and to act for the common good.[27] Beyer acknowledges that it is difficult to achieve solidarity at the highest levels of policy and institution,[28] and he concedes that this ethic may not truly occur outside crisis situations (dictators, natural disasters).[29]

Solidarity commits persons to act on behalf of the dignity of the other, even when those actions may not yield the result one hopes for. To embody solidarity in deed, even in the midst of a crisis and with no certainty that one will succeed, expresses the conviction that the other, whose participation I seek to enable, has inherent dignity and that we belong to a greater whole.

Thus solidarity can be configured as a fact, an attitude, a duty, a principle, culminating in its formulation as the virtue oriented to the common good that disposes its possessor to the good of the whole of which she is a part, and which impacts the agent's character, actions, affections, social identity, perceptions, and religious awareness of the world. Given the framework of the cosmic common good, I next explore how these features of solidarity must expand to become Earth solidarity.

III. Solidarity Expanded: Earth Solidarity
III.1. Earth Solidarity: Foci

Earth solidarity has three foci: (1) all human beings, and in a particular way those most affected by environmental degradation; (2) all plant and animal species; and (3) the ecosystems themselves that sustain and support a diversity of creatures. While solidarity can be enacted on behalf of any member of the Earth community, Earth solidarity entails a special focus on those most imperiled.

Though the cosmic and planetary common good demands solidarity with non-human animals and the ecosystems we all rely on for life, Earth solidarity legitimately sets its first focus on human beings. Earth solidarity acknowledges and affirms differentiated creaturely dignity and the elevated status of human dignity and so differing levels of injustice for threatened creatures. I envision all forms of solidarity among and on behalf of humans, such as concern for violations of human dignity due to an authoritarian government, as types of Earth solidarity. Yet in a particular way my ecological expansion of solidarity means that Earth solidarity with human beings must focus on the poor and vulnerable who suffer most from human-induced ecological disaster. In conjunction with the preferential option for the poor, Earth solidarity points us to the injustices that humans face as a result of a degraded and imperiled Earth. The US Bishops elaborate, "Working for the common good requires us to promote the flourishing of all human life and all of God's creation. In a special way, the common good requires solidarity with the poor who are often without the resources to face many problems, including the potential impacts of climate change."[30] The various effects of climate change—including flooding, more intense storms, a widening range of infectious diseases, and so on—will disproportionately affect indigenous populations[31] and those in poverty,[32] and solidarity alongside the preferential option for the poor demands a response. Solidarity with the Earth must therefore include and accentuate the preferential option for humans as a critical component of a full Earth solidarity. Earth solidarity must not stop, however, at addressing only ecological harm that impacts fellow human beings, whether those presently threatened or future generations.

Earth solidarity that truly responds to the cosmic common good includes two other foci: solidarity with plants and animals, both as individuals and as species; and solidarity with the ecosystems they inhabit. At times, tensions between and among these three foci are inevitable. Some may even juxtapose them, citing rising human population and consumption as an impetus to abandon solidarity with humans and instead defend only nonhuman creatures and their ecosystems. By contrast, Earth solidarity demands a commitment to the well-being of individual creatures and species, human and nonhuman, and in particular of those most distressed or at risk from human activity. Feelings of anguish at the plight of a single animal or tree, or at the prospects of survival for a species, are the initial stirrings of the virtue of Earth solidarity, and they deserve to be cultivated into the kinds of dispositions that shape humanity's planetary and cosmic identity. In addition, Earth solidarity must also include a concern for ecosystems. Just as the cosmic common good seeks not only the flourishing of individual dignified parts but also the flourishing of the wholes of which they are a part, Earth solidarity must display an overriding concern for wholes, for the ecosystems upon which creatures rely for survival. Pope Francis explains, "each organism, as a creature of God, is good and admirable in itself; the same is true of the harmonious ensemble of organisms existing in a defined space and functioning as a system."[33] Earth solidarity calls humans to develop solidarity for the Earth in all these dimensions—humans, plants, animals, and whole ecosystems—in service of the planetary and cosmic common good. Distress at the injustice of ecosystem contamination due to pollution, or dwindling biodiversity and the struggles of plants and animals to survive amidst rampant habitat loss, or those human communities endangered by rising sea levels and intensifying drought and disease all exemplify Earth solidarity and represent the determination to work for the flourishing of fellow members of a cosmic common good.

Earth solidarity is also a reminder that acting in solidarity with the Earth is an act of solidarity with the entire cosmos. Expressing solidarity with nonhumans testifies to the inherent goodness of a diversity of creatures and to the bonds that sustain them. If there are any other planets on which living and perhaps self-conscious creatures dwell, Earth solidarity witnesses to their goodness and acknowledges their contribution to the cosmic common good. Since we have no evidence of anything even remotely approaching the florescence of life on Earth, this only heightens the cosmic import of Earth solidarity.

Various ecological disasters demonstrate the potential for Earth solidarity and its three foci. Solidarity can rightly be directed not only to impacted human populations, but also to individual creatures, populations of species, and to their ecosystems as a whole. For example, following the Deepwater Horizon spill in the Gulf of Mexico in 2010, popular anger at British Petroleum focused not only on the impact on local economies or the threat to species of animals but also on the Gulf as a whole and its ability to sustain diverse forms of life. Pictures abounded of the suffering, including empty tourist communities and fishers waiting listlessly on the docks; dead fish floating in the water; birds covered in oil; and aerial shots of the Gulf waters with miles-long trails of oil. These images intermingled, stoking indignation and resentment on behalf of all who were affected, human and nonhuman alike. Public concern for the Gulf and the creatures who depend on it represented a kind of implicit Earth solidarity. Moved by compassion at the suffering induced by this spill, thousands of Americans made donations, volunteered to clean beaches, spent hours trying to wash oil off wildlife, and consoled the people living nearby, all in related attempts to protect the Gulf. In one notable example, one organization collected over 400,000 pounds of animal fur and human hair in order to make natural, homemade booms to absorb the oil.[34] Whatever the efficacy of this endeavor, it was clearly motivated to respond to this disaster on multiple levels. Various dimensions of Earth solidarity emerge here: a sense of crisis, feelings of anger and distress, moving people to act and commit their resources and energy, not only on behalf of people, but to the entire common good of the ecosystem and its various interdependent creatures.

IV. Dimensions of Earth Solidarity

Drawing on the multifaceted nature of solidarity, I propose a range of various dimensions of Earth solidarity:

IV.1. Earth Solidarity as Reality, Attitude, Moral Duty, and Principle

While interdependence among humans is steadily growing and intensifying, in fact creaturely interdependence has been a cosmic fact from the beginning. Our evolutionary relatedness and ecological interdependence are the bedrock of human existence and of any living creature, making Earth solidarity a natural and fitting corollary to the cosmic common good. Indeed, Earthly interdependence is truly the more prior and foundational reality, the ground that makes human interdependence possible.

At the same time, Catholic social thought notes not only the growing interdependence of nations but also distressing levels of planetary inequality and injustice, of atmospheric and oceanic perturbations that inordinately and unequally affect certain species and populations. The distress of an imperiled Earth has already given rise to feelings of distress at Earth's suffering and has awoken stirrings of the attitude of Earth solidarity. In addition, everyday actions on behalf of the imperiled Earth are increasingly perceived as a moral duty, rather than supererogatory; and Earth solidarity constitutes a potent principle to judge national and international structures, most notably the failure of the international community to adopt and enforce adequate regulations to address climate change.

IV.2. Earth Solidarity as Virtue

Solidarity is foremost a virtue that channels into action our feelings of compassion at the suffering of others with whom we are interdependent. As John Paul II realized, a simple recognition of interdependence does not necessarily lead to a transformation of moral choices. Solidarity with the Earth and especially its most threatened species must not be some "feeling of vague compassion or shallow distress at the misfortunes" of nonhumankind, such as when we see the extent of climate change, oil spills, ocean acidification, and other dynamics that endanger and may extinguish entire species and ecosystems. Rather, it must be marked by a "firm and persevering determination" to preserve the various sensitive and interconnected ecosystems that support manifold species, on behalf of the planetary and cosmic common good. Pope Francis confirms that in providing an overview of global ecological problems, "our goal is not to amass information or to satisfy curiosity, but rather to become painfully aware, to dare to turn what is happening to the world into our own personal suffering and thus to discover what each of us can do about it."[35] The virtue of Earth solidarity converts our distress into concrete moral action for the good of nonhuman nature and for the planetary and cosmic common good.

Given our planetary and cosmic interdependence, Earth solidarity is a fitting social virtue to describe humanity's participation in the cosmic common good. Solidarity corresponds to the part-whole relationship, to our being members of and participants in various and encompassing wholes. As a result, solidarity has three ends. First, like any virtue, solidarity aims at the good of the agent and the transformation of one's own character and identity as a member of the whole. Earth solidarity affirms the human person as part of and belonging to the planetary common good. It requires a personal commitment, a dedication of self to be in relationship with other nonhumans in appropriate ways.

Second, solidarity aims at the well-being of another part, especially those parts suffering an injustice. The other is not conceived of as simply the passive recipient of aid, but as one with whom we are called to be in relationship. In the case of solidarity with humans, it is based on equal dignity and the intention for the other to participate fully in the human common good, which includes the full range of economic, social, and political dimensions; solidarity with nonhumans has a similar structure, based on the shared substratum of creaturely dignity and aimed at the other's full participation in the cosmic common good.

Third, the ultimate end of solidarity is the whole, to which oneself and the other belong. The end of Earth solidarity is the participation of all creatures and their ability to contribute to the cosmic common good. Here our explorations in the doctrine of creation via Augustine, Aquinas, and Berry are useful: solidarity leads us to promote creatures pursuing and having the opportunity to fulfill their innate inclinations; to allow them to rest in the activity that their nature orients them to; to allow the innate cosmic processes of differentiation and subjectivity to unfold, in order that the impulse to communion can be realized.

Earth solidarity should be considered the fullness of the virtue of solidarity, rather than a mere partner virtue. Earth solidarity as an ecological virtue highlights the fact that commitment to the Earth is done in light of humanity's interdependence with the Earth but for the benefit of nonhuman nature. Earth solidarity contributes to the growing field of ecological virtue[36] because, unlike other ecologically focused virtues such as temperance or justice, Earth solidarity corresponds to the essentially social and communal nature of human action and to our membership as part of a broader community. It encourages us to see ourselves as parts of a greater whole and therefore to affirm our essential belonging to a cosmic common good, and to enact those relationships with justice.

There are two complementary ways of positioning the virtue of Earth solidarity between opposing ecological vices, and they regard the perception of the moral scope of the common good and of humanity's power and responsibility toward the Earth. Solidarity must avoid the vice of deficiency, which refuses to acknowledge that interdependence means including nonhumans in the common good. This is found in ethical anthropocentrism, a form of excessive individualism that evaluates nonhuman creatures according to a strict utilitarian calculus.[37] Similarly, solidarity must repudiate the "dominant technocratic paradigm"[38] which presumes that humans can adequately control nonhuman creatures or planetary systems through our abundant technological prowess. Solidarity must also avoid the vice of excess, which views the human person as so radically integrated into creation that it fails to recognize differing levels of creaturely dignity. This could be a nature adoration that prosecutes the human person for participating in the evolutionary dynamics of the cosmic common good and disallows any instrumental or consumptive use of nonhumans.[39] I recognize both extremes as problematic, but I also identify the former as much more prevalent and pernicious than the latter. Hence my articulation of Earth solidarity moves closer to this pole.

Instead, the properly ordered virtue of Earth solidarity must be guided by the virtue of prudence, or right reason, which over time comes to an understanding of what truly constitutes the flourishing of the planetary common good. Earth solidarity allows the exercise of human responsibility, but it does not presume to trust in humanity's superior skill and wisdom in managing nature. On the contrary, it acknowledges the interdependence of humans with the Earth and sees that the good of plants and animals requires the responsible action of human beings who, by and large, have demonstrated a paucity of prudential judgment and humility when it comes to assessing the ecological impact of economic, political, and social decisions. The vice of deficient concern for nonhumankind represents the overwhelming threat, while the vice of excess must be acknowledged but not exaggerated.

As a virtue, solidarity leads to practices that embody these norms in all dimensions of human life. Earth solidarity must be personal and communal: "Social problems must be addressed by community networks and not simply by the sum of individual good deeds. . . . The ecological conversion needed to bring about lasting change is also a community conversion."[40] This entails acts that support a reduced human consumption and extraction of goods from nature; acts that support structures of virtue that preserve and safeguard creatures and the habitats they need to exist and pursue natural inclinations; acts of frugality and satiety that can temper human consumption and leave room for other creatures to exist. Though solidarity will not reverse the tide of climate change or many of the other ecological threats facing Earth, it offers the impetus to act on behalf of those people and species whose immediate survival depends greatly on human intervention.

Earth solidarity means making choices for the good of all biota and abiota, as well as the ecosystems they inhabit, now and into the future. In her own formulation of Earth solidarity, Jame Schaefer persuasively voices the worldview shift it signifies, corresponding to the shift that recognizes the cosmic common good. Earth solidarity, Schaefer contends, moves us from an anthropocentric and instrumental view of nonhuman creatures and ecosystems to valuing them intrinsically as fellow "contributors to and benefactors of a life-sustaining climate."[41] Earth solidarity expresses a geocentric and cosmocentric appreciation of creaturely dignity. As a virtue, it works in collaboration with other virtues and should thus guide us to think more intelligently, decide more prudently, act more justly, consume goods more moderately, and live more courageously in ways that contribute to the planetary common good.

IV.3. Earth Solidarity as a Preferential Option for the Poor

Earth solidarity indicates a similar expansion of the principle of the preferential option for the poor. The poor are understood to be those who are marginalized, who are excluded from participation in the cosmic common good. Similarly, Earth solidarity represents a moral commitment to the cosmic participation of every creature. As Schaefer argues, extending the preferential option for the poor "demonstrates our inseparability from them in this life," and so she advocates a "preference for all poor and vulnerable members of the Earth Community."[42] Pope Francis echoes Earth solidarity when he contends that "a true ecological approach always becomes a social approach; it must integrate questions of justice in debates on the environment, so as to hear both the cry of the earth and the cry of the poor."[43] Again, drawing on Augustine, Aquinas, and Berry, we might say that Earth solidarity commits oneself to liberate those creatures most removed from the opportunity to fulfill their natural inclinations, or to restore those beings hindered from exercising their inherent powers of differentiation and self-creation.

IV.4. Earth Solidarity and the Affective Dimension of the Cosmic Common Good

Earth solidarity is an affective virtue that affirms the feelings of distress that people experience when they encounter injustices against the Earth. The traditional "catalog of woe"[44] that begins many books on ecological ethics, then, is not simply a form of rhetoric designed to impel action. Instead, stories, statistics, and images of ecological disaster are designed precisely to help stoke a sense of anxiety at what is happening. These feelings can lead to an attitude of solidarity, which may then blossom into a stable and consistent virtue of Earth solidarity.

Expanding solidarity to include nonhuman nature helps clarify and validate a moral response already present and justifies the feeling of distress engendered by ecological disturbances. Outrage at the Gulf oil spill illustrates an emergent common consensus, across religious and cultural boundaries, that the Gulf and the many creatures it supports have suffered some kind of injustice and hence can be seen as a manifestation of Earth solidarity. Solidarity names the suffering that many already feel in light of ecological injustices, and it calls forth our energies to re-envision our ethical commitments anew for the good of human and nonhumankind together.

IV.5. Earth Solidarity as Perceptual Virtue

Following John Paul II, Earth solidarity has a perceptual component. It calls us to see the neighbor as a helper, one with whom we are meant to share life. Moreover, solidarity enables people to recognize those upon whom they are dependent as more than simply resources that can be abandoned when they have served their purpose. Earth solidarity then can incline us to contemplate reality more clearly, to be more perceptive of the cosmic common good, and thus to "learn to see ourselves in relation to all other creatures."[45] Solidarity orients us to perceive ourselves as indeed embedded in Earth, as cosmic participants in the "journey of the universe."[46] Just as solidarity stands as a challenge to nationalism, and relativizes any loyalty we might have to any subgroup within our greater common good, so too should it contravene any sense of humanity being radically separated from nonhumans. Earth solidarity inspires us to see the depth and meaning of our relatedness to others and to affirm it as good.

IV.6. Earth Solidarity as Theological Virtue

As John Paul II writes in *Centessimus Annus*, solidarity is linked to recognizing value and grandeur in others. In a Christian context, it will lead us to see God as the "universal common good" of all creation,[47] but it also directs us to the sacred worth of every creature. Without Earth solidarity, one loses sight of the grandeur of those creatures with whom we are created to live in communion. Earth solidarity seeks to "reawaken the religious awareness" of the goodness of creation and thereby follows the example of St. Francis, who "invites us to see nature as a magnificent book in which God speaks to us and grants us a glimpse of his infinite beauty and goodness." Such a virtue might help us "discover the worth of each thing, to be filled with awe and contemplation, to recognize that we are profoundly united with every creature as we journey towards [God's] infinite light."[48] Through Earth solidarity, humans may redefine our relationship to nature and our shared orientation to the cosmic common good.

IV.7. Earth Solidarity as an Ethic of Hope

Earth solidarity is also a response to the fact of an enormous crisis, and it can be categorized as an ethic of hope. Hope is distinct from an environmental optimism that trusts that degradation can be reversed or most species can be saved. Instead, Earth solidarity encourages acts of solidarity that entail a commitment of oneself to the full participation of other creatures in the cosmic common good based simply on the fact of creaturely dignity and the cosmic common good and the possibility of a degree of mutuality and relationship between us. These actions may succeed or they may fail, but as they habituate in us as a virtuous disposition to treat nonhumans with justice and compassion, they shape us as moral actors. Earth solidarity reinforces our membership in the cosmos and affirms both the goodness of nonhuman creatures and the inherent moral goodness in acting with prudence, justice, and love.

IV.8. Earth Solidarity as an Expression of Human Dignity

Earth solidarity does not indicate that humans are meant to share our lives as equals with nonhumans. There remains a unique potential for mutual and reciprocal love among human beings. Yet Earth solidarity reminds us of the goodness of all Earth's creatures apart from human use, and honoring that goodness does not diminish the elevated dignity of the human person. Rather, human dignity is elevated when humans act with reason and will to contribute to the greater common good.[49] Indeed, to display indifference to the plight of suffering nonhumans and ecosystems represents a greater denigration of human dignity. "Reusing something instead of immediately discarding it, when done for the right reasons, can be an act of love which expresses our own dignity."[50] Thus the extension of solidarity is based on creaturely dignity, and it is not necessary for dignity to be equal.[51]

IV.9. Earth Solidarity and the Local Cosmos

Earth solidarity forms an important counterpart to the cosmic common good because it gears us not only to the cosmos as whole, but to the Earth, which is our local site of engaging the cosmos. John Paul II was right to conjoin solidarity to the growing interdependence of peoples and the possibility of feeling distress at injustices suffered by those in "distant countries." Similarly, Earth Solidarity unites us with the biota and abiota who share our Earthly home, and especially with those most imperiled. Yet there is also a distinctive link between Earth solidarity and cosmic subsidiarity. As an affective virtue designed to foster a commitment of our entire selves into relationships with others, solidarity has a special meaning for those with whom we come into direct contact. Thus Earth solidarity must orient us not only to the good of the Earth, but also to the bioregions and specific places on Earth where we live. The habit of Earth solidarity must be forged primarily via encounters with our local habitat.

V. *Conclusion*

Extending the virtue of solidarity to include nonhuman creatures represents a vital contribution to the cosmic common good. It enfolds an intrinsic valuation of nonhuman creation into our moral vision by underscoring the development of ecologically oriented virtues as a main focus for our moral development. Earth solidarity provides a name and a context for attitudes, feelings, perceptions, and actions that are already active, both in the Christian community and across religious and cultural boundaries. Earth solidarity raises up and highlights them as good and morally praiseworthy, and it incites us to search out ways in which our relationship to God may be deepened and strengthened through our relationships to our fellow creatures. A vision of the cosmic common good and the virtue of Earth solidarity offer a rationale and a way of directing human commitment to the greater good of all creatures. To complement this, we turn now to a discussion of rights, which stress the demands of justice and outline the concrete commitments that solidarity entails.

6

Earth Rights

THE VIRTUE OF Earth solidarity acknowledges the interdependence between humans and the rest of the cosmos and inclines people toward the cosmic common good. As a social virtue directed to the common good, solidarity is linked to justice,[1] which is intricately bound up with rights. Thus a vital corollary to Earth solidarity is to demonstrate and codify commitment to the cosmic common good through the bestowal of Earth rights. Earth solidarity directs compassion for nonhuman nature to become a disposition to act. Rights inform this impulse by establishing a negative barrier, the minimum requirements of justice, that render violations of the common good more difficult to justify. Rights specify whether or not we have embodied our solidarity with the Earth and the most vulnerable creatures.

To explore the feasibility of Earth rights, this chapter begins by outlining the salient features and justifications for human rights in Catholic social teaching and thought. Then I address some of the objections to extending rights to nonhuman creation, before turning to my specific proposal for Earth rights. Just as Earth solidarity channels human emotions and dispositions to the good of nonhuman creatures, Earth rights safeguard the goodness of nonhuman nature by imposing human duties.

I. Rights in Catholic Social Thought
I.1. Dynamics of Human Rights

I focus here on six important features of the Catholic understanding of human rights. The first and most authoritative exposition of human rights in Catholic social thought remains John XXIII's 1963 encyclical, *Pacem in Terris*, so I refer primarily to this document.

First, rights are grounded in a theological understanding of human dignity such that God is the ultimate source of rights.[2] Rights are based on intrinsic human dignity, which, as we have seen, stems from the theological doctrine of the *imago dei*, the proclamation in Genesis 1:27 that all human beings are made in (or to) the image and likeness of God. At the same time, Catholic social thought also appeals to the natural law. Human beings as perceived by reason have certain needs, and as social beings have rights that correspond to their membership in society.[3] Human dignity is inherent in the human person prior to any choices, actions, or manifestation of faculties associated with human beings. Dignity is inviolable and inalienable. One's dignity can be violated, by another or by oneself, but it can never be renounced or withdrawn completely.

Second, rights entail and cannot be separated from responsibilities, and both flow from human dignity. The possession of a right leads to duties for oneself, to exercise it well and in appropriate and fitting ways. Indeed, the common good is safeguarded when personal rights and duties are protected.[4] So, for example, John XXIII enumerates the corresponding duties involved in certain rights: "The right to live involves the duty to preserve one's life; the right to a decent standard of living, the duty to live in a becoming fashion; the right to be free to seek out the truth, the duty to devote oneself to an ever deeper and wider search for it."[5]

Third, rights entail duties not only for the subject of a right but for others as well. The possession of a right gives rise in others to the duty "of recognizing and respecting that right,"[6] to enable the other to fulfill her duty and thereby demonstrate respect for the person and her human dignity. Thus there is a twofold duty arising from a natural right: the subject must exercise that right both to the benefit of herself and to the common good; and others must recognize and respect that subject's right, in light of her inalienable human dignity.

Fourth, rights and duties are situated within human communities and in the context of the common good. That is, rights and duties pertain not just to the individuals' flourishing, but they also include social obligations, in light of the inherent value of the common good and the social nature of the person. Rights represent the objective norm of justice, and they are the chief means by which the common good is safeguarded. While rights may belong to the person and are irrevocable, they still maintain an interpersonal and communal orientation.

Fifth, the most fundamental and core human right is the "right to live," and foremostly to live in such a way that persons are able to participate in human society.[7] Thus it is not a right simply to survive and exist, but it includes all that is necessary for "the proper development of life." The right to live must be adequately safeguarded in the various dimensions of social life, including "food, clothing, shelter, medical care, rest," and "the right to be looked after in the event of ill health," old age, and unemployment.[8] John XXIII demonstrates that the right to live is the right to participate fully in the life of the community. Other rights are meant to facilitate and further this capacity.[9]

Sixth, there is an organic and integral connection between rights and the virtue of solidarity. Solidarity with others means minimally not violating their rights and more positively promoting their rights, most particularly the lynchpin right of participation. Moreover, rights must be supported at all levels of human society, from personal acts to coordinated international movements, and from advocacy to the articulation of legal norms. Advocacy for rights is a key way for a community to cultivate the virtue of solidarity.[10]

I.2. Concerns with Extending Rights to Earth Rights

While the cosmic common good and Earth solidarity have precedents in Catholic social thought, the notion of Earth rights poses greater conceptual challenges. Some Catholic social theorists have noted that conditions of ecological degradation may require a reformulation of rights discourse. An ecological application of human rights could then include the right to a healthy environment for human beings to live, the right to be free from toxicity and a radically unstable climate, or the right to reasonably clean water, soil, and air.[11] Similarly, an ecologically informed view of human rights logically extends to future generations, who will be impacted by the environmental consequences of the choices we make today.[12] Yet these do not yet qualify as Earth rights. As we saw, an obvious expansion of solidarity and the preferential option for the poor includes primary concern for those human beings in the present, and all future generations, who are negatively impacted by an imperiled Earth. Yet true Earth solidarity directly includes plants, animals, ecosystems, and the wholes of which all creatures are a part. Similarly, the human right to a clean Earthly habitat may be an ecologically oriented right, but it is not yet a right for nonhumans themselves. Thus the question emerges: To what extent can this category of rights be extended in order to articulate nonhuman rights, or indeed Earth rights?

As we have seen, traditional Catholic social thought has a basic anthropocentric presumption, but the Catholic conception of rights is so connected to specifically human traits that it makes the extension of rights to nonhumans problematic. First, most of the content of human rights stems not from our humanity as biological creatures but from our identities as moral and rational agents, capable of responsible and self-directed participation in the political life of society. Which human rights can reasonably be applied to nonhumans? Second, if only the basic right—the right to live—is affirmed, how is that feasible in a world that depends on trophic relationships? The violation of an innocent person's right to live is considered a crime, while the violation of an innocent creature's right to live is absolutely necessary, and on a daily basis.

Third, the Catholic tradition links rights and duties such that rights are defended in order that people fulfill certain social duties. Without sufficient rationality and free will, animals and plants cannot fulfill duties as humans can, so it seems that they cannot possess rights. Contrarily, if one were to suggest moral duties for non-humans, that would render them morally culpable for their actions, which could lead to a ludicrous conclusion, such as punishing a predator for hunting prey.

Fourth, there remains the concern that expanding rights to include nonhumans could weaken an already lethargic commitment to human rights. Even trying to establish a global and trans-religious consensus on human rights continues to prove challenging.[13] Could rights for mollusks further undermine the urgency for prosecuting violations of human rights?

On the basis of these and other concerns, some theologians and philosophers oppose rights for nature. Thomas Sieger Derr, for example, argues that rights are "applicable only to human society."[14] Renowned environmental philosopher Holmes Rolston III, who vigorously defends the concept of nature's intrinsic value, dismisses the idea of biotic rights, urging instead "universal human benevolence."[15] Cartesian philosopher Richard Watson argues that rights only exist for moral agents, because rights entail reciprocal duties. Some animals may have self-consciousness, but the majority do not, and so most are not part of the moral realm.[16] For Bryan Norton, a theory of rights is meant for moderating disputes between competing interests. Thus only an individual with interests can have rights.[17] Finally, John Passmore calls it "mystical rubbish" to argue for a new ethical framework in which it is "intrinsically wrong to destroy a species, cut down a tree, clear a wilderness."[18]

While I am sympathetic to concerns about undermining human dignity, and though I recognize the validity of the tradition that links rights to duties, I counter that an extension of rights is indispensable if we are to perceive the real demands of Earth solidarity.[19] Certainly, the expanded principles of a cosmic common good and Earth solidarity justify some form of Earth rights. Earth solidarity disposes us to act in ways that honor our relationships to nonhumans in their own right, and the virtue of solidarity is strengthened and habituated through the recognition of and respect for rights. Minimally, rights establish a negative barrier that makes violations of a cosmic common good more difficult to justify. Earth rights become a practical formulation of human duties to the Earth, and in fact they are theologically defensible, ethically meaningful, logically coherent, and even politically practical.

II. Rights Expanded: Justifications for Earth Rights

Clearly, if the scientific and theological grounds for a Catholic cosmic common good are persuasive, then Earth rights are a logical outgrowth of this cosmocentric ethical vision. The true basis of rights is the doctrine of God the Creator who lovingly creates, forms, sustains, and values all creation, humankind and non-humankind alike.[20] Rights for nonhumans, however, need two additional justifications: to demonstrate the logical intelligibility of such rights; and to explain why they are a beneficial and necessary addition to the moral vision of a Catholic cosmic common good.

II.1. Intelligibility of Rights

Despite the link between rights and defending the intrinsic value of creatures, there remains the need to defend the basic intelligibility and non-absurdity of discussing rights for nature. Indeed, as we have seen, many oppose it, even calling it "mystical rubbish." There are two primary sources for confusion regarding the coherency of nature's rights and the impetus to restrict rights solely to humans. The first seeks to point out a putative logical inconsistency by imagining the impossibility of assigning certain human rights (the right to vote, the right to exercise religious freedom) to nonhumans. The second related confusion regards the basic fact of existence in a world of predatory relationships: there is no way to uphold a creature's or a species's or an ecosystem's rights without also the need to perform some actions that weaken or destroy creatures.

Before responding to this concern, it is instructive to note the ways in which theologians and philosophers typically limit rights to humans. Often this conclusion follows a perverse form of circular reasoning or descends into a *reducto ad absurdum*: first, define the meaning of rights in reference to specifically human characteristics; second, use that basis to legitimize assigning rights only to human beings; third, legislate laws that apply only to humans. For example, some claim that rights must be grounded in moral agency, since rights require reciprocity and mutuality among equals. Since only humans possess agency (and so can enter into relationships of reciprocity), only humans can possess rights. Or, rights require the capacity to fulfill duties, and since most nonhumans cannot actively choose to perform such duties, they cannot possess rights.

This kind of circular reasoning can be considered "species-ist," similar to racist and sexist forms of exclusion. Preferring one's own species to another in the interest of self-survival is a basic and natural impulse, and so it does not deserve the moral opprobrium of "species-ism." Yet species-ism emerges when differences between species are used to justify domination and exploitation, just as racism and sexism mean the domination of certain races and sexes.[21] Thus John Hart calls upon people to recognize and acknowledge the self-contradictory and species-serving origins of the belief that rights belong only to humans.[22] By contrast, in the context of a Catholic cosmic common good, and in the narrative of an evolutionary universe, rights are perfectly plausible. To demonstrate this intelligibility, I outline five factors of Earth rights.

First, rights are based on the intrinsic and essential dignity of creatures. Like human rights, Earth rights are inextricably linked to the value of their subjects, and so in this way human rights are a kind of subset of Earth rights. Earth rights highlight and defend the dignity and value of all creatures, while human rights address the specific and unique character of human dignity. Human rights may require the capacity for mutual relationships among equals, but this anthropogenic moral criterion need not be extended to nonhumans in order to argue against Earth rights. The bedrock of creaturely dignity, and the possibility of this dignity being violated, makes it conceivable that nonhumans may suffer injustices, and hence are subjects and possessors of rights. Rights for nonhumans "deny exclusivity of human values and rights" while acknowledging a different degree of value.[23] Contrary to Norton, rights refer not to a creature's desires or intentions, but to one's essential dignity and human recognition of who or what has value. Without Earth rights, the value of Earth may be overlooked or disdained. As James Nash argues, God has endowed creatures with "biotic kinship, which entails human obligation."[24] Without a discussion of Earth rights, exhortations to protect the Earth, respect nonhumans, or even inculcate Earth solidarity may remain anemic moral claims, individualistic and needlessly anthropocentric.

Second, while all Earth creatures deserve Earth rights, creatures may possess differentiated dignity, and so corresponding rights must be understood as egalitarian, rather than equal. Equal rights would denote identical rights for all beings, while egalitarian rights would indicate rights that are equivalent and appropriate to the kind of creature it is. All creatures are in some ways equal, since they are equally created and sustained by and ordained to the same God. All are entitled to consideration, but not to the same degree.[25] Human rights are grounded in the fact of human equality, while Earth rights can operate according to a descending scale of value. While lists of human rights are extensive and diverse, befitting the complexity of human relationships, the list of Earth rights is more humble and constrained. Earth rights do not diminish or minimize human rights because they allow for differing values of creatures while upholding the worth of all creatures and the ecosystems they inhabit.

Third, a complementary way of distinguishing human rights and Earth rights is to acknowledge a difference between rights, not of degree but of kind. Rights are not cumulative, such that humans receive the most rights, with a decreasing number for each "lesser" creature. Rather, differences between rights are qualitative. As Thomas Berry explains, "Rivers have river rights. Birds have bird rights. Insects have insect rights. Humans have human rights. . . . The rights of an insect would be of no value to a tree or a fish."[26] Rights are limited and relative to each species and fitting for the capacities of that species. Earth rights need not trivialize or diminish human rights, since they avow a qualitatively different form of rights for each species.

Fourth, a way of clarifying inevitable conflicts between rights is to understand Earth rights as *prima facie*, or the presumption that they must be honored. They can be overridden for a stronger moral reason, but the burden of proof resides on those who would wish to contravene them. Moreover, the principles of proportionality and discrimination in Catholic social thought can also guide choices in individual cases.[27] Humans have human rights, including a right to habitat and food, and satisfying these rights will mean the death of some other creatures. Within the finite limitations of resources and the evolutionary pressures of survival, some individuals and perhaps some species will need to perish. Humans may be justified in driving an entire species into extinction, such as particular diseases or pathogens. Yet in general, as human activity nears the destruction of a species, let alone whole ecosystems, the violation of Earth rights becomes nearly impossible to justify, and so the rights become nearly absolute.

John Hart engages an interesting question in this regard: could a nonhuman species that does more good for a particular ecosystem, or at the least less bad, displace human beings as the most morally significant species? Hart suggests that, under the right conditions, another species may deserve a moral preference for inhabiting a specific habitat, such as a species that proved to have more neutral regard for other species; whose predation had more compelling motives; and that proved a better fit into the ecological niche. While human beings, through their technology and creativity, have demonstrated themselves able to survive under almost any ecological conditions, this does not grant them the moral authority to do so. The right to life for nonhumans, then, can reasonably contextualize or take precedence over other human rights.[28]

Given that Earth rights differ from human rights, initial concerns about impossible conflicts of interest between competing rights are less worrisome. All creatures have the most basic right, to live, but this cannot be absolutized because it is not an equal right. Moreover, we must recall that creatures possess simultaneously both intrinsic and instrumental value. The seeming absurdity of a right to life for every creature vanishes when one considers not only a creature's intrinsic value but also its instrumental value—to other creatures, its ecosystem, and creation as a whole. Rights, then, are based not on equal dignity or the capacity for social and political relationships, but on one's intrinsic value as a creature as well as one's instrumental value for the benefit of the common whole. In this light, Earth rights are not impractical, because they do not affirm an absolute right to life or a complete prohibition on killing. Humans, and all creatures, still participate in the trophic relationships that require killing when necessary; rights language holds a mirror up to our presumptions of what actually constitutes necessity. In a similar way, the fact of a dilemma or difficult situation does not negate a creature's intrinsic dignity or its rights. Rights are different, but they do signify a kind of equality and point to real intrinsic worth and dignity.

Fifth, Earth rights still maintain a connection between rights and duties, but here the emphasis is on human duties to honor the rights of others. Following John XXIII, the reality of rights gives rise within moral agents to the duty to respect that right in others. The attribution of Earth rights indicates the justice owed to nonhumans by moral agents due to their dignity, the inherent value of their sheer existence, and their contributions to the common good.

Thus advocating for Earth rights is intelligible, logically coherent, and meaningful, as long as they are not reduced to an absurdity. Rather than minimize human rights, holding up rights for creatures that are far less sophisticated than humans should make instances of injustice to humans even more pronounced. Values and rights are not logically contradicted simply by the necessity of conflicts that require sacrificing one creature's rights on behalf of another's. James Nash's definition of biotic rights proves applicable to Earth rights as well: *Morally justified and prima facie claims or demands on behalf of nonhuman organisms, as individuals and collectives (populations and species), against all moral agents for the vital interests or imperative conditions of well-being for nonhumankind.*[29]

II.2. The Necessity of Rights

Rights for Earth and all Earth creatures enhance a Catholic cosmic common good because they distinguish the call to love and reverence nonhuman creation from the duty to do it justice. Rights ground respect for creatures by making the cosmic common good not only morally and intellectually compelling but also legally defensible. Without rights codified into legal code, there is no platform on which to defend the dignity of vulnerable creatures. Legal rights are natural rights codified into human law, so that without this, nonhumans lose the moral standing that their intrinsic value deserves. Rights expressed through law give nonhumans some protection against human abuse and exploitation.[30]

In addition, Earth rights offer a critical support for inculcating Earth solidarity in human agents and communities. Solidarity represents a form of love for Earth, but as a virtue it still remains an internal dynamic. It must be habituated through external acts, and as we saw, the promotion of rights and in particular the right to participation is one of the key ways that persons and communities can cultivate the virtue of solidarity. Rights, the objective norm of justice, become part of the moral landscape outside the agent's interests or concerns. As opposed to love or solidarity, which can only be requested, justice can be demanded, since it is owed to the other. Rights define the boundaries of human responsibility, and they ground the dignity of creatures and our obligations to respect it—not via human self-interest or charity but through the demands of justice. Promoting and defending legally enforceable rights can be a way that individual agents can contribute to "structures of virtue" that orient the human community to their responsibility to contribute to the cosmic common good. Earth solidarity requires acts of generosity and beneficence, but it also encourages advocacy and supporting the institution of international and domestic norms. By enacting and embodying solidarity by the defense of Earth rights, agents cultivate the virtue of Earth solidarity in themselves and in the various communities in which they live.

Not only are legally enforceable rights for nature an important aspect of a Catholic cosmic common good, but they are also in fact politically feasible and realistic. Inspired by Thomas Berry, the emerging disciplines of "Earth jurisprudence" and "wild law" are legal theories that outline specific Earth rights and conduct international surveys in order to identify legal cases in which these rights are protected.[31] The American legal system already recognizes some kind of rights for nonhumans. If animal rights means "legal protection against harm," then many already have them. The American Animal Welfare Act, for example, contains an incipient bill of rights for animals. And in 2002, Germany included animal rights in its constitution when it added the phrase "and animals" to a clause about the state's duty to respect the dignity of the human person.[32] Unfortunately, these animal rights are often in actuality limited, whether through the lack of enforcement (public prosecution is rarely important enough to justify) or large exceptions (for example the cases of hunting, scientific experimentation, and food).[33]

Earth jurisprudence also identifies an emerging movement to attribute rights not only to nonhumans but also to ecosystems. Figuera and Mason note the Kootenai Tribe of Idaho case,[34] in which a US Court of Appeals upheld the "Roadless Area Rule," a national forest regulation approved in 2001 that defends old growth forests. The legal logic demonstrates an incipient sense of nature's rights, the right not only of creatures but of their ecosystems as well.[35] The establishment of national wilderness areas is not for any one species but for the interconnected whole. In 2010, the nation of Bolivia passed the "Law of the Rights of Mother Earth," which invests nature and natural systems with certain rights, such as "the right to continue vital cycles and processes free from human alteration; the right to pure water and clean air; the right to balance; the right not to be polluted; and the right to not have cellular structure modified or genetically altered."[36] The recently confirmed Constitution of Ecuador, which asserts that nature has "the right to exist, persist, maintain and regenerate its vital cycles," suggests that these rights may even become enshrined in a nation's most foundational document.[37] Finally, an excellent example of a global and cosmocentric recognition of Earth rights is *The Earth Charter*,[38] an international document generated over a decade-long drafting process and involving thousands of people. Radically inclusive of all religious and non-religious traditions, it parallels the ethical expansion I propose through the cosmic common good and was lauded by Francis for its challenge to all humanity to develop a new global awareness.[39] It is a "soft law" document, outlining general principles, that is complemented by the "hard law" of binding international agreements.[40] Together, these domestic and international examples suggest the political potential for Earth rights. If solidarity with other human beings leads to the promotion of human rights, then Earth solidarity ought to lead to the promotion of Earth rights, in particular the enforcement of those incipient rights already present in national and international law, and to the expansion of those rights in order to reflect adequately the intrinsic value that those nonhuman creatures and habitats already possess.

II.3. Earth Rights in Catholic Social Thought

This overview of nonhuman rights suggests the compatibility of Earth rights and Catholic social thought. Rights are grounded in the dignity and intrinsic value of subjects, so Earth rights affirm a value in nonhuman creatures apart from their benefit to human beings. As Francis confirmed, "the establishment of a legal framework which can set clear boundaries and ensure the protection of ecosystems has become indispensable."[41] Similarly to human rights, Earth rights not only affirm the intrinsic dignity of nonhumans but draw our attention to instances when their dignity is violated. Safeguarding rights is a critical component of protecting the common good, and one can still distinguish human rights and the human common good from Earth rights and the planetary common good.

Solidarity and rights form an important pair: if solidarity is the virtue that leads us to feel appropriate distress at the injustices suffered by another, rights are the principle of justice that alerts us to the fact that what is occurring is a situation of injustice. Solidarity and love are the high point of our relationality, the fullness of our interconnectedness. Rights form part of the substance of justice, which signifies obligations for moral agents. Laws themselves are insufficient to safeguard the planetary common good: "if the laws are to bring about significant, long-lasting effects, the majority of the members of society must be adequately motivated to accept them, and personally transformed to respond."[42] Thus solidarity calls for the maximum of relationality and inspires the promotion of rights, while rights delineate the minimum of our relationality and further validate Earth solidarity. Rights are not the only way of indicating the dignity of a creature, but they form an integral and persuasive way of affirming it. Rights for nonhumans form a succinct and powerful reminder that "being human" is not the only morally relevant criterion. Rights entail duties, but in the case of Earth rights, the primary responsibility turns to moral agents, who have the duty to safeguard the rights of non-moral agents, in light of their intrinsic value and their participation in the common good. Advocating rights for all Earth creatures represents a moral response to the proper size and scope of the planetary crisis. For the planetary common good and Earth solidarity to have real implications, Catholic social thought requires more than a mere moral exhortation to care for the Earth. Rights are needed to engender and enforce human responsibility.

II.4. Preliminary Considerations

I offer here a few preliminary considerations regarding my formulation of Earth rights and how they differ from previous proposals.[43] First, while James Nash develops a bill of rights only for wild creatures and not domesticated ones,[44] I would counter that the overall foundation of creaturely dignity applies for both. Hence it is important to outline rights that can pertain to both, as well as specific ones pertinent to either wild or domesticated nature.

Second and more importantly, my formulation of Earth rights applies not only to living creatures (biota) but to nonliving creatures (abiota) and ecosystems as well. Moreover, these rights apply not only to species, but to each individual member of that species. Rights exist not only generally, as a generic right for a particular species to exist, but also for the individual creature, so long as the species still exists.

Admittedly, there are logical problems in associating rights for abiota. There is no center of integration in abiota, as there is for biota. Abiota can be amassed without making multiples: water plus water is water, not two waters. One can cut away a piece of a mountain with minimal change to its core integrity, while the same act on a living creature poses a significant threat. Living creatures can die and suffer injustices, while this is uncertain for abiota, except for the ways in which living creatures are affected. For living creatures, there are species and individuals who belong to that species, while abiota can merge and separate at ease. Rights for water clearly pertain to the services it provides to living creatures, but it is less clear how water itself may possess rights. Indeed, what is a "healthy river," except one that supports the flourishing of living creatures?

Yet, in light of my retrieval of Augustine, Aquinas, and Berry, there is a way to posit a kind of integrity, even to nonliving creatures and certainly to habitats and ecosystems. Berry and Swimme describe the autopoiesis of a star and its internal integrity, even if it does not qualify as living. At some point, there is an observable integrity and unity to a river and a mountain.[45] Can we speak of the health or ill status of a particular river, ocean, or valley, without reference to the specific creatures who depend on it?[46] Berry suggests as much when he speaks of the right of a bioregion to engage in its own self-healing, self-education, and self-governance.[47]

By excluding abiotic rights as merely the blended rights of biota,[48] theologians threaten to lose the "both/and" approach that balances ecocentric holism and biocentric individualism, as a Catholic cosmic common good and Earth solidarity strive to do. Instead, I propose expanding the category of rights to include ecosystems as well. Instances of ecological degradation, such as climate change, toxic spills, and barren landscapes, remind us that we must not focus solely on living creatures but also on the conditions of the habitat on which they depend. A Catholic cosmic common good declares that the greatest aspect of creation is its interconnections and the order among its mutual parts. Images of ecological disaster confirm this: when we see the waste of a fracking pit that has spilled onto adjacent land, Earth solidarity gives rise to feelings of distress that are directed not only to the living creatures affected by this but to the good of the whole, including abiota. A proper sense of the cosmic common good emphasizes not only individuals but their contexts—the whole of a species, of an ecosystem, of a bioregion, of Earth, and ultimately of the cosmos. Earth solidarity may rightly channel feelings of loss into action primarily on behalf of the creatures who will die as a result, but it will still maintain a sense of the greater conditions of the whole that must be healed and ordered to bring life and flourishing to biota and the wholes of which they are a part.

Therefore Earth rights should include the right of ecosystems to participate in the natural dynamics of existence, evolving in ways that may bring an end to particular species, or even to the ecosystem itself.[49] While clearly it is a major ethical advance to advocate for biotic rights, relegating abiota to purely instrumental use smacks of the same exclusionary trajectory that marks anthropocentrism as problematic. A Catholic cosmic common good argues not only for the good of individual creatures and various species, but also for the contexts in which they live. There is a good to the diversity of creatures that occupy a particular place and to the nonliving elements that provide the space and nutrients for them. Their common living together is an intangible and non-reducible good, and rights language must identify and acknowledge this as well. As Holmes Rolston argues, the intrinsic value of a creature cannot be separated from the holistic web in which it lives. Intrinsic value "requires a corporate sense where value can also mean 'good in community.'"[50] Befitting the holism of the cosmic common good and the communal orientation of rights in the Catholic tradition, "community" in this sense includes creatures such as water, minerals, and stars. As a living creature, I am of course partial not only to humans but to all creatures that live and die, and I admit I would be perplexed to envision the flourishing of a mountain or a river apart from living creatures that live on them and in them. Yet I believe there is a crucial dimension of fullness in the conception of Earth rights, which includes biota, abiota, the synthesizing context of bioregions, and the overall integrity of the Earth for their mutual interactions and flourishing. Earth rights highlight the interconnected webs of life, from individual creatures, to ecosystems, to Earth as a whole. This is the planetary common good, the good of our planetary commons and the local instantiation of the cosmic common good, to which Earth solidarity directs us.

I argue for Earth rights rather than cosmos rights, because I agree with Hart, Berry, and Nash that these rights should be not only philosophically and theologically coherent but also legally defensible, capable of being enforced within human legal codes. Thus while I do believe that Alpha Centauri is part of the cosmic common good, and in some ways can rightly be included within humanity's Earth solidarity, I restrict rights to Earth and Earth's creatures, as the immediately affected subjects of human legal systems.[51]

III. Earth Rights

Thus I propose the following Earth Rights.

For Earth

1. *The right of the Earth to exist as Earth*: as the single and integral community of all Earth creatures, comprising ecosystems, species, and individual creatures, in their manifold interactions; to be the commons in which all these creatures interact in both conflictual and peaceful order; and as such to host an unparalleled diversity and complex ordering of life, both for itself and as its contribution toward the cosmic common good.

For Biota and Abiota

2. *The fundamental right of all Earth creatures is to cosmic participation*: all entities, from the smallest microbes to the largest ecosystems, have the right to participate in the evolutionary development of life on Earth; all other rights, for abiota and biota, flow from this basic right to cosmic participation. Cosmic participation is both a right and the primary "duty" incumbent upon all creatures, and it grounds all other Earth rights. While human beings may fail to exercise this and other rights in appropriate ways, nonhumans fulfill this duty without abdication, if allowed the proper conditions and opportunities.

3. *The right to fulfill the basic creaturely inclinations* one possesses as a member of one's species; in line with an Augustinian and Thomistic theology of creation, to fulfill one's natural inclinations and to rest in the place to which it is drawn by the Spirit, as its way of imitating the divine likeness and glorifying God; following Thomas Berry, this right is the opportunity to participate in one's genetic inheritances and to engage the power of one's autopoiesis to one's

fullest extent, in balance with the rights of other creatures to do so as well. This correlates with the right to participate in predatory and trophic relationships in order to live.

4. *The right to be free from excessive interventions* by humans or any other moral agents in the ability of this creature, species, or ecosystem to perform its cosmic participation. This includes the right to be free from anthropogenic extinctions and severe degradation; to be free from prodigal and unnecessary consumptive use; to be free from cruelty and abuse; and to live and to die (and to be killed) with dignity in encounters with moral agents. Since humans participate in the natural dynamics of competition and cooperation, they too have the right to participate in predatory relationships and to structure their natural environment in accordance with their needs. This human right highlights the gross disparity between current levels of destructive human interventions, and the modifications and consumption governed by actual necessity.

For Biota

5. *The right to reproduce one's kind naturally*, free from human-induced adulteration or manipulation, including pollution, radiation, and genetic engineering.

6. *The right to habitat*, to a place to be and exist, including the right to seek and occupy adequate shelter, which enables creatures to fulfill their cosmic participation. This ecosystemic place should be governed by the historical evolutionary development of these creatures and of their ecosystems, rather than determined by human preference.

7. *The right to sustenance and to self-defense.* The common goods of the Earth, including water, nutrients, and space, belong not just to humanity but to all Earth creatures. Biota have the right of access to these goods, their "fair share" of the Earth's bounty as members of the planetary common good. This includes the right, for humans and for all creatures, to participate in trophic and predatory relationships, in balance with the rights of other creatures to pursue these same rights.

For Degraded Nature

8. *The right to restoration* such that degraded ecosystems and their creatures are brought back, as far as possible, to their ability to participate in cosmic and evolutionary processes. This right recognizes that ecosystems are always in flux and that "habitat integrity" is a shifting norm. Yet it also acknowledges that human activity can diminish or bring to near collapse ecosystems and can endanger the survival of creatures far before natural and evolutionary processes could typically do so.

For Wild Nature

9. *The right to designated habitats free from human occupation.* Recognizing the complexities of the category of "wilderness," this right acknowledges that non-domesticated creatures still have the right to live in settings that befit their evolutionary developed inclinations and that are relatively free from human control. This may include (1) habitats accessible to humans only as visitors, and only in manageable numbers; and (2) habitats that restrict human presence, in order that biota and abiota may survive during this apoplectic moment of planetary extinction.

10. *The right to fulfill creaturely inclinations in ways perceived as destructive* by human beings or other creatures. This recognizes the moral legitimacy of competition, predation, and overall disruptive activity by microbes, diseases, insects, plants, nonhuman animals, weather systems, and any other subsets/members of the cosmic common good. Creatures retain the right of self-defense, but wildness remains a facet of cosmic integrity.

For Domesticated Nature

11. *The right for domesticated creatures to be treated as humanity's companions*, rather than merely tools or property. Those creatures who have been domesticated over the course of their interactions with humanity deserve a special focus because humans and these creatures form a kind of "mixed community," as these creatures became part of families and communities by establishing individuals bonds with humans.[52] As such, these creatures deserve special freedom from unnecessary human experimentation, cruelty, and abuse.

IV. A Catholic Cosmic Common Good, Earth Solidarity, and Earth Rights: Conclusion

I have argued that expanding and reorienting ecologically Catholic social thought to include nonhuman nature is paramount. While other terms could be developed to describe these forms of concern for the imperiled Earth, one reason to invoke these core principles is due to the scope and severity of ecological degradation. A Catholic cosmic common good, Earth solidarity, and Earth rights attempt to reflect morally on the scope and significance of the ways in which humanity is reshaping the planet. They are ethical terms that adequately address the scale of human activity and of the interdependence between humans and other living creatures.

The common good establishes the moral vision, while solidarity and rights each draw on a critical dimension of our moral lives: rights evoke our sense of justice, and solidarity is a powerfully affective virtue that inspires us to see the depth and meaning of our relatedness to others. Solidarity and rights respond to human interdependence with other dignified creatures and orient us to the common good.

A Catholic cosmic common good, Earth solidarity, and Earth rights call for the inclusion of the Earth as a whole, its sundry ecosystems, and the myriad plants, animals, and creatures that live in them within the circle of moral consideration. I do not impose a rigidly egalitarian solidarity or sense of rights, where humans are equated with any and all living creatures. I do challenge, however, any construal of Catholic ethics where concern for environmental degradation flows simply and merely from a concern for its effects on human beings such that the right to a healthy Earth belongs to humanity alone. This is too narrow an interpretation of a Catholic cosmic common good, and it hides from view the real and lasting effects of human activity on the living systems of the Earth.

The forces that imperil Earth threaten present, permanent, and dramatic effects to the conditions of life on the planet. Ecological disasters are immediate lessons in the interdependence of humans and the Earth and the ramifications of human choices on plants, animals, and the interconnected whole of an ecosystem. The virtue of Earth solidarity and the affirmation of Earth rights help us to name the suffering that many already feel in the light of ecological injustices, and they call forth our energies to reenvision our ethical commitments anew for the good of human and nonhumankind together. Together they spell out in more detail how Catholics may embody their commitment to the cosmic common good.

Now, I take this moral foundation and bring it into dialogue with non-Christian traditions. How do they understand the value of nonhuman nature and the place of the human, and how might this confirm, challenge, or modify a Catholic vision of the cosmic common good?

PART TWO

The Cosmic Common Good and Interreligious Ecological Ethics

7

Comparative Theology and Ecological Ethics

IN THE NEXT three chapters, I test these ecologically expanded and reoriented principles of Catholic social thought for their adequacy and relevance in developing an interreligious ecological ethic. Before engaging Hindu, Buddhist, and American Indian traditions, I offer a brief introduction to the methodology of comparative theology. Scores of theologians and ethicists, in numerous books and anthologies, have brought religious perspectives to bear on the ecological crisis, and it is time to develop a more deliberately comparative conversation regarding an imperiled Earth and the prospects for planetary flourishing. I draw on two main founders of the recent emergence of comparative theology, Francis Clooney, S.J., and James Fredericks, to adumbrate the contours of the field.

I. Overview of Comparative Theology

Like Catholic social thought, comparative theology has precedents and roots in Scripture, in the Patristic and the medieval eras, and, for comparative theology, most notably in the missionary period of the fifteenth and sixteenth centuries.[1] Yet also like Catholic social thought, the impetus for comparative theology today reflects on and responds to shifting cultural conditions, in particular two contemporary developments. First, globalization has led to the "de-territorialization [of religions] as cultural systems"[2] and the increased proximity of religious communities, affording people the opportunity to live in religiously diverse settings and more frequently encounter worldviews different from their own. Clooney comments that comparative theology attends to the fact of diversity, both around us and within us. Attentiveness to other traditions can influence how we think and how we see the world, and it can make a simple exclusive choice for one's own tradition nearly impossible.[3] Just as the growing interdependence of nations led to an expansion of Catholic social thought, the increasing connectedness among various cultural communities has in part spurred the growth of comparative theology.

Second, scholars have now made available an unprecedented number of theological texts from multitudinous traditions, giving people across cultural boundaries access to other religious ways of thinking and viewing the world. There is a stunning amount of knowledge that was not accessible even two hundred years ago. Francis Clooney explains that increased contact between religious traditions and the opportunity to investigate religious diversity through the preponderance of available texts make it "nearly impossible to justify not studying other traditions and taking their theologies into account."[4]

The term "comparative theology" could suggest merely a comparison of two theological or doctrinal systems, as one might find in a traditionally academic and disinterested approach to the history of religions.[5] It is certainly worthwhile to compare how Catholic, Hindu, and Buddhist theologians have understood the ecological crisis, as well as the ethical vision and moral principles they articulate for how humanity should respond. Yet merely becoming acquainted with the beliefs and practices of other religions is not yet comparative theology. While there are a variety of features of comparative theology, I will highlight three key elements: (1) it is dialogical and dialectical; (2) it is constructive and truly theological; and (3) it is composed of limited experiments that are attentive to details and to differences between the traditions.

First, comparative theology proceeds by way of a specific kind of interreligious dialogue. The proximity of religious traditions to each other makes it abundantly clear that the Christian concept of faith seeking understanding, or of intellectual reflection on inherited texts and concepts, is a practice that transcends religious boundaries and can be found in many places.[6] Comparative theology begins with the critical study of another tradition, either through personal dialogue or through the rigorous study of texts, or ideally both. However learned and focused this conversation is, however, it is not yet comparative theology. The approach is not only dialogical but dialectical, with an interplay back and forth between the traditions. It aims not just to identify similarities and differences, but to put different traditions into a fruitful encounter that may lead to new insights. Importantly, however, the key components of the other religious tradition—its major figures, principles, images, and so on—become part of the conversation of the home tradition. In other words, the theologian begins to understand the meaning of the other tradition for herself, and thereby the other religious tradition becomes an integral part of the self-articulation of the home tradition. One theologizes "from both sides of the table."[7] Comparison can be either positive or negative, revealing profound similarities or differences, and often both. Comparison does not seek unanimity or irreconcilable alterity; it seeks specificity and clarity.[8]

Second, as a result of this dialectical process, comparative theology moves beyond mere comparison to become a properly and thoroughly theological, constructive, and revisionist project. It is properly theological because it does not result from a form of disinterested scholarship but proceeds from a theologian rooted in and committed to a home tradition, who then begins to learn from one or more traditions in order to gain "insights that are indebted to the newly encountered tradition/s as well as the home tradition."[9] Comparative theology is constructive and revisionist because interreligious thinking becomes intrinsic to the theological enterprise itself. "Comparison ... now takes place *within* Christian theology, *while* it is being formulated, *not* as an appendage or corollary to an already formed theology."[10] One does not compose a perfect Christian ecological ethic, and then note areas of similarity and difference with a Buddhist or Hindu ecological ethic. Rather, Hindu and Buddhist ethical precepts, metaphors, and commitments become part of the Christian theologian's formulation of a proper and adequate ecological ethic. Again, comparative theology is not merely a comparison of religious systems; it is fully and thoroughly a form of theology, a confessional and normative enterprise, done on behalf of the theologian and her home community.[11] While the theologian remains personally rooted in a particular tradition, the conceptual foundation for comparative theology bridges religious traditions.[12] A good comparativist seeks to point out both similarities and differences, not merely in order to catalog them, but rather to construct a theology that does not decide on the conclusion in advance but rather "occurs truly *only* after comparison."[13]

As a constructive enterprise, comparative theology is a rigorously hermeneutical project that requires interpretation, at both poles. Engaging with texts and practitioners from other religious traditions requires an appreciation for the alterity of the other, for the ways in which other traditions will never be fully understood and must remain at least partially opaque to the outsider. Fredericks critiques the old category of "theology of religions," in which Christians interpret the meaning of other religions and their classic texts according to Christian doctrinal standards.[14] This marks the "domestication of difference,"[15] in which predetermined conclusions about the meaning of the religious other can operate as a cognitive shield, protecting the Christian believer from the danger of needing to change her mind.[16] At the same time, the comparative theologian also makes herself vulnerable to the beauty, intelligibility, and truth of that other religious tradition,[17] and thus open to the invitation to amend her theological positions as a result of that conversation.

Comparison also requires nuance for understanding one's own tradition. On the one hand, the theologian remains rooted in and committed to her home tradition. I, for example, aim to speak as a Catholic Christian, as a representative of that tradition. On the other hand, comparison also makes one sensitive to the multiple voices present in the other tradition. Rather than seeing the other religious tradition as a monolithic and unvarying whole, the perceptive comparativist recognizes disagreements, divergences, and ongoing development. Recognizing the complexities of the other tradition, she can then become sensitive to the presence of difference and otherness within her own tradition. Comparative theology then leads to "a heightened appreciation of the ambiguity and poly-vocality" of one's home tradition.[18] Clooney terms this "dialogical accountability": to ensure not only that one accurately understands and represents the views of the traditions one encounters, but also that one gives an accurate and faithful account of one's own community, and thus develops a broader community of conversation.[19] Fruitful comparison lies in the tension between the rootedness and the vulnerability of the comparativist.

The rootedness of comparative theology distinguishes it from comparative religion, which aims for detached and objective descriptions, and whose primary audience is the academic community.[20] By contrast, comparative theology begins with someone with particular faith commitments who intends to speak to her particular home community. As Clooney explains, comparative theology is grounded in autobiography and the practitioner's reflective and contemplative engagement with the other. It begins with the "intuition of an intriguing resemblance" that calls us to place ideas, texts, and so on in comparison.[21] Indeed, as a constructive and personally engaged discipline, comparative theology even views with some incredulity the possibility of remote and disinterested scholarship, seeing all scholarship as directly autobiographical.[22] The fruits of comparative theology are directed back to one's own community, in order that the home tradition may reap the benefits of a more intense conversation.[23] Comparative theology is "participatory," leading the comparativist "from the truth of one's own tradition through the other" before returning home. If comparison involves judgments, they usually pertain only to one's own tradition.[24] The autobiographical nature of comparative theology means that the newness of comparative theology lies not simply in the generation of novel content but in the change in the theologian. As a result of comparison, the theologian may read familiar documents of her own tradition much differently, or may articulate foundational concepts with a subtly different nuance.[25] Rather than dissolving all religious faith, comparative theology "grounds a deeper validation and intensification of each tradition."[26]

Third, most agree that comparative theology functions best in specific and limited "experiments" that are attentive to details and that accentuate differences. In light of the concern to allow the religious other to remain in some ways mysterious and beyond understanding, comparative theology cannot engage in mere generalities. The comparativist must attend to the poly-vocality of the other tradition and must remain always aware of the limitations and shortcomings of any comparison. There is no single and monolithic Hinduism or Buddhism, but rather a range of Hindu and Buddhist thinkers, who may exhibit ambiguity and poly-vocality in their own individual writings. Thus a good comparative theology delves into specifics and particularities, trusting that comparison is more fruitful when diversity is "most evident and most intensely felt."[27]

As it is customarily done, comparative theology limits itself in three ways. First, generally the comparative theologian puts two, rather than multiple, religious traditions into conversation. Given the vast amount of knowledge on theological traditions we now have, it seems unadvisable to attempt a broad conversation among many religious traditions. Rather, most comparativists prefer to begin from a home tradition, and venture into one other tradition.[28] Second, given the poly-vocality of both one's own and the other tradition, many comparativists focus on a single theologian within each tradition to put into conversation. Thus comparison emerges not between Christianity and Hinduism, but between one outstanding representative from each.[29] Third, comparison does not attempt an overview of every aspect of that thinker's work. Rather, comparison focuses on one question or set of questions and themes that each thinker engages. In this way, comparison becomes ever more specific and limited: a tradition, a thinker, and a particular question.

II. Comparative Ecological Ethics

Comparative theology provides a provocative approach that deserves use for ecological ethics, and here I explain my choice of traditions and interlocutors. Most comparative theology proceeds via classical texts, theologians, and certain concepts/categories that are well established, either in both traditions or at least in one tradition. Questions of human flourishing,[30] or divine embodiment,[31] or the limits of human reason in discussing the divine,[32] have established legacies in various religious traditions.

The ecological question, though, is unprecedented and therefore poses questions that traditions have not asked until quite recently. Instead, thinkers from multiple traditions, including myself, are engaging in a creative and critical retrieval of concepts, themes, and principles that may prove fruitful in addressing ecological concerns. Thus an approach to comparative ecological ethics might proceed a bit differently. This project cannot engage a long line of authoritative texts and theologians who address ecological ethics specifically.[33] Instead, I turn to representatives in these traditions who employ a similar hermeneutic: a retrieval, reconstruction, and ecologically focused expansion of classical theological concepts in order to address ecological degradation and reframe humanity's proper relationship to the cosmos and to the Earth.

I do not suggest that these traditions are essentially ecologically friendly or more ecologically compatible than Christianity. There is a healthy debate regarding whether and to what extent all these traditions are ecologically friendly. Donald

Swearer offers a helpful typology of Buddhist approaches to ecology, which could be applicable to other religious traditions as well: eco-apologist, which assumes that an environmental ethic flows naturally from the tradition; eco-critic, which argues that such an ethic does not; eco-constructivist, which contends that a plausible eco-logical ethic can be constructed from concepts, traditions, and texts; eco-ethicist, which argues that a viable ecological ethic should be rooted from its ethical tradi-tion rather than derived from a general worldview; and eco-contextualist, which seeks not a general ethic but effective responses to a particular situation.[34] My approach, and that of my interlocutors, is basically "eco-constructivist": we begin with the presumption that religious traditions grow by developing organically, re-envisioning traditional concepts and texts through ecological lenses. Thus I will note at times the criticisms regarding the ecological interpretation of these terms, but coming from my Catholic tradition, I do not presume to argue whether or not this eco-constructivist application is authentic or not. It is sufficient, for my pur-poses, that recognized theologians and teachers use it in this way, and that it offers a common ground for the cosmic common good.

Some Christians have rightly argued that Hindus, Buddhists, indigenous peo-ple, and others must do the work of outlining how these traditions should think through ecological ethics.[35] While this work is not complete, many of my dia-logue partners have done so and have generated significant insights. So I believe the time has come for a comparative approach that puts these traditions into dia-lectical conversation with each other. Ecological ethicists from various traditions should begin to "compare notes." In this sense, the comparison is not primarily between outstanding representatives of two traditions. Rather, the comparison lies between theologians drawing on principles from their traditions: I, coming from my Catholic tradition, and others, whom I accept as guides, who also look to ori-ent their traditions ecologically. What is being compared are classical theological principles as they are applied to ecological ethics. Because the work of creatively applying this principle to ecological ethics has already been done by the contem-porary practitioner(s), I believe it is justifiable to establish a multi-traditional con-versation on the prospect of looking at the cosmic common good as a ground for ecological ethics. After all, the ecological crisis is so pressing and the effects so dire that all traditions must work fervently to establish as broad and as shared a foundation among themselves as possible in order that all religious traditions might make some impact.

In light of Fredericks's and Clooney's claim that experiments in comparative theology must be limited and focused, a few words about necessary limitations are in order. First, I do not attempt to dialogue with every possible religious tradi-tion. While there are many overlaps among the Abrahamic faiths, and thus I pre-sume a conceivably strong parallel with the cosmic common good, I choose not to engage Judaism and Islam. To test the potential for the cosmic common good as a ground for interreligious ecological ethics, I have selected three traditions that do not share a common historical root or set of texts and doctrines.

Perhaps more important, I have chosen these three traditions for autobiographical reasons as well. While I separate Catholic social thought and non-Christian traditions in this book for purposes of clarity and convenience, in fact my methodology has been dialogic and constructive from the beginning. My sense of the cosmic common good has emerged through my contact with the traditions and teachers I present here. They have influenced and shaped how I read the Catholic tradition and how I think it must develop and extend ecologically. These non-Christian traditions form further theological grounds for my contention that the cosmic common good represents a theologically authentic moral framework for envisioning humanity's place and role in the universe and on an imperiled Earth.

Second, within each tradition I will not attempt to provide an inclusive overview of its potential for ecological ethics, or the range of texts, images, ethical principles, practices, and so on that others have drawn on for articulating its ecological promise. Just as I have limited myself to select principles of Catholic social thought and their potential to be revised and extended ecologically, rather than the entirety of the Catholic tradition, I do not intend to offer an exhaustive catalog of possible points of conversation between Christian ecological ethics and Hindu, Buddhist, and Native American traditions. Indeed, much like Christians who have debated and struggled to determine what aspects of the Christian tradition are helpful, these traditions are multifaceted in their approach and continue to evolve and develop. Instead, it is a focused application: What aspects of these traditions bear an "intriguing resemblance" to the vision of the cosmic common good thus explored? What principles and concepts seem analogous? And, by exploring these concepts in some detail, how might the cosmic common good be further revised, expanded, and deepened? How might Catholic Christians hear the call to contribute to the cosmic common good differently as a result of conversation with these traditions? For each of these traditions, I identify a principle or node of principles that I think form an adequate conversation partner with the cosmic common good. In particular, I focus on the Hindu tradition's understanding of dharma (cosmic order), the Buddhist tradition's understanding of *pratītyasamutpāda* (interdependence), and the Lakota (American Indian) understanding of "mitakuye oyasin" (all my relations).

Third, I will not pretend to provide a comprehensive historical and theological analysis of each principle—dharma, interdependence, and balance with all my relations—in all its complexity and variation. Thus while I contextualize each term in the broader tradition in which it is found by locating how that principle functions, including classical texts, theologians, and practices, I have also selected limited representatives from that tradition who draw on these principles to fashion a distinctively ecological ethic. At times these figures may even be controversial or disputed within their traditions; this only underscores Clooney's point about "diversity within." Still, the concepts they employ have been a major force in articulating ecological ethics in each of the three traditions I explore here. In this way, I hope to have narrowed my focus enough that a meaningful discussion can arise between a Catholic cosmic common good and these other traditions. As a result, each chapter introduces a theme of "intriguing resemblance" to my presentation of a Catholic cosmic common good that is yet also distinctively different, and it alerts us to possible implications of the cosmic common good that were not apparent prior to this dialogue.

The method of comparative theology provides a ground for conversation with other religious traditions by drawing out similarities and differences. The following three chapters demonstrate not only that other non-Christian traditions contain analogues to the cosmic common good within them, but that by exploring them in depth, Christians might develop an expanded and new vision of a Christian cosmic common good. The cosmic common good emerges as a thoroughly Catholic and Christian concept that yields a point of dynamic and fruitful convergence with multiple religious traditions. In light of Clooney's and Fredericks's injunction to seek and highlight dissimilarities, I do not mean to suggest that the cosmic common good elides all significant differences between traditions. Rather, I think it could stand for a kind of "overlapping consensus"[36] in ecological ethics regarding ethical non-anthropocentrism, the simultaneous intrinsic and instrumental value of nature, and the human role to contribute to a sustainable and flourishing Earth community.

Comparative theology represents the kind of interdependent, global conversation we need to have about the great questions facing humanity, and few questions concretize that better than the ecological crisis in all its dimensions. The dynamics are complex, the effects are planetary, and the burdens are disproportionately placed on those nations and peoples that played the smallest role in creating them. Ecological crises embody the global proximity of peoples to each other, and ecology is an issue that touches adherents of every religious and cultural tradition. A comparative approach to ecological ethics may deepen the burgeoning ecological consciousness within these varied traditions, and undergird and support the activities that are already underway. Perhaps equally important, I hope that initiating this conversation can widen the circle of religious intellectuals who are concerned about the fate of Earth and the possibilities for a transformed human-Earth relationship.

Hindu Traditions

DHARMIC ECOLOGY

HINDU TRADITIONS COMPRISE a staggering number of theistic and non-theistic intellectual traditions, including multiple philosophical schools, thousands of sacred scriptures and theological commentaries, and myriad popular religious practices, making them perhaps the most difficult to generalize of the "world religions."[1] No one text or religious school is supremely authoritative, so to speak of "the" Hindu tradition on ecological ethics is clearly misleading.[2] Christopher Chapple outlines three general approaches to ecological degradation in India, the birthplace of Hinduism: tribal and indigenous relationships to the land; Brahminical models that look at classical texts and traditions to emphasize the intimacy between humanity and the cosmos; and the renouncer traditions of Yogis, Buddhists, and Jains that stress nonviolence and the limited consumption of material goods.[3] The latter two are prominent streams of Hindu traditions that could support an ecologically sustainable India and are especially valuable dialogue partners for Christian ecological ethics: the ascetic tradition, which emphasizes limiting the consumption of goods; and the devotional tradition, which praises the divine in all creatures. Pankaj Jain notes that while rural villagers respect the austerity of the ascetics, religious and devotional rituals still dominate their lives, making those a more effective ecological lens than renunciation.[4] Among the Brahminical approaches, the principle of *dharma* has figured prominently. In addition, dharma permeates nearly every strand of Hinduism, making it a suitable way to unite rural, urban, and diasporic expressions of Hindu faith.

Unlike the principles of Catholic social thought, which have been elaborated only recently dharma has long had a central position in Hindu scriptures and Hindu theology. This asymmetry notwithstanding, there are a variety of "intriguing resemblances" that suggest compatibility between the cosmic common good and dharma, as well as interesting points of contrast. To explore the links between the cosmic common good and dharma, I begin with an overview of the concept of dharma and then the recent development among Hindu theologians and scholars[5] of *dharmic ecology*, which attempts to extend dharma ecologically. Drawing on their work, and amplifying it through passages of two prominent and classical Hindu texts, the *Laws of Manu* and the *Bhagavad Gītā*, I will note both resonant and dissonant themes. First, the similarities: theocentrism; the intrinsic value of nonhumans and their unique creaturely contributions to the cosmos; and the cosmocentric context that unites humans and nonhumans into one family of Mother Earth. At the same time, the Hindu tradition also includes other principles that form notable points of contrast with the Catholic tradition: the principle of *ātman*, or the sameness of self across species; rebirth, and the fluidity of creaturely identity; and an ethic of *ahiṃsā*, nonviolence, or noninjury. Finally, I will assess some of the implications for a Catholic cosmic common good.

I. Dharma in Hindu Traditions

Dharma has a dense and complicated role in Hindu scriptures and theological traditions, and the variety of translations for it suggests its broad implications.[6] Derived from the root *dhr*, "to sustain," "to support," or "to uphold," dharma can be conceived as law, righteousness, religion,[7] justice, proper action, merit, and more generally as the "fulfillment of social and religious duties."[8] Dharma represents the origin of world order, the actions necessary to maintain and promote social well-being, and a path to personal flourishing, both now and in eternity.[9]

At the cosmic level, dharma refers to how all that exists is supported and ordered. The dharma of fire is to burn, and the dharma of humans is to act in a dharmic way. "Anything that upholds an individual, a society, a polity, even the cosmos, is its dharma. Dharma is what makes a thing what it is, either descriptively or prescriptively."[10] Dharma, as both personal and social ethics, flows from this cosmic ordering, since justice and religious duty support and uphold human society. Dharma encompasses a theory of virtue and personal development, as well as stipulating detailed ethical rules and the religious obligations one must fulfill. In the *dharmaśāstras*, or dharma texts, the term primarily signifies the responsibilities that people have according to their position in society (related to *varṇa*, or social class) and their stage of life (*āśrama*). The dharmic moral code sustains human society by outlining the social duties that are mandated for particular classes: "[Dharma is] an all-encompassing ideology which embraces both ritual and moral behavior, whose neglect would have bad social and personal consequences."[11]

At the personal level, there is a "subjective" component, consisting of the "inner purification" of the mind, and two objective components, those duties that are universal and common to all (*sanātana dharma*), and those that are particular to one's position in society and one's stage of life (*svadharma*). Dharma entails responsibilities and duties, but these are not conceived of as abstract and universal principles. Instead, they are flexible guidelines that direct but do not enjoin, and the ethos of dharma encourages persons to particularize the rules to her situation so that injunctions may shift in value.[12] From epic stories, one learns the general ethical rules that lead to social cohesion, as well as examples of heroes and villains who embody dharma (or *adharma*), but one must still decide how to apply these rules in one's own personal context. This flexibility of dharma is underscored by the multivalent nature of Hinduism. Hindus generally prefer local traditions, and local custom often supersedes the stipulations in the authoritative texts.[13] Dharma thus begins as a holistic and cosmic concept, establishing order and law for all creatures; it underscores one's responsibility to contribute to the common good and to fulfill duty for duty's sake, correlated to that person's position in society; these duties are not only for temporal well-being but can also lead people to *mokṣa*, or liberation;[14] and, significantly for ecological ethics, it even includes a moral template delineating the proper treatment of nonhumans.

While dharma clearly has a central religious and social meaning, it has not necessarily claimed supreme importance in the Hindu tradition. Classical Hindu texts from around the beginning of the common era outline four *puruṣārthas*, or goals of human life. The first is *artha*, political and economic prosperity; second is *kāma*, sensual pleasure; third is *dharma*, the moral and ritual duties that constitute righteousness; and finally *mokṣa*, liberation from the cycle of death and rebirth and all the attendant struggles and dissatisfactions of this world (*saṃsāra*). *Mokṣa* texts typically focus not on ethical practices but on *tattva*, the truth about ultimate reality, including the identity of the supreme being and the nature of the human person, the goal of human life, and the way to achieve that goal.[15] *Mokṣa* texts avoid making strong dharmic or ethical statements, and they even configure liberation in contrast to the goals of dharma, encouraging devotees to be detached from this world.[16]

Hindu traditions that privilege *mokṣa* as superior to dharma have proven influential among eco-theologians for the way in which they describe a pervasive divine presence through all reality. Arne Naess, for example, drew on the renowned philosophical school of Advaita Vedānta (strict non-dualism) to argue for the intrinsic value of nature and to formulate the principles of "Deep Ecology."[17] Since Advaita sees all beings "as inseparable from ultimate reality," this inspired the idea "that Hinduism sees all of nature as sacred and worthy of reverence."[18]

Yet there are ways in which dharma and the texts and traditions that transmit it are more conducive to constructing a robust ecological ethic. First, *advaita vedānta* achieves its non-duality, in which ultimate reality and the cosmos are inseparable, not simply by divinizing nature but by calling it *māyā*, or unreal.[19] All things derive from Brahman the imperishable, grounding a certain equality between humans, animals, and insentient creatures. Still, that does not indicate that all these creatures are different and yet intrinsically valuable; rather, having the appearance of a distinct and individual identity is fundamentally false.

More important, these philosophical traditions are not widely known except by the greatly learned and are more pertinent to seeking *mokṣa* than guiding everyday behavior, rendering them less helpful in reforming Hindu ecological ethics.[20] By contrast, texts that explore and extol dharma—not only the law books, but more famously through the *Puranas* (stories of creation) and the epics (most notably the *Mahabharata* and the *Ramayana*)—are widely popular, instructive for daily life, and accessible to most people.[21] Since religious devotions dominate the lives of most Hindus,[22] this further justifies the turn from *tattva/mokṣa* texts in philosophical traditions to dharma texts and popular practices.[23]

Thus many Hindu theologians see the concept of dharma as the optimal lens through which to view ecological ethics. There is a close connection between dharma and ecological degradation. As dharma declines, human greed becomes obsessed with consumption and decimates nature, while eras in which dharma is honored are characterized by the thriving of living beings.[24] Some have expressed a concern that the promotion of dharmic ecology functions as a kind of "Trojan horse" that right-leaning Indian nationalists will use to hijack ecological concerns for their own ideological purposes.[25] Still, others hold out the hope that, just as Gandhi used traditional Hindu symbols, texts, and myths to support the cause of Indian liberation from British rule, Indians today could be inspired to adopt more ecologically sensitive practices if the message is rooted in dharma.[26] Indeed, Pankaj Jain claims that unless environmentalism is translated in dharmic terms, it will not succeed in Hindu communities.[27] Swami Vibudhesha Teertha, for example, explains dharma in this way: "According to Hindu religion ... that which sustains all species of life and helps to maintain harmonious relationship among them is dharma. That which disturbs such ecology is adharma."[28] Vasudha Narayanan concurs that while philosophical Hinduism could not prevent ecological disasters, Hindus today employ numerable dharmic texts in diverse ways: as inspiration to plant gardens, to revive wisdom on the medicinal uses of plants, and through song to protest attacks on women and nature.[29]

II. Dharmic Ecology: Theocentrism and the Intrinsic Dignity of Creatures

The first major similarity between a Catholic cosmic common good and dharmic ecology is its theocentrism and the pervasive presence of the divine within the cosmos. O. P. Dwivedi develops four principles that form his vision of dharmic ecology. The first is *Vāsudeva sarvam*—the Supreme Lord or Supreme Being resides in all beings and is the innermost reality of any creature. Myriad passages from sacred scriptures such as the Vedas, the Bhagavad Gītā, and the *Puranas* affirm that the divine is everywhere and dwells within all beings, and therefore all elements of creation are to be respected. The *Bhagavata Purana* (2.2.41) declares that water, air, fire, animals, trees, and all creatures are organs in the Lord's body, and so a devotee respects them all.[30] Drawing on this divine and theocentric foundation, dharmic ecology leads humans to see the divine presence in all things, and as a result to treat all creatures with respect, and without harm or exploitation.

An exploration of the *Bhagavad Gītā* helps to underscore the theocentrism of dharmic ecology. The *Gītā*, certainly the most widely known of Hindu scriptures, is a key source to identify traces of dharmic ecology in classical Hindu scripture.[31] The *Gītā* is part of the renowned and vast Hindu epic the *Mahabharata*, and it consists of a dialogue between the warrior Arjuna and his charioteer Krishna. On the eve of the final great battle between the Pandavas and Kauravas, cousins by birth, Arjuna is devastated by the prospect of having to fulfill his duty as a war-rior to fight and kill his family members. Krishna reveals himself as the *avatar* (incarnation) of the supreme Lord Vishnu, and he explains subtle mysteries, such as how he relates to the universe and that all things exist in Krishna, and how humans can find liberation from the bondage of suffering and rebirth and find release through him.

Dharma clearly plays a central role in the construction of the *Gītā* overall. The first word of the entire epic is *dharma-kṣetre*, "On the field of justice" (1.1).[32] Later, when Arjuna complains of his inability to act, he laments that his mind is befuddled with questions of "right and wrong" (*dharma-sammudha-cetah*), of justice and injustice (2.7). Just as dharma frames the battle between the two great families (it is a war that will be decided on the field of justice), it also precipitates the spiritual crisis that paralyzes Arjuna and necessitates Krishna's extensive teaching.

Dharma integrally relates to the theistic vision of Krishna as the source of the entire universe and the inner nature of all beings. Krishna explains to Arjuna the mode and justification of his many incarnations into the world:

(6) Unborn am I, changeless is my Self, of [all] contingent beings I am the Lord! Yet by my creative energy I consort with Nature—which is mine—and come to be [in time]. (7) For whenever the law of righteous-ness [*dharmasya*] withers away and lawlessness [*adharmasya*] arises, then do I generate Myself [on earth]. (8) For the protection of the good, for the destruction of evildoers, for the setting up of the law of righteousness [*dharma-saṁsthāpanārthāya*] I come into being age after age. (4:6–8)

Dharma, or its antithesis *adharma*, appears three times in just two lines, making this a central site for understanding dharma's relationship to the divine. The Lord is changeless and timeless, the Lord of all beings. The universe arises because of Krishna's "creative energy," but it does not exhaust his power because it belongs to him. The intention behind Krishna's incarnations (*avatāra*) is to re-establish dharma, the law that governs the universe he created. Krishna's identity as the primeval seed of the universe is melded with his task of protecting the virtuous and upholding righteousness. These lines establish two foci for understanding dharma: it is intimately joined with the almighty Krishna who exists in all contingent beings; and its purpose is to establish and protect the good, in human affairs and beyond. Already we see the roots of an ecologically oriented dharma: dharma is a dynamic reality that, through the omnipresent Lord, binds all finite beings together; and this interdependency has a moral force, such that dharma ought to promote the welfare and flourishing of this interconnected whole.

Interestingly, often when the *Gītā* discusses dharma, it is immediately preceded or followed by a text that asserts the panentheistic vision of Krishna abiding in all creation. Krishna is the protector of dharma, just as he is the Lord of all contingent beings. In explaining some of the essential features of his divinity, Krishna begins with a discussion of two natures, a lower one that comprises eight elements, and a higher one that is "developed into life by which this world is kept going" (7.5). He continues to offer a holistic notion of the Lord's natures and the intrinsic connection that links the universe to the Lord: "To all beings these two natures are as a womb; be very sure of this. Of this whole universe the origin and the dissolution too am I. / Higher than I there is nothing whatsoever; on Me this universe is strung like clustered pearls upon a thread" (7:6–7). These lines establish the continuity and discontinuity between Krishna as creator; the universe finds its origin as it emerges from the Lord's womb, and it ends by the Lord's decree. The simile of the world as a necklace of pearls connotes the Lord's centrality but also hiddenness, the form and structure that remains occluded behind various clustered entities. It also suggests a robust affirmation of this world and its value, as a beautiful and precious good that exists to glorify the Lord.

Krishna continues to explain how he penetrates everything, forming the essential core of all created things, and yet is not emptied by the process. His description is a poetic reminder of the pervasive indwelling of the divine in creation: "In water I am the flavour, in sun and moon the light . . . pure fragrance in the earth am I, flame's onset in the fire: [and] life am I in all contingent beings" (7:8–9). Krishna emerges not merely as the pure stuff (*prakṛti*) out of which these beings are made, but as the dharmic essence that gives them identity and their most appealing attribute. Nevertheless, he is not pure spirit (*puruṣa*) that dwells within them as a foreign entity. Rather, Krishna is the "primeval seed of all contingent beings," the origin of that which makes them most unique: "Insight in men of insight, glory in the glorious am I" (7:10). Krishna's indwelling is still rooted in dharma: "Power in the powerful am I—[such power] as knows neither desire nor passion: desire am I in contingent beings, [but such desire as] does not conflict with righteousness" (7:11). Krishna forms the various grounds of being for all creatures, yet this power and desire for life within contingent beings must not interfere with the proper fulfillment of dharma, or righteousness. One of the central themes of the *Gītā* is the purification of desire, of moving beyond self-centered desire by fulfilling one's dharma with no attachment to the fruits of one's actions (*karmayoga*, 2:47).[33] If dharma orders the world, then Krishna cannot tolerate unruly passions that might upset the social, and thus cosmic, order. Instead, Krishna is the origin of all creation who animates creatures in accordance with cosmic law.

In chapter nine, Krishna again discloses himself as creator and as source of the moral law, and he reveals to Arjuna the secret wisdom of righteousness, which abides forever and brings true joy. Next we see the intimate connection between this law and the constitution of the universe:

(3) Men who put no faith in this law of righteousness fail to reach Me and must return to the road of recurring death. (4) By Me, Unmanifest in form, all this universe was spun: in Me subsist all beings, I do not subsist in them. (5) And [yet] contingent beings do not subsist in Me—behold my sovereign skill in works (*yoga*): my Self sustains [all] beings. It does not subsist in them; It causes them to be-and-grow. (9:3–5)

This passage underscores both Krishna's transcendence and the essential distinction between Krishna and all contingent reality, and also Krishna's immanence in creation, since all contingent beings emanate from Krishna. All beings subsist and are upheld by Krishna, yet the Lord is not a passive agent within them. Rather, Krishna causes all beings "to be and grow." The Supreme God is the "the beginning and the end and the middle too" (10.32), the creator, preserver, and ultimately destroyer of the entire universe. In both transcendence and immanence, the law of dharma that humans must obey derives from the same source as the entire universe. In this law people find joy, and without it they are condemned to ceaseless death.

At the magnificent transfiguration, when Krishna reveals his true self to Arjuna, we find another pairing of dharma and the structure of all creation. Arjuna sings the wonders of Krishna and adores his infinite body, which contains multitudes upon multitudes. He exclaims, "Oh, who should comprehend it? You are the Imperishable, [You] wisdom's highest goal; You, of this universe the last prop-and-resting place, You the changeless, [You] the guardian of eternal law [*dharma*], You, the primeval Person" (11:17–18). Again, within this paean to Krishna's glory we understand dharma's integral role in structuring the universe.

The source and rest of the universe, the goal of wisdom, and the security of the eternal law all derive from Krishna.

The *Gītā* depicts dharma as a cosmic law emanating from the supreme Creator Krishna, and this cosmic force is the ground for human social order. Krishna emerges as the source not only of the Earth's existence but of its unique beauty. He is the vivifying principle within the world, giving all contingent beings (which is everything but Krishna) what is intrinsically worthy and valuable about them. Just as Krishna gives power and glory and austerity to humans, he also gives flavor to water, light to the sun, and life to all beings. The Lord underscores that he is the source of their being as well as of their life, which he depicts in terms of vigor and excellence.

III. The Ātman (Self) and the Transmigration of Souls

While there is a remarkable parallel between a theocentric Christian doctrine of creation and the indwelling of Krishna depicted in the *Gītā*, the Hindu tradition diverges sharply in its understanding of the human person. Dwivedi adds to his understanding of *Vāsudeva sarvam*, the Supreme in all beings, the Hindu conception of the *ātman*, or Self, and the belief in rebirth and the transmigration of souls (*punar bhava*). Hindus distinguish the *jīva*, the living or embodied creature, from the *ātman*, the stable, changeless self that resides at the foundation of each living creature. The *ātman* is the true self of all creatures, distinct from our bodies, our senses, and even our thoughts. The *ātman* is understood to be an indifferent, untouched, and unaffected observer, beneath and beyond the vicissitudes of pain and pleasure. The *ātman* is deeper and more fundamental than our identity based on *varna* (caste), gender, or even our species identification. The *jīva* combines the *ātman* with various material constituents (e.g., earth, fire, water), which results in the diversity of species we experience, such that the *ātman* has been reborn as a *jīva* over and over again in multiple kinds of bodies; in the famous words, "from [the creator god] Brahmā to a blade of grass." Thus the *ātman* could exist as a god in a heavenly realm, a human, an animal, or even a blade of grass. A human rebirth is clearly superior to rebirth in nonhumans lifeforms, in part because a human existence allows advancement toward liberation (see later discussion in this chapter), yet all living creatures share a common dignity and goodness. While there is debate between those like Rāmānuja who see many equal but distinct *ātmans*, and advaitins like Śaṅkara who would argue that there is only one metaphysical reality that is identical with *ātman*, still both would agree, "all beings ultimately have the same spiritual potential."[34] Dharma is the moral framework for every *ātman*, because by being what it is, each (nonhuman) *ātman* necessarily performs its dharma. For Dwivedi, the fact that a human being has been an animal in a past life and may return to Earth someday as an animal again means that we ought to show reverence to those nonhumans now. Transmigration of lives across species boundaries establishes a link between the "lowest" life forms and humanity, and it connotes a fluidity to our creaturely identity. If a human life is superior to a nonhuman life, that superiority is a temporally contingent reality, since ontologically each *ātman* is fundamentally equal to another.

The *Gītā* is an important source that represents the general Hindu conceptions of the *ātman*. Here Krishna explains how the *ātman* can never perish: "Never was there a time when I was not, nor you, nor yet these princes, nor will there be a time when we shall cease to be,—all of us hereafter. (13) Just as in this body, the embodied [self] must pass through childhood, youth, and old age, so too [at death] will it assume another body: in this a thoughtful man is not perplexed" (2:12–13). The human person may die, but truly there is never a time when the deepest and most fundamental identity of the person—the *ātman*, the self—was not, since the *ātman* cannot die. Since the *ātman* may assume another body and experience rebirth, that life may easily be nonhuman: "[These] wise ones see the self same thing in a Brāhman wise and courteous as in a cow or an elephant, nay, as in a dog or outcaste" (5:18). The true *ātman* is identical in all these creatures. While this verse has not historically led to the ethical implications for ecology or social justice that it might imply, nevertheless it emphasizes the fluidity of creaturely identity. In a contemporary reconstruction, it is clear how the principle of *ātman* and the transmigration of lives modifies the sense of the divine in all beings and hence of our dharmic duties. Dwivedi concludes that perceiving the Supreme Lord in all beings leads to a variety of conclusions: (1) all creatures, and the universe as a whole, are the proper abode of the Supreme God; (2) the Lord intends the universe for the benefit of all; and so (3) each species must enjoy the benefits of the Earth as parts and members of it, in relationship with other creatures.[35]

IV. Common Good of Mother Earth

Dwivedi offers two further principles of dharmic ecology that connect the common good with the sense of the divine in all creation. The first is *Vasudhaiva kuṭumbakam*, which proposes to see all creatures on Earth as part of one extended family, with the Earth as Mother. Perceiving the Earth as Mother Goddess finds its scriptural roots in the *Pṛithvī Sūkta* of the Atharva Veda, and its 63 verses in praise of Mother Earth. These passages honor all creatures both for their beauty and their utility:

O Mother Earth! Sacred are your hills, snowy mountains, and deep forests.
Be kind to us and bestow upon us happiness. May you be fertile, arable,

and nourisher of all. May you continue to support all races and nations. May you protect us from your anger [in the form of natural disasters]. And may no one exploit and subjugate your children.[36]

Just as Krishna in his transcendent Self is the source of all contingent beings, Mother Earth is the source of all nourishment. This text clearly suggests a dual intrinsic and instrumental valuation for the family of Earth's creatures: it sees all creatures as valuable and beautiful because they stem from the Mother who supports all creatures, but it also recognizes the utility of creatures for the nourishment of others. The attributes of Mother Earth are not for any one people, or indeed for any one species. Instead, dharma demands that we see all cosmic creatures as valuable and part of one extended family.[37] Dharma affirms the underlying unity of all life and the cosmic body that forms the foundation for human society.[38] In this way, dharma already includes nonhumans in the greater good to which humans must contribute.

Dwivedi's final principle of dharmic ecology is *Sarva-bhūta-hitā*, which contends that dharma means working for the welfare of all beings, or in other words the common good. Similar to a Christian notion of the cosmic common good, dharma begins with Brahman, the Supreme Being, who as we have seen undergirds and supports all creation and is thus the universal good of all creatures. Dharma therefore orients people to care for the common good, such as protecting the poor and defending living beings, before they choose a merely private good. A member of the family of Mother Earth who wishes to be a dharmic member of this community acts for the *sarva-hitā*, the common good of all.[39] Dharma outlines duties both to oneself and to the community, and it impels us to do acts of service and to avoid exploitation. A dharmic act provides for the sustenance of the universe, while an *adharmic* act focuses on the good for oneself: "It is I who is powerful." Dwivedi cites the *Mahabharata* for a general sense of the duties entailed in dharma: "That by which the *welfare* of all living creatures IS sustained, that for sure is *Dharma*."[40] Classically, it was the king's or ruler's dharma to protect the Earth, and epithets such as "husband of the earth" and "protector of the earth" expressed the king's duty to safeguard the well-being of the land for all people.[41] Dharmic ecology, then, begins with the divine presence in the entire cosmos and the welfare of all living beings to outline the kind of moral vision that humanity must espouse and the kinds of duties they should uphold. As *ātmans* with profound power, and yet fundamentally equal to nonhuman *ātmans*, human beings have no absolute authority over other creatures. Dharma enjoins obligations to maintain the fabric of moral and social order, contributing to planetary order and healthy relationships with all creatures.[42]

V. *Dharmic Rituals as Embedded Ecology*

In his study of various Hindus groups in India who engage in devotional practices that protect nature, Pankaj Jain singles out dharma as a concept that combines and synthesizes religious faith and ecological practice. For example, the Bishnois, a small community in the state of Rajasthan, follow the teaching of Guru Maharaj Jambaji (born 1451 C.E.), the first guru to offer teachings that we might now recognize as ecological.[43] During a drought in his youth, Jambaji noticed that the destruction of trees led to increased numbers of animal deaths as the drought continued. So he formulated twenty-nine rules for his disciples, eight of which deal with preserving biodiversity and encouraging the beneficent treatment of animals.[44] Over time, this area turned into a lush forest, so verdant, in fact, that three hundred years later, the king of Jodhpur sent officers to the Bishnoi area to procure timber for a new palace. The Bishnois resisted by circling the trees, and the soldiers responded by attacking them, in the end killing 363 people. When the king heard of this sacrifice, he ordered his soldiers to cease and offered them protection, and today the Bishnois continue to adhere to Guru Maharaj Jambaji's injunctions.

In his observation of the Bishnois, Jain concludes that most traditional groups continue their nature worship and ecologically meaningful practices with little understanding of ecology. These groups do not espouse an "environmental ethic" per se, as those in the West might understand it.[45] Similarly, groups in India that do promote environmentalism are inspired more by human needs, rather than a theologically rooted ethic of the divine in all creatures and nature's intrinsic value.[46] Instead, traditionally rooted groups like the Bishnois adopt ecologically praiseworthy choices based on dharma, which weaves theology and religious practices, ecology, and ethics into one coherent whole.[47] When the Bishnois save and protect an animal like the blackbuck, they do so because of the dharmic teachings of the guru.[48] Thus they embody a form of environmental conservation simply as part of their religious observances. Jain agrees with Dwivedi that Hindu traditions intertwine humanity, divinity, and ecology, and he adds to dharmic ecology the dimension of religious ritual: dharma means virtue for humans, cosmic order for ecology, and rituals for spiritual life.[49]

Dharmic devotionals thus function as "embedded ecologies," "where cultural, aesthetic, and religious conceptions orient perceptions of natural spaces."[50] An ecological awareness may not have existed as such, but in the context of certain religious practices, devotees enact a concrete relationship to the Earth and to non-humans that can support ecologically sustainable lifestyles. We may never know the original intentions of why some of these traditions developed eco-friendly practices like tree worship, but what is significant now is to support those practices as they are embedded in daily life.[51] Devotees experience themselves simply as living out their dharma and expressing devotion to God, and it is precisely this organic connection between the embodied practices of faith and the practices that lead to a sustainable human society that dharmic ecology must uphold. "Their *duty, virtue, cosmic ecological order,* and *spiritual* aspects of their lives are all intertwined" because dharma extends outward into all of those dimensions.[52]

VI. Ahiṃsā and Vegetarianism

An innovative feature of dharmic ecology is the extension of the ethic of *ahiṃsā* (noninjury, nonviolence) and the practice of vegetarianism. Together, they point to intriguing possibilities for a nonviolent Earth solidarity. *Ahiṃsā* is not originally a Hindu ethic, but due to the influence of Jains and Buddhists, it became a central feature of Hindu dharma. The principle of *ātman* expresses a level of sameness among creatures, while the principle of karma states that the individual reaps the consequences of her choices.[53] The *Mahābhārata* exclaims, "Ahimsa [nonviolence; noninjury] is the highest dharma [duty or righteousness]. Ahimsa is the best austerity. Ahimsa is the greatest gift. Ahimsa is the highest self-control. Ahimsa is the highest friend. Ahimsa is the highest truth. Ahimsa is the highest teaching."[54] Of course, *ahiṃsā* is not purely an ethic of concern for nonhumans. In the classical era, the ascetic ideal of *ahiṃsā* derived from anxiety about the personal karmic consequences of one's action "more than out of an alleged democracy of all creatures," though communion with other creatures may emerge as result.[55] Still, if Hindus avow a belief that life is interconnected and fundamentally equal, *ahiṃsā* is a logical conclusion.[56] *Ahiṃsā* emerges as a central way to express the belief in the divinity within all creatures and the fluidity of the *ātman* over time.

A related aspect of *ahiṃsā* is the continued prevalence of vegetarianism in Indian culture, even amidst the rise of modernity and globalization. Given the evident links between meat production and climate change, Jain laments the hypocrisy of the developed world for failing to link global problems to personal lifestyle choices. Western conservationists champion the preservation of nature but continue to engage in rampant consumption, and this is obvious in those who devour vast amounts of meat.[57] Jain charges that vegetarianism is "one of the most important dharmic lessons inspired by Indic traditions" that can reduce climate change, as well as better honor the intrinsic value of nature and the human responsibility to treat animals virtuously.[58]

Still, *ahiṃsā* is not an immediately applicable ecological virtue. Lance Nelson problematizes the Hindu principle of *ātman* as a basis for Earth solidarity by showing how classical authors presumed a view of the world that was not only anthropocentric but also androcentric, and even Brahmin-centric, excluding both certain animals and certain marginalized humans together. The Vedic worldview "conceptualized nonhuman animals as 'lower' forms of existence and allowed for animal sacrifice."[59] The basis for a hierarchical anthropocentrism is not a metaphysical distinction between humans and others, but a moral and religious one: only humans can accept revelation, have access to liberation from rebirth (*mokṣa*), and perform dharma in the form of correct religious rituals.[60] The principle of *ātman* seems to form the basis for an egalitarian ethic of respect, yet the way traditional sages interpret this passage reveals a pronounced anthropocentric hierarchy. Rebirth as a dog or an outcaste are clearly regarded as punishments, demonstrating the tight connection between oppressing nonhumans and marginalized humans. For this reason, Nelson concludes that the doctrine of *ātman* and rebirth do not really form a proper basis for a true communion between humans and animals because *ātman* is an ontological category that transcends the realm of emotional and cognitive exchange; and at the level of mind, there is a low estimation of nonhumans, "hence, any powers of, or potential for, *communio* would be limited."[61]

Edwin Bryant portrays an alternative development of the ethic of *ahiṃsā* based on the principle of the same *ātman* in all creatures. While Vedic religion necessitated, and even made obligatory, the sacrifice of animals, later post-Vedic texts exhibit a marked discomfort with this. Commentators upheld the importance of animal sacrifice, distinguishing them from the Jainas and Buddhists who discounted them outright, but they also modify or minimize the sacrifices in the direction of *ahiṃsā*. In particular, Bryant sees the development of vegetarianism, based on *ātman* and rebirth, as an evolving sense of communion between animals and humans.[62] The author of the *Laws of Manu*, for example, upholds the inherited sacrificial system but also creates "efficacious alternatives," which demonstrate a sensitivity for animals as subjects.[63] Post-Vedic authors "envisioned a universe where, at least in theory, all beings were accepted as living subjects with the same rights to life as their human companions" because they all embodied the same *ātman*.[64] More importantly, Bryant raises up the exegetical and hermeneutical strategies that later theologians used to contextualize and reformulate inherited principles. While Nelson is right to express suspicion about the sense of communion with nonhumans in classical texts, Bryant highlights the theological task of reinterpreting the tradition, which is precisely the approach that dharmic ecology adopts. *Ahiṃsā* and vegetarianism may have arisen for different purposes, but they remain a potent facet of Indian culture, capable not only of guiding Hindu approaches to ecological ethics but also of challenging Western and Christian ones as well.[65]

One of the foremost texts on dharma, *The Laws of Manu*, provides an excellent focal point for teasing out the relationship among dharma, *ahiṃsā*, and vegetarianism. *The Laws of Manu* is the most prominent and authoritative legal text on dharma with explicit rules for human activity.[66] It establishes a critical role for dharma: "Stricken, Justice [dharma] surely strikes back; defended, Justice defends.

Therefore, never strike at Justice, lest Justice, stricken, wipes us out" (8:15). Broader than mere justice, dharma as social and religious order is something that, when protected, protects us. As Patricia Mumme notes, if we read dharma here as "ecological order," then it is clear that dharma is a source for the modern concern for ecological stability: "For surely it is ecological order and stability which is the foundation of the whole biosphere and which sustains all species."[67] The temple at Tirumala-Tirupati, in Andhra Pradesh, urges its devotees to plant trees, and it plays off of this verse: "Trees, when protected, protect us."[68] Here the perduring cultural resonance of Manu and the ecological ramifications of dharma are evident.

For Manu, dharma is a cosmic force that applies to all creatures and unites humans to nonhumans in a shared cosmic order, such that damage to nonhuman life must be taken seriously. For example, under the category of punishments for physical assault, Manu contends that one must pay for the promiscuous treatment of other creatures: "For injuring any kind of tree, a fine should be imposed proportionate to its utility—that is the fixed rule. If someone strikes humans or animals in order to inflict pain, the king should impose a punishment proportionate to the severity of the pain" (8.285–286). Here Manu expresses an interesting mixture of what we might identify as intrinsic and instrumental value. The measure of the fine for injuring a tree is based on its utility, while the punishment for inflicting pain is based not on the animals' utility, but on the degree of pain. This implies a kind of intrinsic value and inherent dignity: no creature should be subjected to pain for no purpose.

Other passages reiterate the protection of nonhuman creatures. Even though society depends on agriculture, which is the dharma of the Vaiśyas, Manu exhorts Brahmins not to engage in it, even during times of hardship. "[Agriculture] involves injury to living beings and dependence on others. People think that agriculture is something wholesome. Yet it is an occupation condemned by good people; the plough with an iron tip lacerates the ground as well as creatures living in it" (10.83–84). Or again, "Except during a time of adversity, a Brahmin ought to sustain himself by following a livelihood that causes little or no harm to creatures" (4:1). Manu stipulates a variety of punishments for those who wantonly kill or injure an animal or vegetation (11:132–145), and for some this even entails losing one's caste status (11:60–67). Manu also displays a concern for ecosystems as well, for example by prohibiting people from polluting the water of rivers with filth (4:56). By including animals and their well-being into the legal code, this text evinces an incipient dharmic ecology.

Though humans and animals share a moral order, Manu depicts a complex relationship between the two. At times, animal life is subservient to human life. Manu describes multiple instances, for example, in which people may engage in hunting or the raising of animals for food. In addition, the force of dharma punishes certain evildoers by reincarnating them as shrubs, worms, dogs, or pigs (12:55–68), proving that some animal life is despicable.[69] At other times, however, Manu implies a total equality between animals and some humans in disturbing ways. For example, many of the punishments for killing animals and vegetation are the same as those for killing a Sudra or a woman (11:60–67). Grouping Sudras and women with animals and imposing stiffer penalties on the killing of a Brahmin or Kṣatriya show how assigning differing levels of dignity in creatures does not demand that the line be drawn at the level of species. Still, in general Manu depicts a hierarchy of dignified creatures: humans and animals share a common and interconnected world, with humans at the top, and Brahmins at the summit of humanity.

A closer examination of his rules for eating food demonstrates how Manu clearly upholds the inherited tradition of Vedic sacrifices, but he interprets the prescriptions in a way that moderates and limits that tradition and strengthens an ethic of *ahiṃsā* toward nonhumans. Manu affirms that in the context of a ritual, sacrificial killing does not qualify as killing (5.39, 5.44), so when plants, trees, or animals die in a sacrifice, they receive a higher birth (5.40). Brahmins are allowed to kill approved birds and animals to feed their dependents, as the sage Agastya did in the past (5.22). Manu states that the "twice-born" may consume meat, when it is consecrated at a sacrifice, ordered by Brahmins, when one is ritually ordered to do so, or when one's life is at risk (5.27). Manu then offers the traditional justification for eating meat, stating that it is written into the order of creation: "Prajapati created this whole world as food for lifebreath ... the eater is not defiled by eating living beings suitable for eating, even if he eats them day after day" (5.28, 30). "The Self-existent One himself created domestic animals for sacrifice, and the sacrifice is for the prosperity of this whole world" (5.39). Indeed, if one is commissioned to perform a sacrifice, then failure to consume the meat leads to rebirth as an animal for twenty-one lifetimes (5.35).

Yet Manu departs sharply from Vedic custom in his strict limitations on the consumption of meat outside the stated Vedic rituals. For example, no Brahmin is permitted to eat animals that are not consecrated by ritual formulas (5.36), and he must curb his desire to kill: "When a man kills an animal for a futile reason, after death he will be subject in birth after birth to being slain as many times as the number of hairs on that animal" (5.38). Killing harmless creatures for pleasure induces sorrow here and after death, while seeking the good of all beings leads to immortal bliss (5.45–46; see also 6.60). A concern for unnecessary death leads to a general ethic of vegetarianism:

One can never obtain meat without causing injury to living beings, and killing living beings is an impediment to heaven; he should, therefore, abstain from meat. Reflecting on how meat is obtained and on how embodied creatures are tied up and killed, he should quit eating any kind of meat. . . . There is no greater sinner than a man who, outside of an offering to gods or ancestors, wants to make his own flesh thrive at the expense of someone else's. (5.48–49, 52)

Manu even correlates abstaining from meat with the auspicious power derived from engaging in the horse sacrifice, one of the most revered Vedic rites, every year for a hundred years. The reward for such an impossibly arduous and exhaustive ordeal and the reward for vegetarianism are identical (5.53). Manu offers a phonetic etymology of the word meat, *māṃsa*, composed of two syllables, *mām* (me) and *sa* (he). Manu develops a traditional Vedic argument that the animal whose flesh I eat now (me) will eat me in a future life (he).[70]

The Laws of Manu thus seems to exhibit a proto-ecological ethic in its advocacy for *ahiṃsā* and the limitations it imposes on eating meat outside the context of a sacrifice. It demonstrates how the basis of *ātman* and rebirth offers a platform for a dharma that honors humanity's responsibility to the family of all creatures through its extensive prohibitions against harming living creatures.

VII. Implications for a Catholic Cosmic Common Good

Noting both similarities and divergences, I propose four implications of dharmic ecology for a Catholic cosmic common good.

First, dharmic ecology reiterates and underscores a theocentric and sacred dimension of the cosmic common good. The divine is thoroughly immanent and present in all beings, and all creatures exist due to and for the Supreme Lord. Similar to my conception of the cosmic common good, dharma is rooted in and derives from the ultimate and so fuses the divine, the human, and the cosmos into a coherent whole. In addition, we see the correlation between cosmic order and moral order, connecting divine presence in the cosmos to social welfare, personal moral responsibility, and universal flourishing. Dharma thus offers a cosmocentric context for human righteousness and happiness. Vishnu incarnates repeatedly in order to uphold and protect dharma, and in fulfilling one's dharma, a person achieves life's aim. Just as the common good aims at justice and peace between creatures for the well-being of the whole, dharma signifies the well-being of the cosmos, directing us back to the divine as its source. Dharmic ecology intensifies the connection between the theocentrism and the cosmocentrism of the cosmic common good. It calls humanity to integrate its ethical responsibility to enact Earth solidarity and to support the cosmic participation of all creatures with our religious and supernatural ends and our ultimate orientation to the Lord. Following Jain, there is an integral link between performing one's dharma as devotion to the Lord, and contributing to the ecological and planetary common good.

Second, the principles of *ātman* and rebirth reinforce the principle of creaturely dignity yet establish a more fluid continuity between humans and nonhumans. The concepts of *ātman* and rebirth validate and justify concern for nonhuman animals because they remove the strict Western distinction between humans and nonhumans (as evidenced by the very term "nonhuman"). *Ātman* proposes a sameness of self across species and therefore a baseline of dignity common to all that ought to be esteemed and valued. Moreover, while the Catholic conception of creaturely dignity allows for an elevated human dignity, the principle of *ātman* implies that any moral differences between creatures are subordinate to a more foundational equal dignity. In addition, rebirth teaches that the divide between humans and other creatures is moral and temporal, rather than metaphysical. For these reasons, Dwivedi can speak of the family of Mother Earth, in which case working for the welfare of all creatures is a natural implication. Clearly, as Nelson shows, classical Hinduism instituted a rigid hierarchical order that not only elevates humans and dismisses nonhumans, but also elevates certain classes of humans above others. Contemporary Hindus, however, can reformulate and employ *ātman* to underscore the commonality between humans and nonhumans. Furthermore, while some gradation of species seems reasonable in crafting an ecological ethic, the dharmic dimensions of *ātman* evoke a stronger relativization of those distinctions than Catholic social thought. There may be elevated dignity, but this is contextual to this lifetime, not ontological, and so the divisions are more relaxed. Finally, given the long-standing debates surrounding anthropocentrism, the Hindu tradition suggests that even if we did not move to a cosmocentric common good but instead to an *ātmanocentrism*, that would constitute a significant shift in moral vision. Additionally, *ātman* and *ahiṃsā* join humans and animals in a common category of protection, again broadening the category of dignity.

Third, dharmic ecology signals the importance of *ahiṃsā* and the practice of vegetarianism. In the *Gītā*, Krishna urges the wise to see Him in all creatures, and for Manu this leads to an ethic of reverence for nonhumans. While a Catholic cosmic common good upholds, and even celebrates, the evolutionary development of the cosmos and the predatory relationships that that process entails, the principle of *ahiṃsā* poses a conceptual challenge. Together, the principles of rebirth and *ahiṃsā* suggest that within the cosmic common good, these trophic dynamics must not only be celebrated and preserved, but also somehow be lamented.[71] Earth solidarity, in conversation with Hindus, may need to articulate a nonviolent solidarity that critiques our own participation in evolutionary trophic relationships, even when these are necessary. More concretely, Dwivedi and Jain observe the critical contribution that vegetarianism as a specific commitment to *ahiṃsā* offers to form a more sustainable world. My conception of the cosmic common good must also be open to critique and conversion, just as Hindus have redefined and reconceived their tradition, subordinating the sacrificial paradigm and making *ahiṃsā* and vegetarianism central.

Finally, the close links that Jain outlines between dharma and ecology indicate the force and value of embedded ecologies. For many Hindus, their ecologically resonant and praiseworthy behaviors are primarily dharmic rather than acts of environmental preservation. As Nagarjan describes, this form of "intermittent sacrality" can pose problems, since it may be inconsistent and may even cancel itself out.[72] Yet the ineradicable link between religious worship and dharmic ecology points to the need for a Catholic cosmic common good to include forms of devotion and prayer, rather than merely a religious analogue for a scientifically grounded conservation ethic. This does not call for the creation or fabrication of Earth-honoring devotions, as much as it means recognizing that the practices of Earth solidarity, the promotion of Earth rights, and the celebration of the cosmic common good must be embedded (or re-embedded) within the worship of God, and that these practices are not peripheral but central to our growth in God.

Dharmic ecology affirms and modifies a Catholic cosmic common good in critical ways: similarly, dharma orders creation and links humanity to other creatures and establishes their goodness and value; it gives humanity a central but not separate vocation; and it arises from an integral relationship between the divine and the material world. Dharma thus also contains similar moral implications because it provides a comprehensive vision of the whole, and it produces a moral mandate to uphold that order. By participating in the human and cosmic community, one not only contributes to a good beyond the good of the individual, but it is the central means by which one can attain one's own salvation.

9

Buddhist Traditions

INTERDEPENDENCE

AS IN CHRISTIAN and Hindu traditions, contemporary Buddhists have engaged creatively with classic principles and texts and have applied concepts ecologically in broad ways,[1] including an emphasis on virtues,[2] a focus on vices (or defilements) that drive unsustainability,[3] narratives that inspire better ethical treatment of animals,[4] and classical figures sympathetic to the aesthetic appreciation of nature.[5] Here I narrow my focus to one principle that is central to the tradition, has been used extensively to address ecological ethics, and I believe correlates to a Catholic cosmic common good: *pratītyasamutpāda* (Sanskrit; *paṭiccasamuppāda* in Pali), translated as "dependent origination," "dependent co-arising," "conditioned arising," or "interdependence"; and the related principle of *anattā*, or "no-self."[6]

Rather than trace the universe back to a primal beginning, Buddhists understand the emergence of beings as the product of a series of mutually influencing processes, a dynamic they label *pratītyasamutpāda*.[7] Since dependent origination accounts for the causes and structure of reality, it correlates well with a Christian theology of creation—Thich Nhat Hanh even calls interdependent co-arising the "Buddhist genesis"[8]—and so is a fit comparison for a Catholic cosmic common good.

I begin with a brief overview of the four noble truths and the standard meaning of dependent origination, which establishes it as a cosmological principle. Then I turn to the ecologically inflected interpretation of dependent origination as interdependence in the thought of Thich Nhat Hanh and Joanna Macy. Next, I examine the principle of interdependence through its metaphorical representation in the classical image of the jeweled net of Indra. The similarities between a Catholic cosmic common good and interdependence include the sense of the human as part of a greater whole, and a consonance between this ecological principle and the insights of the evolutionary and ecological sciences. Interdependence and no-self stretch the cosmic common good in its formulation of the relationship between part and whole, the stronger connection between interdependence and the goal of the four noble truths, and by offering a non-theistic and non-teleological common good. Interdependence yields creative possibilities for a reimagined cosmic common good.

I. Pratītyasamutpāda/Dependent Origination as a Cosmological Principle

The heart of the Buddhist tradition is the teaching of the four noble truths, in which the Buddha encapsulates his insight into the nature of reality. First is the noble truth of *dukkha*, translated as uneasiness, discontentment, unsatisfactoriness, or the absence of perfect peace. The second noble truth (*taṇhā*) expresses the origin of *dukkha*: thirst, or self-centered craving, which wants other than what the world offers. The source of life's discontentment is the mind and how it reacts as it does; the second noble truth is also associated with the three mental poisons of greed, anger, and delusion, especially the delusion regarding who we are. The third and fourth noble truths address ending this discontentment: the reality of the cessation (*nirodha*) or "blowing out" (*nibbana*, or *nirvāṇa* in Sanskrit) of craving; and the eightfold path (*magga*), the Buddha's central teaching for liberating people from suffering. The eightfold path comprises right actions (steps 3–5), meditative practices (6–8), and wisdom into the nature of reality (steps 1–2). The first step, "right view," takes aim at the spiritual ignorance that powers the dependent origination of *dukkha*. Right view constitutes "knowledge which penetrates into the nature of reality in flashes of profound insight, direct seeing of the world as a stream of changing, unsatisfactory, conditioned processes."[9] Dependent origination is thus central to the Buddha's teaching of the four noble truths.

The principle of dependent origination represents the Buddha's insight into how the world is arranged and functions, which when experienced helps to end the unsatisfactoriness of customary existence. The scriptures offer a succinct four-line summary of dependent origination, which appear multiple times: "This is, because that is. This is not, because that is not. This comes to be, because that comes to be. This ceases to be, because that ceases to be."[10] Dependent origination stresses the contingency and evanescence of phenomena and the dependency of anything on other factors for its emergence. What a thing is, depends on myriad past and present factors. Nothing is entirely separable from anything else: everything exists as it is because of its connections to innumerable others, which allows us to see our existence as bound up with the existence of everything else. In the earliest scriptures, dependent origination was configured as a causal circle of linked factors. The exact number and specific factors varied, but over time the tradition codified these elements into a series of twelve steps.

Dependent origination accounts for the *dukkha* one experiences in this life by relating it to the development of karma through the choices one has made in the past. More broadly, it also explains the continuing cycle of rebirth. A fundamental ignorance of the nature of reality affects the cravings for pleasant feelings in one's sensory body, which impacts unenlightened intentions and choices, all of which help to generate the state of *dukkha*, the process of suffering, death, and rebirth in various worlds.[11]

Two related principles help to elucidate dependent origination: impermanence (*anicca*) and no-self (*anattā*). We saw above that right view entails a direct insight into the true nature of reality as "changing, unsatisfactory, conditioned processes." Impermanence highlights the shifting nature of reality and the fact that in a ceaselessly changing world, suffering accrues from misunderstanding reality and developing attachments to it. Essentially, impermanence contends that "nothing exists absolutely, with an absolute nature; 'things' only arise in a mutually conditioning network of processes."[12] Right view leads the practitioner to experience and to know as true the impermanence and the sheer emptiness of self-subsistence. Like the Hindu tradition, most Buddhists express a basic belief in rebirth, and thus a fluidity to human identity softens any hard distinction between humans and non-humans. The Buddhist notion of no-self liquefies this distinction further. In direct opposition to the Hindu principle of *ātman*, and the notion of a permanent self that can be reborn through multiple life forms, the Buddha's worldview denies any such self. There is, instead, no stable solid self beneath our physical and mental processes. Not only are all things that humans crave impermanent and fleeting, but so is the very sense of self that most humans take for granted. "What [humans] crave is not, most important, the union with or satiation by something they desire but instead the notion of a self that can experience satisfaction at all. They crave to be selves, able to be completed and fulfilled by unchanging things."[13] A world structured by dependent origination is an impermanent one, and it indicates the lack of any permanent or substantial self. There exists no "thinker of thoughts, feeler of sensations, receiver of rewards and punishments for all its actions good and bad."[14]

Buddhist traditions in East Asia extended the principle of no-self even further, arguing for the radical emptiness (Sanskrit: *Śūnyatā*) of all phenomena, not just human existence. All things are empty of their own independent being, such that there are even no self-existent "things" to be impermanent. Any strict and strong distinction between self and other, or the attempt to locate an unchangeable "essence" apart from anything else is ultimately incoherent. Dependent origination underscores how attachment to the fiction of self versus other, or we versus them, leads to suffering. To separate myself from another, or an "us" from an objectively and ultimately separate "them," is a delusional act. Buddhist practice shifts people from an egocentric viewpoint to an objective one that places nothing in the center. All things lack a core of stable identity, and the goal of Mahayana practice is to experience this.[15]

Dependent origination, impermanence, and no-self function together to provide an explanation for the nature of reality and for the source of human dissatisfaction without reference to any external or divine cause. My identity, my experience of the world, and the nature of all phenomena that I encounter are the product of a host of interconnected and dynamically related factors. The emergence of any creature, including myself, is due to other factors, which in turn are impacted and affected by other factors. Thus *pratītyasamutpāda* has a cosmological bearing, but in a way critically different from a Catholic cosmic common good or Hindu dharma. It accounts for the emergence and order in the world, but there is no appeal to a creator or a transcendent source of the world. Rather, *pratītyasamutpāda* offers an internally relative and non-theistic ground for cosmological order.

The original intent of the teaching of *pratītyasamutpāda* was to provide insight into the nature of craving, the emergence of *dukkha*, and its source in the delusion of a permanent self. As a law of causality, its primary focus is karma and the destructive effects of clinging within a mutually conditioned world.[16] Some contemporary Buddhists, however, see this vision of mutuality and relationality itself as a basis for ecological healing and enlightenment.[17] They have reinterpreted dependent origination to affirm the intrinsic goodness of the interconnectedness of all beings within the universe. Rather than escaping the conditioned world, interdependence teaches us to attune ourselves to ecological interdependence. The law of dependent origination becomes a healing vision of cosmic interdependence that can itself decrease clinging and discontentment both for ourselves and for all beings.

Two aspects of the traditional teaching of dependent origination have become central to its ecological application. First, dependent origination, especially in its Mahayana forms, undermines attempts to establish dualisms between creatures. Just as no-self denies any absolute distinction between self and other, no-self underscores that no one, and no species, is at the center of the universe. Second, as a result, all things as they arise are relative and interdependent. Sallie King argues that through dependent origination, Buddhism recognizes not only the instrumental value of nature, but also the intrinsic value of things. All things are instrumental in that they are factors that condition others, but all things are intrinsically valuable since they do not exist simply to be used for and by another. Instrumental valuation of nature is not inherently bad, but it is only partial. To see things always in terms of instrumentality is a form of egocentrism. For King, it is objectively true that things do not exist for humanity alone, or that they can be well understood only in relation to us. Indeed, to think this way is "a manifestation of our fundamental ignorance."[18]

To explore interdependence further, I turn to two prominent Buddhist teachers and practitioners, Thich Nhat Hanh and Joanna Macy. Nhat Hanh and Macy are central figures in the movement known as "engaged Buddhism," which is a "contemporary form of Buddhism that engages actively yet nonviolently with the social, economic, political, social [*sic*], and ecological problems of society."[19] Engaged Buddhism is not a centralized movement that is led by a single or specific set of leaders, nor is it confined to one geographic area or any single Buddhist tradition (Theravada, Mahayana, Vajrayana, or non-sectarian). Instead, engaged Buddhism is united by the efforts of various Buddhists across sects "to apply the values and teachings of Buddhism to the problems of society in a nonviolent way," as an expression of concern for others and as a direct outgrowth of their Buddhist practice.[20] Indeed, Nhat Hanh himself coined the term "engaged Buddhism" in the 1960s to describe the kind of social awareness and political involvement that he believed Buddhists ought to foster.[21] He sought to disseminate Buddhist ideals of wisdom and compassion for the benefit of all beings. In Nhat Hanh's teaching, Buddhism must be socially engaged because Buddhist practice must lead to love and concern for the entire universe precisely because one learns to recognize oneself as an interdependent part. In their exploration of interdependence as an ecological principle, both Nhat Hanh and Macy model the goal of engaged Buddhism to address ecological devastation from the ground of Buddhist teaching and practice. Macy and Nhat Hanh envision the universe in terms of ceaseless and ontological interdependence, which supports and further extends a Catholic cosmic common good.

II. *Pratītyasamutpāda/Interdependence as an Ecological Principle: Thich Nhat Hanh*

Thich Nhat Hanh is a contemporary Buddhist monk and teacher whose writings and life revolve around the teaching of mindfulness, being in the present moment, and interdependence. Trained primarily as a Zen monk in Vietnam, Nhat Hanh later became the founder of a new order of Buddhist monks and laypeople, called the "Order of Interbeing." Nhat Hanh places interdependence at the core of his teaching and practice in a way that renders it explicitly ecological.

For Nhat Hanh, the principle of interdependence is central to the Buddha's teaching and is rooted in a conventional Buddhist understanding of impermanence and no-self. Impermanence, he explains, is neither positive nor negative. Impermanence is simply the nature of reality that makes life possible. "All things are in endless transformation and without an independent self."[22] Impermanence and no-self are the basis of interdependence. Since everything changes, all beings depend on other factors for their present existence. To see impermanence and no-self clearly is to perceive the truth of interdependence. In fact, all Buddhist teachings are based in some way on interdependent co-arising.[23]

Nhat Hanh translates *pratītyasamutpāda* literally as "in dependence, things rise up." Earlier Buddhists understood this as "interdependent co-arising," but he prefers "interbeing."[24] As we shall see, another popular expression of dependent origination is the "interpenetration" of beings, which expresses the mutual dependence and interrelatedness of creatures. Interpenetration, however, has the connotation of some kind of divide between creatures, of an external force somehow entering into the internal reality of a being. Instead, Nhat Hanh argues, interbeing expresses the reality that there is no ultimate distinction between external/internal. Instead, creatures simply "inter-are."

Following the Buddha's death, Buddhist schools and teachers elaborated multiple ways of interpreting the principle of interdependence. For example, the standard form outlines twelve links, and some interpret these twelve links according to past, present, and future lives, or to two levels of cause and effect. Nhat Hanh argues, though, that the links are not to be understood as a linear or causal chain because causality is omnidirectional. The number of links and their relationship are meant to be a guide for meditative practice and to help put an end to our suffering. Indeed, the Sarvāstivāda school teaches that dependent origination can be expressed via one, two, three, four, five, or up to twelve links.[25] The first link, ignorance, is taken by some to be the foundation for all the others, but Nhat Hanh counters that in the Buddha's teaching there is no first cause that is not conditioned by the others.[26] Instead, the links are empty and impermanent. None exists except for the presence of the others, and each link conditions and is conditioned by all the others.[27] "Each link in the chain of Interdependent Co-Arising is both a cause and an effect of all the other links in the chain. The Twelve Links inter-are."[28]

The interdependence of all things and the reality of impermanence do not necessarily negate differences between creatures. Nhat Hanh's view of interbeing insists on both unity and diversity, since they themselves are interdependent.[29] Interdependence describes the fabric of the entire cosmos that links diverse creatures together because every entity is formed through the coordination of other phenomena. The unity that interdependence creates, however, does not revolve around any one creature, or a species of creatures, or even the universe itself. "The universe is a dynamic fabric of interdependent events in which none is the fundamental entity."[30] The principle of interdependent origination teaches that "the one comes about because of the all, and the all is present in the one."[31]

For Nhat Hanh, interdependence and the truth of no separate self are not only Buddhist principles, but they are also attested to by the insights of modern Western science. For example, the science of genetics shows that there is no "I" here apart from my ancestors, who continue to live in me through my genetic inheritance.[32] Indeed, "'Myself' is nothing more than an appellation for a whole line of ancestors whom I represent."[33] Extending this more broadly, he draws on evolutionary theory and the biological sciences when he posits that human beings are composed of various nonhuman parts such as rocks, plants, and animals. Echoing Thomas Berry, Nhat Hanh contends that nonhuman creatures form part of us because in an evolutionary worldview we could only have arisen due to the emergence of these other creatures: "As I look more deeply, I can see that in a former life I was a cloud. This is not poetry; it is science." Nhat Hanh circumvents the question of belief in the Buddhist principle of rebirth by remarking that one's existence as a cloud is a scientific and historical fact. "Everyone of us has been a cloud, a deer, a bird, a fish, and we continue to be these things, not just in former lives."[34]

Nhat Hanh also appeals to modern physics and the science of atomic particles to illustrate the principle of interbeing. Scientific discovery reveals that each entity that we can observe actually consists of innumerable little particles, which in turn comprise smaller elements. At this unfathomably miniscule level, every particle depends on the others for its stability and existence. Each particle in fact is an interconnection between other particles, which are interconnections for other particles. This for Nhat Hanh becomes a synecdoche for the entire universe and a nearly perfect metaphor for interbeing.[35] Our bodies and minds have arisen from the soil of countless other beings, and so in a way we continue to be these things. If there exists no central and eternal "I" within me, argues Nhat Hanh, then I may equally profess to be the countless beings that conditioned my emergence.

Nhat Hanh famously offers tangible examples to explain interdependence that not only express the teaching but are also explicitly ecological. A flower, for example, is always receiving "non-flower" elements, such as water, air, and sunshine, to sustain what it is. Just as a flower is a stream of change, so is human life, which also cannot be separated from water, air, sunshine, and flowers.[36] Similarly, when one looks deeply at a table, one can see all the causes necessary for it to exist (sunshine and trees); and when one looks deeply into these causes, one perceives the table.[37] The interdependent relationship between a tree and its leaf helps to explain the interbeing of the twelve links of interdependent co-arising, because a tree gives birth to the leaf, but the leaf provides nourishment to the tree and so is mother to the tree.[38] The dynamic and mutual interdependence of the various links of the principle of dependent origination are mirrored in the dynamic and reciprocal relationship one can witness between trees and leaves.

As his examples demonstrate, Nhat Hanh does not view the teaching of interdependence as a cautionary explanation of the factors that lead to suffering, but also as a wholesome worldview that can lead to wisdom and compassion. Previous Buddhist teachers, he thinks, have missed the positive mental states that interdependence can induce.[39] Consciousness itself, for example, is only dissatisfying when it is watered by unwholesome seeds such as ignorance and craving. The seed of awakening is present in each link of interdependence, and again Nhat

Hanh employs an earthy, ecological metaphor to depict this positive dimension: "In compost there are flowers; and in flowers there is compost. If we know how to make compost, it will quickly become flowers."[40]

One of Nhat Hanh's greatest contributions to Buddhist ecological ethics is the development of a series of mindfulness practices and meditations on interbeing. These concrete meditative practices enable practitioners to acquire a direct insight into interdependence and to experience its beneficent power. In turn, they help people reinhabit their body and the world and thereby express an explicitly ecological ethic. For example, Nhat Hanh invites us to eat an orange mindfully and to bring our attention to all the senses involved:

> Peel the orange. Smell the fruit. See the orange blossoms in the orange, and the rain and the sun that have gone through the orange blossoms. The orange tree that has taken several months to bring this wonder to you. Put a section in your mouth, close your mouth mindfully, and with mindfulness feel the juice coming out of the orange. Taste the sweetness.[41]

The purpose of the meditation is mindfulness, waking up to the miracle of the present moment. Attending to the reality of ecological interdependence heightens one's sense of wonder and reduces clinging. Observing the color and shape, the smell as we peel back the rind, the taste of the orange as we chew one bite at least fifty times[42]—these details sharpen our awareness of the present moment and decenter our self-centered preoccupations, which cause suffering. Nhat Hanh extends this by meditating on all the ecological conditions that made this orange possible: the rain, the sun, and the months of effort expended by the tree will soon become a part of us as we eat the orange. Eating an orange becomes a path to experiencing the truth of interbeing and the reality of no separate self.

Nhat Hanh presents similarly ecologically oriented versions of the traditional Buddhist mindfulness meditations on the body. In the "Touching, Healing" exercise, Nhat Hanh invokes a number of Earth images in order for the meditator to touch and come into contact with various phenomena, and then to extend thoughts of healing toward them. These include the pure mountain air, a clear stream, the arctic ice fields, the clouds, and the trees.[43] Meditating on aspects of these, such as their clarity, their freshness, or their freedom, helps the meditator to develop those capacities in herself. This meditation also awakens, however, the ecological realities affecting the imperiled Earth: "When we visualize the arctic ice fields, we may recognize that this is a wonder of nature that is disappearing as global warming increases. This will help us be in touch with impermanence and also strengthen our deep aspiration to do all we can to reverse global warming."[44]

Perhaps his most famous example of interbeing, however, is his invitation to ponder deeply a white piece of paper and to see the cloud within it. This is not poetic whimsy, or an abstract philosophical principle; rather, by contemplating the paper's origins, we see in fact that it comprises multiple other entities. The paper arises because of previous conditions, and as such it exists in interrelationship with everything that precedes it and follows it. "You will see clearly that there is a cloud floating in this sheet of paper. Without a cloud, there will be no rain; without rain, the trees cannot grow; and without trees, we cannot make paper. The cloud is essential for the paper to exist. If the cloud is not here, the sheet of paper cannot be here either."[45] Nhat Hanh continues and discovers within the paper the presence of the sun that made the tree grow, the logger who cut the tree, the bread that fed the logger, the parents who gave birth to the logger. Just as this paper contains a multitude of other beings, there is no way we can annihilate this piece of paper. "This sheet of paper has never been born, and it will never die. It can take on other forms of being, but we are not capable of transforming a sheet of paper into nothingness."[46] By extrapolation, everything in the universe is like this piece of paper, including human beings. We contain a host of other beings within us; there is no time when a separate "I" began, and there will be no time when a separate "I" dies. Meditating on the principle of interbeing by peering deeply into reality allows an unmediated experience of oneself as connected to the universe and can awaken latent powers of compassion and healing that enable us to appreciate our connectedness to all beings. Thus realizing interdependence is the expression of "right view," and key to the cessation of *dukkha*. Nhat Hanh's meditation on the piece of paper has a dual purpose: as a reflection on the reality of interbeing, it is meant to pierce delusion, to empower people to see reality, and thereby to reduce their suffering and eliminate fear. At the same time, it also contains a potent ecological message: without healthy clouds, healthy water, and healthy soil, there may be no paper, or worse, no food.

When one comes to an awareness of the interbeing of things, one discovers that the well-being or suffering of any being cannot be indifferent to us. Mindfulness of interbeing leads to spontaneous compassion, the expression of the second aspect of the eightfold path.[47] Compassion must not only be felt but expressed.[48] Moreover, this action is not on behalf of the other, but for oneself as well. Everything is interconnected, and so damage to one sphere of reality endangers my own well-being. "We humans are made entirely of non-human elements, such as plants, minerals, earth, clouds, and sunshine. For our practice to be deep and true, we must include the ecosystem. If the environment is destroyed, humans will be destroyed too. Protecting human life is not possible without also protecting the lives of animals, plants, and minerals."[49]

The lack of any individual substantial self means that every person contains many selves, most of which are nonhuman. To act on behalf of nonhuman nature, then, really reveals an act of wisdom and compassion that also protects oneself. To protect rivers, we must be our true larger selves, which includes rivers. "Because we inter-are with the trees, we know that if they do not live, we too will disappear very soon."[50] For Nhat Hanh, enlightened awareness means both recognizing one's interdependence with trees, clouds, arctic ice fields, and the entire Earth, and then acting compassionately to protect them. By drawing on the Buddhist principle of interbeing, Nhat Hanh unites the ethical concern to protect the Earth with the central religious ends of the Buddhist tradition. Interdependence is a theological principle that explains the origins of *dukkha*, but it is also an ecological principle that provides the foundation for mindfulness and peace.

The doctrine of interbeing prompts the Buddhist practitioner to dispel delusion and extinguish some of the sources of suffering by drawing closer to those parts of the cosmos that constitute her own existence. The classical doctrines of dependent origination and right view acquire a new thrust: "There is nothing which is 'more real' beyond the interdependence of everything in nature."[51] Interdependence represents both a liberating insight into the karmic causes of suffering and a gateway to liberation by enabling people to experience non-conceptual reality in the infinite connections among beings in the universe. In one sense, engaging in ecologically responsible behavior represents an expression of enlightenment. At the same time, expressing fundamental principles in an explicitly ecological way encourages people to see reality more truly. Mandating a concern for the Earth and for the welfare of nonhumans prepares the soil of the mind for adherents; they may begin to see themselves and the world more clearly.

III. Pratītyasamutpāda/Interdependence as an Ecological Principle: Joanna Macy

Joanna Macy is a prominent lay Buddhist and scholar-activist in the West whose ecological interpretation of interdependence has also been a guiding force for contemporary engaged Buddhists. Macy combines her understanding of dependent origination with the philosophical school of general systems thinking.

Like Nhat Hanh, the principle of interdependence has been foundational for Macy, and she likewise argues that it represents the central doctrine of the Buddhist tradition. She even calls interdependent co-arising the "deep ecology of all things."[52] Based on her reading of the earliest Buddhist texts, Macy argues that dependent origination represents the unique and distinguishing insight of the Buddha. It underlies everything that the Buddha taught about suffering, the nature of the self, and the means of liberation from suffering. The radical relativity and impermanence of reality itself provides the moral grounding and the rationale for the four noble truths and the steps of the eightfold path.[53] The doctrine of dependent origination, while it can seem abstruse, helps us to see the deep intricate web of all beings and the reciprocity of thought and action, of self and other. Dependent origination prompted Macy to understand her feelings of despair at the ecological and social devastation all over the world as a natural and healthy pain that arises due to our mutual belonging together, and in turn she has developed and led many "despair and empowerment" workshops to assist others.

The flow of reality, Macy explains, is continual, but it is not merely random flux. Instead, things are determined by factors of conditionality. Reality is a "web of mutual causality," each creature being both cause and effect.[54] Certain factors help others to arise by providing the context for them, and in turn they are affected by that relation. Macy thus detects a "reciprocal dynamic" among beings, such that power does not belong to any one cause, but inheres in the relationship between causes.[55]

A deeper understanding of interdependence can occasion an expansion of our sense of self. As we have seen, the Buddhist tradition denies the Hindu concept of an abiding self and instead argues that there is no stable or permanent self to be found. The self is simply a "metaphoric construct of identity and agency," a concept we use for self-preservation, self-approval, and self-interest.[56] Macy detects a cultural shift, however, whereby people are extending their sense of self to become co-extensive with other beings and with the life of the planet. She describes this process as the "greening of the self." Human beings are meant to experience the world as an extension of our self, and the story of the universe as our own story.[57] The larger cosmic self is not undifferentiated; just as leg, liver, and lung are differentiated within our one human body, so are the various beings of the world.[58] Differentiation does not lead to hierarchy, though, and an appreciation for human interdependence with nonhuman beings will lead people to work for the Earth, as it constitutes their very selves.

Macy sees in systems theory a good analogue for interdependence. General systems theory views cognitive activity as a circuit, which embraces both the external world and that which perceives it.[59] Feedback forms a causal circuit, making perceptions conditioned by previous experience. There is no such thing as an uninvolved observer. Instead, the self is an open, self-organizing system that draws on the world to constitute itself. Thus systems theory sees the human person as a "flow through," a conduit of matter, energy, and information. Mind or consciousness, then, is immanent in nature, since the human capacity to know is simply an intensification of a wider natural process. Human beings are "resilient patterns within a vaster web of knowing."[60] The process of knowing is interactive and relative to the perceiver. Thus it is difficult to speak of ultimate truth, or of a transcendent and perfect object of knowledge. The Buddha, Macy claims, did not teach a supreme object to know, but rather a supreme mode of knowing.[61] Macy draws on Gregory Bateson, who argues that the abstraction of a separate "I" distinct from others and the world is an "epistemological fallacy" of the West. The process by which humans incorporate information and materials in the course of deciding and acting is much larger than individual subjectivity. The separate self in the Western mind is really a "false reification" of only one part of a larger self-corrective feedback circuit.[62] Like systems theory, Buddhism also undermines the distinctions between self and other, but more importantly, it also demonstrates the pathogenic character of any reification of self, and it offers methods for healing this suffering. The principle of interdependence, the co-arising of phenomena, reveals the convention of a separate continuous self as a dangerous fiction that leads to suffering for oneself and for the Earth.

For Macy, the principle of interdependence helps us to heal the Earth in three ways. First, it demonstrates our embeddedness in the web of life. All things exist because of the presence of other factors around them. Even our human capacity for knowledge is a form of being embedded in the world, since our process of perceiving the world incorporates the world into our act of knowledge. Interdependence thus reveals not only the illusion of a separate self, but also the illusion of human flourishing at the expense of a degraded Earth. Second, interdependence highlights humanity's distinctive capacity for action. Consciousness pervades all existence and so does not set humanity apart, but consciousness is not uniform. Nonhuman creatures have their mind events, but their mind doesn't loop back in complexity as human minds do. Macy configures humanity as integrally related to everything else: "We exist in nested hierarchies of natural systems, from the molecules and organs that comprise our bodies to the social systems and ecosystems that sustain us from without."[63] Human consciousness is a privileged site of interdependence, one that can recognize it and respond accordingly. Actions based on the delusion of a separate self or on the solely instrumental value of nature will lead to suffering, while actions that embody interdependence will lead to compassion. Third, Macy argues that the sense of a greater eco-self can support the kinds of sacrifices that ecological ethics calls for. Moral exhortations and guidelines in themselves are insufficient, while a broadened and deepened sense of self would naturally lead to a change in self-interest and a desire to benefit nonhuman beings.[64] Theological contributions to ecological ethics are based on a proper sense of humanity's place and role on Earth, rather than merely impassioned rhetoric or more detailed social and personal prescriptions.

IV. The Jeweled Net of Indra

For both Nhat Hanh and Macy, a classical metaphor discussed in the *Avataṃsaka Sūtra* and elaborated in the teachings of Hua-Yen Buddhism (in China; Kegon Buddhism in Japan) poignantly expresses the ultimate meaning of interdependence: the jeweled net of Indra.[65] Far away in the heaven of the great god Indra, there is a net that stretches out in infinite directions. At each juncture of the net lies a jewel, and each jewel is infinitely faceted. So, within each of the infinite jewels sits the reflection of every other jewel, leading to an endless series of inter-connected reflections.[66] These glittering jewels are not only related and connected, but internally interrelated. The light that pervades one jewel enters into and con-stitutes the light that illuminates all the other jewels as well. A change or alteration in one jewel would instantly be reflected everywhere. Configuring every jewel as a representation of an individual life form, cell, or unit of consciousness, the net of Indra depicts a universe composed of beings existing in a complex interdependent matrix.

In Kegon Buddhism, two doctrinal formulations express the meaning of this image: *riji muge*, the interpenetration of part and whole; and *jiji muge*, the interpen-etration of part and part. Not only are all things marked by extensive relatedness and dependent on each other for existence, but they are also "interpenetrating," meaning that things are literally constituted by and constitutive of others. Nothing exists that does not in some way depend on its conditions; observable beings exist only because the surrounding conditions permit it, and in turn these conditions become part of what that creature is. This interpenetration exists between each part, and between each part and the whole. A change in one being will affect all the others and will alter the flux of the universe. Thus in Hua-yen Buddhism, "there is nothing which is not of value in the great harmony of nature."[67] Since all things are empty of a separate and stable self, this also means that all things are deeply interrelated. When one is harmed, all is harmed; one restored, all improved. Everything is related, but each also makes its contribution to the whole.

The interpenetration of parts means that nothing can be considered separate or extricable from the whole, but it does not deny the distinctiveness of the parts. The net of Indra entails "neither a monistic dissolution of the self into Indra's net nor a transcendence of the net."[68] Interpenetration denies any objective standpoint by which one could judge the universe in its entirety. Every being may remain in some way distinct from the rest of the universe, but it cannot claim to occupy a position separate from the universe. The origins of any being are dependent on external conditions, but that dependent origination remains distinct from oth-ers. The net of Indra thus leads to the loss of any "perspectiveless perspective,"[69] because there is no way to stand apart from the remainder of the cosmos.

This image sheds light on the non-theocentric, non-teleological, and non-hierarchical dimensions of this Mahayana Buddhist tradition's relational and "cosmic ecology."[70] Beings rely on nothing else but themselves and thus consti-tute "a self-creating, self-maintaining, and self-defining organism." There is no theory or concept of a creator or a beginning time, or an explanation for the pur-pose of the universe. The net, or the universe, simply is as it is. The principle of dependent origination and the image of the net of Indra critique all notions of self-existence and reaffirm the teachings of emptiness and impermanence. In the net of Indra, the interpenetration of parts means that no part is intrinsically inferior to another. Any supposedly superior entity is composed of the lower, and likewise the superior is contained within the lower in complete reciprocity. The jeweled net of Indra deconstructs the mind's tendency to arrange a hierarchical universe comprised of substantial beings who deserve their status because of who they are. By contrast, here each part possesses value because it is contained within everything else. In this image, the human person "cannot be considered the crown of creation, because there is no hierarchy and no center."[71] Or, if there is a center, "it is everywhere."[72] There is no telos or ultimate purpose to the net, either in the Creator or in humanity. The net of Indra depicts the dynamic of interdependence in which all beings participate, but no individual creature or subset of creatures can purport to be the true purpose for the dynamic.

One clear ecological implication of this image is the danger of environmental degradation and the moral imperative to restore and rehabilitate a degraded Earth. As Stephanie Kaza explains, "If any jewels become cloudy (toxic or polluted), they reflect the others less clearly. To extend the metaphor, tugs on any of the net lines, for example, through loss of species or habitat fragmentation, affect all the other lines. Likewise, if clouded jewels are cleared up (rivers cleaned, wetlands restored), life across the net is enhanced."[73] There is a certain self-interest in restoring cloudy jewels to a more brilliant state, but following Macy, it is an expanded self that includes rivers and wetlands as constitutive of our very being.

V. Implications for a Catholic Cosmic Common Good

Contemporary eco-Buddhists like Thich Nhat Hanh and Joanna Macy offer a profound support to a contemporary interreligious ecological ethics through their understanding of interdependence. Here I trace out some of the similarities and differences between interdependence and a Catholic cosmic common good.

I note at least six similarities between interdependence and the cosmic common good. First, both employ part/whole images and concepts to provide a moral framework by which human beings are part of a greater cosmic whole. The human person is inextricably related—and insufficiently understood without reference to—nonhuman nature, to the entirety of Earth, and indeed to all beings. There is an "interpenetration" of part and whole, such that the human person and the entire human community are formed by their relationship to the whole, and the whole is impacted by the participation of each part. Or, following Nhat Hanh, all creatures are already mutually implicated, and so "inter-are."

Second, interdependence also argues for a parallel description of the intrinsic/instrumental valuation of nature. A host of dynamically related factors contributed to my own emergence, making them instrumentally valuable to me, yet in turn I am a factor in their emergence, making me instrumental to them. The net of Indra provides another model for the cosmic common good, allowing for the distinctiveness of each part and its radical connection to the whole, as well as the simultaneous instrumental and intrinsic value of every being.

Third, both interdependence and the cosmic common good privilege relationships over discrete subjects. Like a Catholic cosmic common good, interdependence teaches that multiplicity constitutes an integral and essential feature of unity; and that relationships are primary, because there is no substantial self that can exist independent of others. The true paradigm of reality, as the ecological crisis currently demonstrates, is one of fields of relationships, not of substantial objects only tangentially affected by their contexts.

Fourth, despite the emphasis on relationships, neither the cosmic common good nor interdependence seeks to destroy or negate all individuation. Interdependence makes the individual more real by seeing her as part of a greater whole. The interpenetration of parts signifies that every part, in itself, is valuable within the overall unity of the universe.

Fifth, in their methodological approach, Nhat Hanh and Macy similarly draw on ecological and evolutionary sciences, as well as contemporary philosophical systems, to reinterpret the classical doctrine of dependent origination as the ecologically oriented interdependence.

Finally, interdependence and the net of Indra provide another support for bioregionalism and drawing closer to the particular locales where we come into contact with the cosmic common good. As Nhat Hanh proposes, to see a flower deeply is to see the entire universe.

At the same time, various dimensions of interdependence pose an opportunity for challenging certain aspects of a Catholic cosmic common good. Here I note five. First, interdependence articulates a non-theocentric and non-theistic cosmic common good. A universe that is completely interdependent does not require an external source for validation. Unlike Christianity, which perceives the universe in terms of its identity as God's creation and as part of a temporal history of salvation, Buddhist traditions do not ground their moral framework on any further source of the universe because there is none to discover. This means, however, that the universe is to be taken as a fact, in its multifaceted entirety. One does not look beyond reality in order to discern a further cause for its goodness, but instead accepts it as a fact to be experienced. In a similar way, the universe is also non-teleological and non-anthropocentric. The universe does not exist to accomplish some predetermined goal, especially the flourishing of humanity. Like Berry's cosmocentric vision, but without any allusion to a "numinous origin," the existence of the Buddhist cosmos is self-justifying.

On the one hand, while this does differ from a Catholic cosmic common good, the aforementioned similarities lend credence to my claim that the cosmic common good presents a common ground among religious traditions. While a Christian cosmic common good will be theocentric, theocentrism is not neces- sary to identifying a moral framework in which all beings are instrumentally and intrinsically valuable and the human person properly belongs to a cosmic commu- nity. Interpreted theocentrically, the cosmic common good leads directly to God; without theocentrism, a cosmocentrism that decenters all subjects remains viable. The Christian may ground each creature's right to cosmic participation in the ontological participation of each creature in God, but this latter dimension is not absolutely essential to arguing for a non-anthropocentric ecological ethic.

Second, interdependence or interbeing offers an intriguing intensification of how human beings belong to a greater whole. Interdependence stresses the Earthly and cosmic dimension of human identity. Humans are in nature, and nature is in us, and to show compassion for oneself, we must also show compas- sion to the Earth. Nothing is more real than interdependence, and nothing will bring us real joy and peace until we recognize the reality of our total, inextricable interdependence with the rest of the universe. The doctrine of the interpenetra- tion of part and part suggests not only that the self belongs to the whole, but that the self is also constituted by and dependent on other selves. To be human is to be composed of nonhuman elements, and to engage in human consciousness is to include the world within us. Nhat Hanh's meditations provide a clear example of how the mind might encounter the truth of this claim, a truth that is both scien- tific and experiential. Or, following Macy, we recognize an alternative intensifica- tion of creaturely dignity by seeing the self as Earth and as the cosmos itself. An expanded sense of self means that humans care for the whole not just because we belong to it, but as our very self. Macy understands the human as "open systems" who are constitutively communal and oriented to a greater good, and even in some way ontologically indiscernible from the whole.

While it seems to lend greater emphasis to the whole, in fact interdependence privileges neither, and so it offers a point of contrast with the Western world's preoccupation with how to balance the individual and the collective. As we have seen, the Western Christian tradition has long feared a collectivism that swallows the individual into the whole. Yet as Nhat Hanh and Macy present interdepen- dence, emptiness stands at the core of the collective as well as the individual. Interbeing provides an alternative relationship of unity and diversity that coun- teracts the threat of dissolving the individual's integrity into the common good. Interdependence does not allow the good of the whole to mask the good of the individual being because there is no stable identity or permanence to the whole that must be preserved either. Interdependence displaces humans as centers, but replaces it with nothing else. Coming from a Western perspective, interbeing pro- vides a helpful corrective: rather than merely balancing individual and commu- nity, interdependence affirms the relative well-being of each while simultaneously negating the ultimate separation of both.[74] Even cosmocentrism, then, is too much; centrisms themselves are suspect. In this way, interdependence is deeply ecological: one pursues a cosmic common good as the matrix of interbeing, the mutual good of each being and each whole, including each planet, and indeed the entire cosmos.

Third, an expanded sense of self, or an intensification of human belonging to the cosmic whole, makes hierarchy or any attribution of proportionate dignity questionable. A Catholic cosmic common good argues for an essential creaturely identity and for the cosmic participation of all creatures, but it also allows for an elevated dignity of the human person. The Hindu principle of *ātman* recalibrates human uniqueness by including all living creatures within the scope of *ātman*. Interdependence, no-self, and the net of Indra further complicate differentiated dignity and offer a profound argument against claims of superior value over other creatures. Attempts to erect barriers between self and other of any kind, including substantial differentiation between human and nonhuman, is grasping at a delusion, which will result in suffering. Anthropocentrism is not only theologically unjustified; it represents a fundamental delusion that leads to uneasiness and suffering, both for those who hold this view and for those with whom they come into contact. Nhat Hanh and Macy seem to be imploring those of us in the Christian West to modify our sense of self and our understanding of humanity's place within the whole of the cosmos. This delusional view that humanity is somehow able to live above or apart from other beings has led to the ecological crisis, and recognizing the fundamental truth of interbeing is the optimal way to lead us out of it.

Fourth, interdependence clarifies and strengthens solidarity between humans and nonhumans. Interdependence establishes the connection between a right view of the world and the right attitude (steps one and two of the eightfold path), making solidarity a natural impulse rather than a moral imperative. The virtue of Earth solidarity flows from a conception of self as related to others, and in turn strengthens this insight. A delusional sense of separate self, or of being a member of a separate species, hinders true solidarity. Insight into the nature of interdependence, however, will more readily lead to self-identification with nonhumans and to the relief of their suffering. A Catholic cosmic common good and Earth solidarity are indeed joined as right view and right attitude. Macy poses an interesting objection to my construal of the virtue of Earth solidarity. Earth solidarity may not develop best by observing injustices suffered by nonhumans that stoke a feeling of distress. Instead, a commitment to the well-being of all creatures flows from deconstructing notions of a separate self and cultivating an expanded self-identification. Compassion for the nonhuman victims of human negligence does not arise because they possess creaturely dignity. Rather, they are constitutive of my own self, and so I care for them as one of them.

Fifth, Nhat Hanh and Macy present interdependence as absolutely integral to the goal of spiritual practice. While Catholics certainly do connect growing in faith and working for the cosmic common good, or see an imperiled Earth as a result of sin, Buddhists enjoy a more direct correlation between caring for nonhumans and the cessation of suffering, and a much stronger link between anthropocentrism and the cause of human suffering. Like dharmic ecology, interdependence presents a causal connection between a cosmic common good and our religious ends, which is less apparent in the Catholic tradition. To sink oneself into Indra's net helps to relieve suffering, and not to do so directly frustrates the cessation of suffering. In a Catholic tonality, such an approach would suggest that attempting to elevate humanity above and beyond the cosmic common good, or to direct the planetary common good solely to human welfare, is a fundamental expression of the sinful rejection of God. Ecological sins are mortal sins, which require repentance and grace. Nhat Hanh and Macy encourage Catholics to consider the cosmic common good not only part of our path to God, but also that not doing so detracts us from our fundamental human longing to rest in God. They encourage integrating the cosmic common good into the heart of the Christian moral and spiritual life, and they validate the call to ecological conversion.

Like dharmic ecology, interdependence affirms and modifies a Catholic cosmic common good in critical ways. Interdependence provides further support for the main vision of the cosmic common good and its decentering of the human in the wider cosmos. Rather than affirming non-anthropocentrism through theocentrism, though, the Buddhist principle of interdependence decenters every being, including the cosmos itself. It echoes Berry's attempt to allow the goodness of the universe to stand on its own, without a further ontological ground or teleological purpose. Nhat Hanh and Macy's emphasis on the emptiness of human uniqueness stretch my principles of creaturely dignity and Earth solidarity further than Catholic social thought may be able to entertain, though they provide even further impetus to question any ecological ethic that depends on barriers between "us" and "them." The human person truly belongs to the cosmos as part of it. Acting in defiance of this ultimate reality brings about suffering, whether through ecological degradation or through the persistent craving after a false sense of self. By contrast, interdependence underscores the mutual flourishing of human and nonhuman, and it offers meditative practices that guide us to perceive our participation in the great net of Indra, in which we are always and everywhere related to every other being.

American Indian Traditions

BALANCE WITH ALL OUR RELATIONS

I. Indigenous Traditions and Systemic Violence

Conversation with Hindu and Buddhist traditions has explored the interreligious resonance of the cosmic common good, but a critical component of its global viability is dialogue with indigenous traditions. Like many other Christian ecological ethicists, I am drawn to the wisdom of indigenous peoples, and as a North American, particularly to that of American Indians.[1] In various ways, their cultures and religious traditions inculcate the sense of cosmic and planetary belonging that the cosmic common good seeks to describe: humanity as part of a whole that flourishes only alongside the flourishing of other creatures. Moreover, their historical interactions with the land have embodied the ecologically sustainable practices that the cosmic common good demands.

There is an equally if not more important reason, however. Scholars of religion and ecology, as well as Christian theologians generally, have too often failed "to integrate analysis of social violence" into their work, namely to incorporate perspectives from oppressed peoples and to acknowledge histories of systemic violence.[2] In engaging in dialogue with the traditions of a marginalized people, I hope not only to explore further the shape of a Catholic cosmic common good, but also to avow the intertwined relationship among the affluence of the developed world, the plight of colonized and suppressed indigenous communities, and ecological devastation. The story of the imperiled Earth is also a story of, and indeed is inextricable from, the story of imperiled indigenous peoples.

In this chapter I initiate a tentative dialogue with an American Indian worldview, specifically the Lakota (also known as the Sioux). Adopting an ethical perspective from the marginalized and excluded is not without danger, however. Western theologians must strive to learn from indigenous traditions in a way that does not co-opt the margins for the center.[3] I write as a white, male citizen of the United States, and a member of the community of "overconsumers" and "uncreators."[4] I am economically privileged, and my economic comfort has been purchased in part not only at the expense of the Earth but also of the majority of peoples around the Earth. I strive to be aware of the dangers of this conversation, and how easily appreciation for a marginalized people can quickly degenerate into a form of intellectual colonialism and voyeurism. Thus I also draw on the work of George Tinker, theologian and citizen of the Osage nation,[5] to guide my dialogue with Lakota religious outlooks and practices and to render my engagement as just as possible. Tinker agrees that Euro-American Christians have much to learn from indigenous traditions and he highlights the ecological promise of Indian cultural and religious practices, but at the same time he criticizes the Euro-American heritage of the cosmic common good. Any member of the privileged class of overconsumers must learn carefully from the Lakota, and not merely use them for predetermined purposes that ignore their contemporary and very real struggles for justice.

I begin my dialogue with indigenous traditions with two presumptions: first, not only do indigenous traditions offer a perspective on humanity's relationship to the Earth from which a Catholic cosmic common good can learn, but traditional indigenous lifestyles have generally been more ecologically responsible than my Western and Christian cultures. Without idealizing the Lakota or indigenous peoples, as if they are exemplars of perfect ecological awareness, the history of indigenous relationships to the Earth still represents the closest examples we have to "sustainability" and to the cosmic common good. Moreover, Western conceptions of the common good were initially anthropocentric and required an expansion and reorientation to make them ecologically applicable. Dharma and interdependence do have some implications for how nonhumans were treated, but they still necessitate a contemporary interpretation to make them appropriate to ecological ethics. Of all dialogue partners, indigenous peoples have been closest to embodying and living out an implicit awareness of ecological connectedness and human responsibility. The history of how Lakota and other indigenous peoples lived on Earth makes them a privileged voice to listen to and to learn from.

Second, there is a link between the cultural patterns that have led to the ecological degradation of the Earth and those that led to the colonization, oppression, and degradation of indigenous societies. Indigenous traditions may not only be able to introduce novel insights into ecological ethics, but they can also expose some of the dynamics in Western and Christian worldviews that have led to ecological degradation in the first place. The history of Lakota-Christian encounter is one of violence and domination, with even the "common good" used as a justification for displacing Lakota and American Indians. This is one reason that even an ecologically and socially sensitive framework like a Catholic cosmic common good must first and primarily listen to the voice of the victim before, or ever, offering a critique. Given the legacy of domination, and the continuing imbalance of power between White Americans and American Indians, I do not find it appropriate to challenge Tinker's presentation of Native American spirituality or the Lakota religio-cultural practices. Instead, I adopt a position of learning from these traditions, and I allow any possible contribution of Christian ecological ethics to American Indians to be something they claim for themselves.

With these caveats in mind, I proceed in four steps. First, I begin with an overview of some features of American Indian religious traditions, beginning with George Tinker's contention for spatiality, rather than temporality, as the cornerstone of American Indian spirituality. Second, I summarize Lakota spirituality and analyze the ecological implications of two prominent Lakota religious and cultural traditions: the Lakota prayer *mitakuye oyasin*—"all my relations," and the *inipi* ceremony, or sweat lodge ceremony. Together, the sweat lodge and this Lakota prayer express a visceral connection to the Earth and the understanding that every creature in the universe is kin. Balance with all relations forms an American Indian cosmic common good. Third, I return to Tinker and locate Lakota spirituality within his distinction between Indian spatiality and Christian temporality to draw out an implicit critique of, and challenge to, my western and christian[6] formulation of the cosmic common good. Finally, I revisit a Catholic cosmic common good as it is inflected with critical insights from a Lakota worldview that remains on the margins of my Euro-American theological project.

II. Four Features of American Indian Worldviews and Their Ecological Implications

Just as there are multiple Christian (and Hindu and Buddhist) religious traditions, so again there are myriad traditions, stories, and rituals among indigenous American Indians. Still, George Tinker contends that there is a common thread among them that allows one to speak of an American Indian worldview. Tinker argues that there are "four fundamental, deep structure differences" between American Indian cultures and the cultures that derive from european traditions: organizing the world spatially and not temporally; the priority of community; the interrelatedness of all creatures; and attachment to particular lands.

First and foremost, indigenous traditions construct their world in terms of spatiality, while euro-americans focus on temporality. Certainly the West has an understanding of space, and American Indians a concept of time, but for each there is a primary category around which other concepts are arranged. Space and the corresponding reality of land have come to dominate American Indian conceptions of reality, while time and the metaphor of history dominate western ones. European christian traditions, for example, privilege concepts and values rooted in the idea of a linear direction of time: "Hence, progress, history, development, evolution, and process become key ideas and narratives" that find their way into all disciplines, from science and economics to theology and ethics.[7]

Examples abound that demonstrate the predominance of temporal thinking in the Catholic tradition. In "The Proclamation of the Date of Easter on Epiphany," the Church declares and promulgates the date for Easter for that year. Particular days, and therefore time, are deemed holy, rather than land and space. In one of his earliest statements, Pope Francis exemplified a focus on time by claiming in *Evangelii Gaudium* that "time is greater than space." Francis links time with fullness, "an expression of the horizon which constantly opens before us," while space points to the limitations that people face in individual moments.[8] For Francis, a concern for space points to a struggle over power, while time unfolds fresh possibilities because it focuses on "initiating processes rather than possessing spaces."[9] Francis provides further evidence that while American Indians may situate themselves "here in a certain place," Christians tend to understand themselves "now in this particular epoch."

Second, American Indians privilege the community over the individual, while the thrust of contemporary amer-european culture emphasizes the centrality of individual freedom and happiness. American Indian culture is a totality and cannot be separated into discrete categories of religion, politics, or economics.[10] "Religious rituals" are therefore not separate cultural productions but one of copious ways that the community organizes its life within the context of its particular space. Even esoteric knowledge, transmitted orally and to a select number, exists for the sake of the community. Indigenous peoples undergo individual rigorous purification rites for the good of the people or even all creatures, rather than as an avenue of self-fulfillment or personal salvation.[11] Thus when western new age individuals, whom Tinker castigates as "new age fetishists," participate in American Indian ceremonies, they fundamentally misunderstand and misuse them by treating them as a commodity to purchase and indulge in.[12] By stressing personal salvation, "euro-missionization" withdrew converts from the collective whole, thereby also eroding ceremonial traditions, which often required the entire community's participation.[13]

Third, American Indians assume the interrelatedness of all living and non-living creatures, while western christian cultures depend on a foundational division between humans and other creatures. American Indians see as part of their community "animals (four-leggeds), birds, and all the living, moving things (including rocks, hills, trees, rivers, and so on), along with all the other sorts of two-leggeds (e.g., bears, humans of different colors) in the world."[14]

Fourth, due to the bases of space, community, and the interrelatedness of creatures, indigenous peoples view themselves as attached to particular lands and places, while euro-americans latch onto individual and private property. Every

Indian nation, Tinker avers, has some sense that spiritual powers placed their people into a relationship with a specific area of land. That people have a lasting responsibility to that land and to all the creatures that reside in it, just as the land has a "filial responsibility" to the people. There is a reciprocity of responsibility, between the humans and that place on Earth, as well as a "spatially related responsibility" for all the animals, waters, mountains, and birds that share that land with them.[15] For Indians, creation stories deal not with the beginning and end of the universe but with "an ecosystem present in a definable place."[16] Thus John Grim observes the moral obligation among the Ojibway to protect the habitat of moose, not simply because human members of the Ojibway wish to continue hunting, but because the moose themselves are also members of the Ojibway community. Responsibility for the land is not simply self-preservation, but a duty stemming from their relatedness to fellow creatures.[17] In this way, even group ownership of land is foreign to Indian nations.

These four categories, or the contrast Tinker establishes between American Indians and amer-europeans, should not be seen as absolutes. Certainly there are ways in which space and commitment to the land could lead to ethnocentrism and a non-egalitarian ethic (e.g., which groups or subgroups within the community occupy the space nearest clean water). Similarly, thinking in categories of time is not purely problematic, but instead is a vital way to address injustices toward Indians, such as a thorough comprehension of the history of European colonization of indigenous peoples. Moreover, Christian ethicists, as well as my own articulation of a Catholic cosmic common good, offer analogous condemnations of Western individualism and human abuses of land and other creatures. Still, Tinker's formulation of the core of American Indian traditions provides distinctive lenses that alter and reshape a Catholic cosmic common good in meaningful ways.

These four cultural differences are interconnected: by privileging spatiality and its associated metaphor of land over time and history, indigenous traditions lend themselves to a worldview that emphasizes communality, even to the point of including within its moral purview nonhuman creatures. For Tinker, an enduring connection to the land and responsibility to all creatures who are considered relatives—whose implications fascinate eco-theologians like myself—constitute American Indians' most valuable gift to amer-europeans, and must be understood as inextricable from a communitarian ethic and a world-structured spatially.[18]

John Grim employs the term "lifeway" to describe the integration of indigenous approaches to the person, society, and the land in a way that echoes Tinker's four categories. Grim identifies four embodiments of lifeways, which are interrelated and form their own kind of body: a personal body, a social body, a land or ecological body, and a cosmic body.[19] Just as there is no correlate to the western category of "religion" as discrete and separate from other cultural forms, there is no parallel to the science of ecology or the study of ecosystems.

Knowledge of the land is woven through these bodies and expresses an indigenous ecological awareness.

Tinker's depiction of American Indian lifeways yields an ecological ethic that stresses balance and reciprocity. Balance connotes harmony between creatures as a constant goal. When any disruption arises, which is inevitable, something must be done to restore the balance. An ethic of balance represents a keen awareness of humanity's place within the whole and humans' responsibility to maintain and further the harmony of creatures that inhabit the land. An ethic of reciprocity underscores the kinship between humanity and the rest of creation and connotes mutuality and corresponding exchanges between parties. Reciprocity does not indicate simple equality, but it does extend beyond other human beings to include all living creatures, and the land itself. Kinship leads to respect, which professes the value of the creatures with whom one shares the space of this particular land.[20]

American Indians realize, of course, the necessity of upsetting that balance and occasionally harming those to whom one is related, such as hunting or going to war. Yet they also recognize that harmony must be re-established and kinship be acknowledged following the damage. In order to renew and regain balance and to honor their reciprocity, American Indians perform certain ceremonial acts that could counterbalance the disruption.[21] For example, both before and following a hunt, many American Indian nations engaged in ceremonies that asked for good fortune for those going hunting and for purification for having killed the hunted. Harvesting cedar bark in the Northwest, or procuring a tree for the sundance among the Lakota, or killing a buffalo—all of these would be attended by prayer.[22] Even arguably necessary behaviors such as hunting were perceived as a kind of warfare and a disturbance of balance. An ethic of reciprocity and balance is based on a fundamental respect for all life and exemplifies the traditional ecological knowledge that bears relevance for ecological ethics today.

III. *The Lakota*

While this overview already has implications for a Catholic cosmic common good, I remain wary of failing to attend to differences among American Indians. More problematically, without some further substantive engagement I fall prey to the euro-american penchant for isolating ideas and peoples from their places and lands, and their "spirituality" from the concrete conditions of contemporary life, including an acknowledgment of the history of systemic violence done to them.

Thus I concentrate here on one Indian nation that epitomizes both Tinker's categories and this painful history: the Oglala Lakota, a subdivision of the Lakota nation. The Lakota prayer *mitakuye oyasin*, and the *inipi*, or sweat lodge ceremony, are cultural and religious traditions that express fundamental features of a Lakota worldview and enable non-Indians a deeper view of its spatial, communitarian, and cosmological vision.

The prayer *mitakuye oyasin* translates roughly into "all my relations" or "for all my relations." Like the Christian word "amen," it is spoken at the end of every prayer, and often *mitakuye oyasin* are the only words that are spoken during an entire ceremony, and so they become an entire prayer unto themselves.[23] Behind the word "relations" stand multiple layers of meaning. "Relations" includes one's close relatives, like parents, aunts, uncles, cousins, and so on. More broadly, it incorporates all human beings, persons of all nations and colors. Yet, in contrast to traditional euro-american christianity, the circle of spiritual relatedness and moral concern does not end there. Rather, as we have seen, the communitarian impulse behind American Indian religious and cultural traditions naturally encompasses the community of place and includes all creatures on Earth, with whom human beings are intimately linked. *Mitakuye oyasin* therefore reflects the abiding sense of solidarity the Lakota strive to experience toward all nonhuman beings, whom they consider their relatives. Tinker cites a Lakota teacher who suggests that a better translation for *mitakuye oyasin* would be: "For all the above-me and below-me and around-me things: That is for all my relations."[24] This more recent translation expresses perfectly Tinker's observation that American Indians tend to configure reality in terms of spatiality rather than temporality. What binds these other creatures to the one who prays is not a common history or even a common root in God or the divine. Rather, it is their location and their proximity to the speaker: all the creatures who exist above, below, and around the one who utters this prayer. It is a spatial, community-oriented prayer that affirms the interrelatedness of humanity with all creatures. Thus the Lakota prayer *mitakuye oyasin* contains in ritual form the core elements of Native American spirituality: reciprocity with the rest of creation and balance with all our relations within the universe.

The sweat lodge is a Lakota religious and cultural tradition that includes this prayer and embodies the four hallmarks of an American Indian worldview. The sweat lodge is a pan-Indian ritual, so people of many tribes can engage in this ceremony as a celebration of common values and beliefs.[25] The sweat lodge is a round, domed structure, customarily built into the ground and covered with willow saps or blankets on the top. One enters and exits the lodge praying the words *mitakuye oyasin*, making "all my relations" the constant focus of the entire ritual. Once inside the lodge, participants assemble in a circle. Rocks are placed in a fire outside the lodge until they are blisteringly hot, and then they are brought into the lodge and placed in the center, where a small pit has been dug. The entryway is covered, ensuring total darkness except for the glow of the rocks. The leader, who has studied and trained with elders for many years, begins with sung prayers and pours water over the rocks, so that music, prayers, and darkness fill the space as participants experience the heat of the steam. The steam, sound, and darkness make the body palpably present; one is viscerally connected to the space of the sweat lodge, and to all who share that experience.

The structure of the lodge, the form of the ritual, and the spoken words all instantiate the Lakota worldview as spatially oriented, with the correlative attachment to the land, the community, and all creatures as kin. The entry and exit both face East, unless there are multiple lodges, in which case they face to the center. The shape of the dome is meant to symbolize Mother Earth, so that participants enter into the Earth, their common Mother, in order to be purified and reborn when they emerge. Since the lodge shuts out all light, time ceases to function as a central component of the ritual. Indeed, there is no set day or time for the ceremony, and the duration of the ceremony may vary. Yet, the location and physical orientation of the lodge are carefully considered, making space central from beginning to end.[26]

The circle in which participants sit is another representation of the Lakota sense of interrelatedness with all creatures. The circle is a fundamentally egalitarian setting, stressing the community over any one individual. The circle is also an embodiment of eternity and unity; the participants are linked not only through inhabiting the same space, but by how they inhabit the space. When they sweat and pray together, those seated represent the wholeness of the tribe, of all people, and indeed of all creatures. Tinker cites the Lakota elder Lame Deer, who claims that "the sweat lodge contains the whole universe."[27]

Tinker identifies religious significance in all aspects of the ceremony and the creatures that make it possible. The burning rocks that generate steam represent the Earth and are considered alive, and so one may pray to them; the water also represents the Earth, and when the steam arises into the air, it expresses the merging of Mother Earth and Father Sky. Steam is the breath of the Grandfather, carrying the prayers of those seated up to the Creator.[28] The humans, the rocks, and the water all comingle in the earthen lodge in order to bring forth greater balance and harmony to all creatures. The "relations" for whom one prays clearly extend to include non-sentient beings as well.

The sweat lodge is a rite of purification, but like all American Indian practices, it is never meant for the benefit of the individual participant alone. Instead, one enters into the prayer and the space of the lodge in order to suffer vicariously for *mitakuye oyasin*—all my relations, all the creatures of Earth. Those who experience this purification together are fashioned into a community, joined together by their common roots in the land. The shape of the dome, the seating in a circle, the sense of solidarity with the land, the rocks, and the water, conceived of as relations, the songs and prayers, and even the darkness itself that encompasses all the participants—they are all elements that reinforce the cosmic and spatial dimension of a Lakota worldview.[29]

The relatedness that one experiences to that portion of the Earth yields a sense of responsibility, both to and from the Earth. The purification that one undergoes is done on behalf of *mitakuye oyasin,* and so this ritual inculcates a sense of responsibility to the land and to all the creatures who dwell in it. It enables and empowers the community to pursue balance and to honor the reciprocity among creatures. As the prayer and sweat lodge rituals demonstrate, a spatial worldview lends itself to a non-hierarchical world that can envelop all things simultaneously and make them instantly interrelated.

IV. Lakota Spatiality as Implicit Critique of amer-european Temporality

Thus far I have contended that the Lakota prayer *mitakuye oyasin* and the sweat lodge illustrate the American Indian ethos of reciprocity and balance, and Tinker's distinction between Indian spatiality and amer-european temporality elucidates why. Clearly many intriguing resemblances, as well as differences, exist between a Lakota worldview and a Catholic cosmic common good. Before drawing these out, however, I want to emphasize two dangers involved when an economically privileged White male like me seeks to learn from American Indians.

First, highlighting the ecologically profound aspects of Native American religious traditions might romanticize them into an exotic other to be used and consumed, all the while utterly neglecting their current political and economic struggles. For example, American Indians are much more likely to be poor and unemployed than the rest of the population; Tinker reports that the average unemployment rate ranges from 40% to 60%, while some reservations experience unemployment ranging from 85% to 92%. Diseases are abnormally common, and life expectancy among Indian peoples trails rates for the broader American population by 15 to 20 years.[30] In looking to the Lakota and Native Americans for inspiration, amer-european christians dare not isolate their religious and cultural traditions from their contemporary struggle for political sovereignty. As Larry Rasmussen has said, "To make marginated peoples truly angry, steal their spirituality without joining their political struggle."[31]

A second and deeper danger is that White north american christians, even when well-intentioned and trying to learn ecological practices and principles from them, might overlook and suppress their complicity in the conditions that exist for American Indians today. It is worthwhile to honor and valorize the Lakota sense of relatedness to all creatures and their respect for life; it is naïve to ignore how White europeans' abusive treatment of the Lakota and their land and subsequent White prosperity are intertwined. For too many, there remains little to no sense of the connection between White privilege and wealth and

Native American struggles, and Whites rarely accept culpability for the legacy of oppression and cultural genocide that endures today. Tinker contends that American Indian poverty is actually necessary for White americans to justify their continuing occupancy of the land.[32] While many White christians might recognize American Indians' tribulations and empathize with them, they lack an intelligible framework in which to contextualize this suffering. In particular, they lack the story that accounts for the recurring history of White violence through colonization and conquest, which lives on today in the lingering struggles of indigenous peoples.[33] Lakota poverty and disease are linked to eco-devastation of the Earth. Together, they stand in stark opposition to the Lakota's prior tenancy of this land and how the Lakota used to live out their sovereignty until the arrival of European settlers.

Like Tinker, John Grim notes that indigenous lifeways stand in opposition to the forces of extractive industries and a global corporate world that views indigenous land strictly as resources. The "holistic wisdom" of indigenous lifeways offers an alternative approach to "development" based on centuries of experience exercising sustainable sovereignty over the land.[34] These lifeways not only differ from the standard modern view of development, but they also often come into direct conflict.[35] Witness the Lakota resistance to the Keystone Pipeline: in February 2014, the Great Sioux Nation adopted resolutions to oppose the pipeline, and President Cyril Scott of the Rosebud Sioux Tribe declared that authorizing it would be an "act of war." "The Lakota people have always been stewards of this land. ... We need to start remembering that the earth is our mother and stop polluting her and start taking steps to preserve the land, water, and our grandchildren's future."[36] The lasting significance of indigenous religious and cultural traditions is not simply their historical example of more ecologically sustainable practices and their connection to local bioregions, but also indigenous peoples' continuing commitment to them amidst their resistance to the ongoing attempts to treat their lands as mere resources.

Therefore Tinker's categories of spatiality and temporality do much more than highlight a broad difference between two cultural traditions. Instead, they can become a lens by which to understand euro-american impulses to domination and ecological rapacity. Tinker argues that spatiality lends itself to a more egalitarian worldview, while temporality encourages hierarchical thinking. Though they acknowledge differences among creatures (two-leggeds, four leggeds, etc.), as well as justify occasional human destruction of these creatures for food (e.g., hunting), American Indians primarily emphasize the commonality among all creatures that inhabit the land as common space. By contrast, the euro-american privileging of time tends to establish unequal power dynamics. A culture that values history (and related ideas of progress and development) tends toward hierarchy and therefore hegemony of some over others. Tinker contends that if spatiality and its associated principles lead to an ethic of reciprocity and balance, the amer-european stress on temporality leads to a predilection for domination and control. The power of the metaphor of Manifest Destiny, or the continuing cult of progress in America—both of which have contributed mightily to ecological degradation and the systematic dismantling of Native American culture— suggest the destructive potential of the Western obsession with time. Tinker poses a challenge to Berry: Can such a stress on the story of the universe, with its universalizing scope, be of use to counter patterns of technological domination of the Earth and marginalized peoples?

By locating *mitakuye oyasin* and the sweat lodge in the category of egalitarian spatiality, in opposition to subjugating temporality, I hope to imbue them with an implicit critique of the history of exploitation, oppression, and domination that have defined european-Indian relationships from the beginning, and the kinds of mentalities that continue to threaten the planetary common good. The greed that conquered and dominated indigenous peoples then is the same greed that imperils the Earth today.[37]

A fine example of non-universalizing openness to difference comes in the peaceable coexistence of differing creation stories. Two neighboring Indian communities may each consider its valley to be the center of the universe, and each has a creation story to account for how this is so. They know each other and their stories well, but neither community presumes that the truth of their story negates the truth of the other. "At no point, however, does any tribal religion insist that its particular version of the creation is an absolute historical recording of the creation event."[38] When tribes encountered other ones with differing origin stories, each was believed "since it was not a matter of trying to establish power over others."[39] "Sometimes a single truth is not enough to explain the balance of the world around us."[40]

This general characterization elides many instances of non-hierarchical and egalitarian practices in the West, and of non-egalitarian and dominating practices among American Indians. Yet by identifying the Lakota prayer *mitakuye oyasin* and the sweat lodge as spatial and therefore egalitarian, in contrast to temporal and hierarchical, Tinker places the Lakota attachment to land and space, and the history of US-Lakota relations, in a disturbing light. *Mitakuye oyasin* expresses an attachment to the land and a desire for harmony, as well as a responsibility for the flourishing of all creatures; but the history of amer-european contact with the Lakota is one of warfare, expulsion, and finally sequestration away from their particular lands and forced settlement on reservations. For a Catholic cosmic common good to respect and learn from *mitakuye oyasin* and the sweat lodge, and thus acknowledge the Native American devotion to space and land, it must also question whether the totalizing scope of a common good that is "cosmic," or its acceptance of some differentiations of dignity, or its valorization of the universe's history, might mask tendencies toward domination and control, of the kind that has marred the relationship between Whites and Native Americans.

Aaron Huey, a White photojournalist, provides a stirring synopsis of the history of the Lakota nation in his lecture, "America's Native Prisoners of War."[41] Huey spent over five years on Pine Ridge reservation—which he also calls prisoner of war camp 334—and chronicles the hardships faced by the Lakota today. Huey's talk exemplifies the kind of historical understanding that White amer-europeans must struggle to attain. He outlines a timeline of dates, of "treaties made, treaties broken, and massacres disguised as battles." For example, in 1851, the United States and the Lakota signed the first treaty of Ft. Laramie. If those boundaries held today, the Lakota would occupy much of Montana, Wyoming, North and South Dakota, and most of Nebraska. In 1868, the United States and Lakota signed the second treaty of Ft. Laramie. In this treaty, the US government guarantees the sovereignty of the Sioux nation and the Lakota's right to the sacred Black Hills, as well as hunting rights in surrounding states. When White settlers flooded into Lakota territories as a result of the Homestead Act, the discovery of gold, and the completion of the transcontinental railroad, tensions boiled until 1890. For Huey, this is the most important date. On December 29, 1890, the US government attacked and massacred over 350 people, the bulk of which were defenseless women and children, at Wounded Knee. After this date, there are no more treaties with the Lakota nation.

Huey asks whether we as White amer-europeans feel connected to this history or not, and whether we feel responsibility for the conditions of the Lakota today. He reminds us that the legacy of colonization he witnessed on the reservation, and White economic prosperity, are conjoined. He offers a chilling indictment of White apathy: "The last chapter in any successful genocide is the one in which the oppressor can remove their hands and say, 'My God, what are these people doing to themselves? They're killing each other. They're killing themselves while we watch them die.' This is how we came to own these United States. This is the legacy of manifest destiny." [42]

Huey exemplifies the kind of historical remembering that Whites, and any member of the privileged class of "overconsumers" in North America, must engage in before they attempt to approach and learn ecological responsibility from Native American nations. Tinker's categories of American Indian egalitarian spatiality and amer-european hierarchical temporality become critical lenses by which to approach Lakota spirituality. Understanding spatiality as an implicit critique of the history of White-Lakota encounters becomes an injunction for White amer-europeans to begin to come to grips with their history of domination and their de-spatialized emphasis on time and progress, which tends toward domination of the Earth and indigenous peoples. The Lakota prayer *mitakuye oyasin* and the sweat lodge ceremony become both a reminder of the legacy of colonization, injustice, and suffering that endures today, and the promise of an ethos that privileges space and inculcates relatedness between human beings and all other creatures. Catholics and Christians may be invited to learn from Native Americans and their cultural and religious traditions, but only if they also cultivate an awareness of how their reverence for progress and time has led to social and ecological devastations.

V. Self-Critical Implications for a Catholic Cosmic Common Good

Even more so than in dialogue with Hindu and Buddhist traditions, I think there is a vital component of self-critique that ought to accompany a Christian appreciation of Lakota traditions and their articulation of the cosmic common good. Christian ecological ethicists can and should engage in critical dialogue with indigenous peoples, and I believe that Tinker's categories of spatiality and temporality allow us to do so more justly.

On the one hand, this encounter has engendered further grounds for the inter-religious resonance of the cosmic common good. Both Catholic social thought and indigenous traditions reject the rampant individualism of euro-american culture. Instead, both seek a communitarian social vision quite different from Marxist collectivism in which the good of the whole outweighs the private interests of the individual, but also one in which the community supports and enables the full freedom and flourishing of the person. Indeed, the similarities between their communitarian vision for human society lends greater validity for expanding the Catholic notion of the common good to include the entire cosmos, as indigenous cultures presuppose. As Grim suggests, the person, society, the land, and the cosmos are intertwined, making a purely human common good unthinkable. Like American Indian traditions and the Lakota in particular, a Catholic cosmic common good envisions the human as one of many intrinsically valuable creatures and as part of a greater whole; it expresses a concern for balance, harmony, and reciprocity among the many interdependent parts of the whole; it acknowledges that disruptions in this harmony are occasionally necessary; it recognizes cosmological forces and anticipates meeting them locally; it encourages the affective and personal connection between humans and the Earth; and it stipulates the importance of responsibility toward nonhuman creatures and the land itself, not solely for the self-preservation of the human community, but rooted in humanity's intimate relatedness to other creatures.

At the same time, common good language, especially derived from the Christian tradition, could be seen as a concept rooted in a colonizer's mentality that appropriates what it wishes from American Indians. Tinker has sound reasons to be suspicious of calls for a "common good," since historically the "common good" of White euro-americans has been predicated on the disempowerment and exploitation of American Indians. Tinker trenchantly notes that truly healthy Indian communities actually pose a threat to White american well-being, since they would be more successful in pressing their legal claims to land and sovereignty.[43] Tinker also observes that, in the history of colonization, European colonists and their american descendants tended toward one of two camps: one that called for the destruction and murder of Indian communities; and the gentler or more liberal one, which insisted that Indians be converted and civilized, and taught the ways of private property. These latter benevolent Whites encouraged a kind of common good that ultimately meant the destruction of an indigenous way of life.[44] In this way, a common good that does not begin from a critique of continuing colonial marginalization is an extension of the conquest mentality.

A vision of the cosmic common good that critically engages American Indian and Lakota cultural traditions must therefore include a plausible account of the history of colonization and oppression. Whites in solidarity with American Indians ought to make a renewed call for the sovereignty of displaced and marginalized peoples, their resistance to global hegemonies, and their efforts for independence. Rather than simple borrowing from American Indians or romanticizing them, engaging in critical dialogue with the Lakota allows a Catholic cosmic common good to develop patterns of self-critique that enable it to avoid some of the worst transgressions of the colonizing euro-american traditions. In turn, it might thus be enriched, expanded, and transformed in ways that are consonant with its core theological roots. *Mitakuye oyasin* and the sweat lodge become visions of possibility for euro-americans as well as a call to conscience.

With this in mind, I wish to propose eight aspects of Lakota and American Indian cultural traditions that may inform a Catholic cosmic common good.

First, the Lakota "lifeway" speaks to the integration of the person, the human community, the land and all its creatures, and the cosmos. There is no separation of "religion" or "culture" from other aspects of human life or indeed from life itself. The sense of relatedness and practices of balance, harmony, and reciprocity are not primarily ecological principles, nor do they arise as a response to an experience of ecological degradation. Rather, they reflect how the Lakota and American Indians structure their entire existence. Similar to dharmic ecology, the Lakota lifeway does not graft ecological principles onto other religious and cultural practices, but instead embodies them as an integrated whole. Even more so than dharma, however, *mitakuye oyasin* is not a theoretical concept, but a prayer that is part of a lived practice of a community. Similarly, a Catholic cosmic common good must strive to be a lifeway, rather than an ecological ethic per se.

Second, *mitakuye oyasin* and the *inipi* teach the importance of being spatially oriented and inculcating a moral vision that encompasses everything, but they also caution against the threat of universalizing tendencies in a cosmic moral vision. I do not think Christianity should, or even could, discard its emphasis on time or the desire to embrace in its purview the entirety of the cosmos. Yet given the connections between temporality and hierarchical domination and colonial exclusion, we must also point to the dangers of temporal thinking. The experience of American Indians contains a fervent warning that a Catholic cosmic common good must not override individual persons, communities, or species in its vision of the good. In this way, spatiality plays a critical counterbalance to the temporal dimensions of a Catholic cosmic common good.[45] Berry singles out cosmic history as a key ingredient of a cosmocentric common good. The Lakota spotlight the spatial dimensions of the cosmic story, and indeed the wisdom of reconciling competing creation stories by allowing them to coexist. A spatially oriented love for the cosmic common good means to love this land below me, this sky above me, the wind and the trees and the animals around me.

Third, *mitakuye oyasin* expresses an ethic of remaining rooted in what is local, and specifically attached to and responsible for the land. Spatial thinking guides American Indians to be attentive to the local land and to all the family members that dwell in it, and to sense how one belongs to the place in which one finds herself. Moreover, the relationship to the land spans centuries, making indigenous peoples the closest model for a sustainable human culture that we have. Filial responsibility for the land suggests alternative ways for conceiving of the intrinsic value of nonhumans and for cultivating a sense of solidarity with them. Solidarity grows not only in recognizing the dignity of nonhuman creatures or by perceiving a common origin in God, but through a common origin in the land. Responsibility for the land and all its creatures is conceived spatially, rather than derived from a divine command. In addition, spatiality offers perhaps an excellent example for attributing goodness not only to nonhuman animals and insentient beings, but also in terms of ecosystems. The common good refers to specific spaces and how all the relations relate to each other in harmony and balance.

In a way, the Lakota stress on the local and one's particular land is decidedly non-cosmic. Spatiality underscores bioregional thinking and validates the moral summons for communities to take responsibility for the part of the cosmos they inhabit. Aspects of a Catholic cosmic common good attempt to balance the cosmic and the local. The virtue of Earth solidarity promotes personal commitment to the Earth but also to a local bioregion, and the story of an emergent universe directs us to the local story of the places where we live. Yet indigenous traditions remind us that while humans belong to the cosmos and the Earth, we do so primarily through the particular lands where we dwell. Cultivating a spatial awareness of the land promotes our awareness of the cosmic common good and urges us to avoid exploiting or taking for granted the space we occupy in the name of some more abstract form of "progress."

Fourth, American Indians offer an alternative way for understanding human interdependence with the rest of the Earth via the category of "relations." A Catholic cosmic common good posits a sense of relatedness scientifically via the theory of evolution and theologically through the doctrine of creation. The Lakota prayer *mitakuye oyasin* intensifies these claims by claiming all creatures as "my relations" and offering the metaphor of family united through the land. They recognize diversity among creatures and promote a sense of kinship between humans and other living beings. Humans ought to perceive our relatedness to the two-leggeds, the four-leggeds, and "all the living-moving things on Mother Earth."[46] The American Indian cosmic common good is not merely the flourishing of parts within a greater whole, but the flourishing of a cosmic and planetary family.

Fifth, American Indians teach Christians that an ethic of reciprocity requires acknowledging and rectifying imbalances. Humans are related to all creatures, and when disruptions of harmony are necessary, as they inevitably will be, they must be attended by prayers of repentance and purification. A Catholic cosmic common good naturally comprehends that some death and suffering are necessary, but Native Americans pose a challenge to Christians: What kind of prayers and rituals will restore the balance when we kill our relatives in order to live? A Catholic cosmic common good must recognize the need for rituals of repentance when harmony is violated. An ethic of balance and harmony reorients Christians away from merely thanking God for providing the means for our survival and toward the creatures who enable us to live and flourish, and who are also our relations.

Sixth, the history of systemic violence between amer-europeans and indigenous peoples imbues a Catholic cosmic common good with an impassioned rebuke of social injustice. The present instantiations of indigenous lifeways today have two dimensions: they maintain traditions and sensibilities that offer the possibility of a more reasonable human-Earth relationship, but the rampant poverty and grueling social conditions of life among Indian nations are also a criticism of euro-american cultures and traditions. They remind us that oppression of the Earth was and remains a simultaneous oppression of indigenous peoples. An indigenous cosmic common good stands as a judgment on the totalizing aspirations of modern cultures. It also points to American Christian traditions that benefited from that violence and thus remain complicit in the perduring conditions of life for Lakota today. When a Christian seeks to learn from the prayer *mitakuye oyasin* or the sweat lodge ceremony, she must hear the Lakota people: their spatial and egalitarian worldview; their orientation to the community; their sense of relatedness to all creatures; and their commitment to the land, from which they were driven by White amer-european christians. North american christians cannot espouse an adequate ecological ethic of the common good in this place, on this land, without recalling the indigenous people who were systematically removed and often

killed. A Catholic formulation of the cosmic common good must include a constant reminder of how the powerful elide the concerns and rights of indigenous
peoples globally.

Seventh and similarly, the experience of American Indians in North America
stands as a continual rejection of false claims to development and progress.
Catholic social thought also voices a critique of development that is purely
economic and technological, focused on consuming material goods. Instead,
it articulates the priority of "integral" or "authentic human development," in
which the multifaceted dimensions of the human person are addressed and
being is privileged over having and possessing.[47] Tinker expands these critiques by bringing into question the West's thirst for development and progress itself.

Eighth, an American Indian cosmic common good insists on political sovereignty, which is the power of self-determination on the land to which a people
belongs. Indigenous peoples everywhere teach the danger and folly of pretending
that humans do not depend on the land, or that the Earth will sustain whatever
level of consumption we desire. Admittedly, political sovereignty over the land
by one people means exclusion from the land by others, and that leads to conflict. Given the UN's projection that the global population will peak at 11 billion
people by the end of this century,[48] the assignation of sovereignty proves contentious. Instead, I take Tinker's promotion of sovereignty in two ways: the return
of political determination to marginalized peoples, and the radical importance of
subsidiarity and of generating solutions to our ecological questions from the local
population. Subsidiarity-cum-sovereignty means that political decisions should
be made at the lowest possible political level, because these people have a right
and responsibility to cultivate a filial relationship to their land. Thus the example
of indigenous nations worldwide in resisting intrusion from without becomes a
model in how to resist the global forces that imperil Earth and the most vulnerable
of Earth's creatures.

Indigenous traditions, explored here through the Lakota prayer *mitakuye
oyasin* and the *inipi* ceremony, offer critical perspectives to the interreligious
ground of the cosmic common good. Like dharmic ecology and interdependence, these traditions underscore certain elements of a Catholic cosmic
common good while also reorienting them even more dramatically around
a nonhuman good. Viewing Lakota traditions through Tinker's portrayal of
Indian spatiality, they provide an example of a common good that is more egalitarian and views nonhuman animals as "relations." The Lakota offer ethical
categories of balance and harmony to the cosmic common good, indeed raising
these categories to the summit of moral reflection as the telos of human flourishing. To seek harmony and balance with all our relations is a fitting American
Indian description of the cosmic common good.

Conclusion

AN INTERRELIGIOUS COSMIC COMMON GOOD

THIS BOOK BEGAN with two thought experiments: a distant planet, "Eden," composed of myriad species in complex arrangements, whose florescence is suddenly and dramatically ended by a random asteroid; and the reader's personal memory of an encounter that evoked the recognition of the goodness and value of the nonhuman world. In the interim, I hope that these explorations and my proposal for an interreligious cosmic common good have provided a moral vision and ground for articulating and expressing the good in these places, and for the good of our participation in them.

Pope Francis exhorts, "We need to sink our roots deeper into the fertile soil and history of our native place, which is a gift of God. We can work on a small scale, in our own neighbourhood, but with a larger perspective."[1] Terms from Catholic social thought, once expanded and reoriented theocentrically and ecologically, can provide that larger perspective and a lens to understand and respond to the imperiled Earth. The cosmic common good envisions the human person as a part of a larger whole, the "splendid universal communion"[2] of the cosmos, who flourishes only in mutual flourishing with other beings. This ecological ethic affirms both the intrinsic and instrumental value of all creatures, and it posits humanity's unique responsibility to contribute to the common good as an integral component of humanity's ultimate end.

Through conversation with other traditions, we have explored analogues to a Catholic cosmic common good in Hindu dharmic ecology, Buddhist interdependence, and Lakota balance with all our relations. Intriguing resemblances between them suggest many areas of consonance among traditions on a broad moral vision that includes nonhumans in its purview directly. Indeed, conversation with non-Christian traditions underscores the importance of reorienting Catholic social thought ecologically and introduces unprecedented invitations to broaden it more.

Areas for further development of the cosmic common good as interreligious ground include continuing dialogue among Christian, Hindu, Buddhist, and American Indian traditions, to verify the extent to which the resemblances I identify in fact hold. As I noted in Chapter 1, each chapter could be its own book, and that holds especially true for the comparative chapters. More extensive engagement between traditions will complicate and enrich my preliminary observations, such as rigorous comparisons between theologians on the doctrine of creation, varying conceptions of self and therefore differentiated dignity, and concrete religious practices that embody these principles in everyday life. Further work needs to move closer to concrete and specific application of this ethical vision to issues like water, biodiversity, hydraulic fracturing, food, and others. This will demonstrate how an interreligious ethical foundation like the cosmic common good can actually motivate common action on particular issues and problems.

The cosmic common good provides a larger moral perspective, but it also exhorts us to "sink our roots deeper" into our native place and to work for the good of our place on Earth. The cosmic common good enjoins us to adopt and intensify the many Earth-oriented personal daily choices and movements for structural change with which we are already familiar, for example reducing consumption and energy use, eating less or no meat, minimizing our dependence on automobiles, enforcing standards to reduce carbon in the atmosphere to below 350 parts per million. The cosmic common good provides the context for these many currents, a vision grounded in multiple narratives and religious traditions that might unify and galvanize these concrete actions and global social movements. In countless simple choices we have made and feelings we already experience, the drive to promote the participation of all creatures in the cosmic common good is present. This book is meant to ratify and synthesize these choices and dispositions, and encourage us that in doing so, we fulfill our deepest human calling.

Sinking our roots in our native place on this fertile Earth, but with the larger perspective of the cosmic common good, may we become like the righteous, "like a tree planted near streams of water, that yields its fruit in season," whose "leaves never wither," and that "whatever [we do] prospers" (Psalm 1:3–4). May the larger perspective of the cosmic common good inspire us to live and to work for the good of all members of this vast and wondrous cosmos:

for the poor, the vulnerable, and all those imperiled;
for the contexts in which creatures flourish, and for the greater wholes of
    which they are a part;
for the order in creatures, by which they glorify the Creator;
for the good that creatures provide to other creatures;
for the good of the order of creatures, by which the cosmos is sustained;
for the emergent universe and the communion of subjects;

for the solidarity that binds us to all creatures;

for the promotion of justice for all creatures;

for the sacred that lies in the innermost being in all creatures;

for greater nonviolence and peace;

for the interdependence that shines like a jewel within all creatures;

for all our relations above, below, and around us;

and for the land and this plot of Earth by which creatures come to discover
the cosmos as home.

Notes

INTRODUCTION

1.   The phrase is David Abram's, *The Spell of the Sensuous: Perception and Language in a More-Than-Human World* (New York: Vintage Books, 1996).

CHAPTER 1

1.   Francis, *Laudato Si': Praise Be To You: On Care For Our Common Home* (2015), 1. Pope Francis released this landmark encyclical, now the Catholic Church's most comprehensive and authoritative statement on ecology, just as this book was going to press. So I have not been able to weave it as thoroughly into my proposal for a Catholic cosmic common good as I would like, but I have included some passages that indicate significant resonances between them. http://w2.vatican.va/content/francesco/en/encyclicals/documents/papa-francesco_20150524_enciclica-laudato-si.html.

2.   It is a sign of progress, I believe, that books addressing theological ecological ethics no longer require an extensive overview of worsening environmental conditions to justify a theological response. For the most comprehensive overview of global ecological conditions, see United Nations Environment Programme, *Global Environment Outlook 5*: http://www.unep.org/geo/pdfs/geo5/GEO5_report_full_en.pdf. For a focus on ecosystems, see the Millennium Ecosystem Assessment's summary report, *Living Beyond Our Means: Natural Assets and Human Well-Being*: http://www.maweb.org/en/boardstatement.aspx. For an overview of climate change science, see the Intergovernmental Panel on Climate Change's most recent Fifth Assessment report: http://www.ipcc.ch/.

3.   See, for example, J. R. McNeill, *Something New under the Sun: An Environmental History of the Twentieth Century* (New York: W. W. Norton, 2000); and James

Gustave Speth, *Red Sky at Morning: America and the Crisis of the Global Environment* (New Haven, CT: Yale University Press, 2004).

4. Witness the rise of programs focusing on the environmental humanities, which foster an interdisciplinary approach to environmental concerns, e.g., the Environmental Humanities Initiative at Princeton University.

5. For statements on ecology from all the world's religions, see the Forum on Religion and Ecology at Yale University: http://fore.yale.edu/.

6. Benedict XVI, *If You Want to Cultivate Peace, Protect Creation* (2010), 4: http://www.vatican.va/holy_father/benedict_xvi/messages/peace/documents/hf_ben-xvi_mes_20091208_xliii-world-day-peace_en.html.

7. Francis, *Laudato Si'*, 216, 62, 201.

8. John A. Grim and Mary Evelyn Tucker, *Ecology and Religion* (Washington, DC: Island Press, 2014), 18.

9. Gifford Pinchot, *Breaking New Ground* (Washington, DC: Island Press, 1998), 505.

10. Michael Agliardo, "Restoring Creation and Redressing the Public Square," in *Green Discipleship: Catholic Theological Ethics and the Environment*, ed. Tobias L. Winright (Winona, MN: Anselm Academic, 2011), 37–59; 39–44.

11. A long-standing and neuralgic debate in ecological ethics is how human beings should perceive themselves in relationship to other creatures and the extent to which nonhumans can possess intrinsic value rather than merely instrumental value. Environmental philosopher J. Baird Callicott has commented that the question of nature's intrinsic value "is the central *theoretical* question in environmental ethics. Indeed, how to discover intrinsic value in nature is the defining problem for *environmental* ethics." J. Baird Callicott, "Intrinsic Value in Nature: a Metaethical Analysis," http://ejap.louisiana.edu/EJAP/1995.spring/callicott.1995.spring.html.

12. For an overview of nature-based ecospirituality and the tension between environmental groups and traditional religions, see Bron Taylor, "Earth and Nature-Based Spirituality, Part I: From Deep Ecology to Radical Environmentalism," *Religion* 31, no. 2 (2001): 175–193; and "Earth and Nature-Based Spirituality, Part II: From Earth First! and Bioregionalism to Scientific Paganism and the New Age," *Religion* 31, no. 3 (2001): 225–245.

13. Agliardo, "Restoring Creation and Redressing the Public Square," 41.

14. Agliardo, "Restoring Creation and Redressing the Public Square," 43.

15. The locus classicus for tracing the origin of this argument is a brief but astoundingly reverberative article by Lynn White Jr., "The Historical Roots of Our Ecologic Crisis," published in the widely read journal *Science* 155, no. 3767 (1967): 1203–1207. White's famous article is not truly a theological argument, but it clearly touched a nerve among Christians and has retained cultural relevance for how people perceive Christian ecological ethics. In an oft cited and exemplary statement, he claims, "Christianity is the most anthropocentric religion the world has seen. . . . Man shares, in great measure, God's transcendence

of nature. Christianity . . . not only established a dualism of man and nature, but also insisted that it is God's will that man exploit nature for his proper ends" (1205). White's article, which focused concern on anthropocentrism and the instrumental value of nature, became a touchstone for the emerging field of environmental philosophy as well. For a critical review of White and his lingering legacy, as well as of the narrative I described earlier, see Willis Jenkins, "After Lynn White: Religious Ethics and Environmental Problems," *Journal of Religious Ethics* 37, no. 2 (2009): 283–309.

16. See, for example, the Harvard conference series on *Religions of the World and Ecology* and the influential collection of books they produced. This work continues in the Forum on Religion and Ecology at Yale University. See also The National Religious Partnership for the Environment, http://www.nrpe.org/. For an overview of this field, see Grim and Tucker, *Ecology and Religion*. Again, I deem it a sign of progress that I need not argue for the legitimacy of drawing on religious principles to address ecological degradation since religion and ecology is now an established academic field as well as an active and growing site for environmental activism.

17. Grim and Tucker, *Ecology and Religion*, 6.

18. Grim and Tucker, *Ecology and Religion*, 35.

19. Grim and Tucker, *Ecology and Religion*, 63.

20. Grim and Tucker, *Ecology and Religion*, 39.

21. See Celia Deane-Drummond, *The Ethics of Nature* (Malden, MA: Blackwell Publishing, 2004), xii; and Christiana Peppard, "Denaturing Nature," *The Union Seminary Quarterly Review* 63, no. 1–2 (Spring/Summer 2011): 97–120, 111. One of White's key points is the relationship between vision and action: "What people do about their ecology depends on what they think about themselves in relation to things around them." White, "The Historical Roots of Our Ecologic Crisis," 1206.

22. Willis Jenkins, *Ecologies of Grace: Environmental Ethics and Christian Theology* (Oxford: Oxford University Press, 2008).

23. Willis Jenkins, *The Future of Ethics: Sustainability, Social Justice, and Religious Creativity* (Washington, DC: Georgetown University Press, 2013), 79. Seth Clippard makes a parallel argument from the Buddhist tradition, preferring the rhetorical power of Thai monks ordaining trees rather than a merely textual approach that looks to classical texts and concepts. Seth Clippard, "The Lorax Wears Saffron: Toward a Buddhist Environmentalism," *Journal of Buddhist Ethics* 18 (2011): 212–248.

24. Jenkins notes how specific communities do turn to cosmologies as part of a larger strategy to address specific problems. Inspired by Thomas Berry, Leonardo Boff develops a cosmic worldview to denounce the destruction of the Amazon in *Cry of the Earth, Cry of the Poor* (Maryknoll, NY: Orbis Books, 1997). Jenkins, "After Lynn White," 299, 301.

25. See Sarah M. Taylor, *Green Sisters: A Spiritual Ecology* (Cambridge, MA: Harvard University Press, 2008); and John Pawlikowski and Richard Fragomeni, *The Ecological Challenge* (Collegeville, MN: Liturgical Press, 1994).

26. See, for example, the focus of CRS on climate change: http://www.crs.org/pope-francis-climate/.

27. CCHD is the domestic anti-poverty, social justice program of the US Catholic bishops, and it offers grants to organizations that work on a variety of development issues, including environmental justice. See the 2013–2014 list of awardees at http://www.usccb.org/about/catholic-campaign-for-human-development/upload/grantee-list-2013-2014.pdf.

28. The capitalized form "Cosmos" refers to our observable universe, within the current cosmological theory of multiple universes (the multiverse). I utilize the lowercase "cosmos" as an analogue for creation, which includes the Cosmos and any other existing universe.

29. In a survey of the field of religion and ecology, Willis Jenkins and Christopher Chapple offer a typology of religious environmentalisms. My own work would fall squarely within their description of a "confessional/ethical" approach that aims at developing an "ecological worldview," in which "scholars reexamine religious traditions with the ecological ideas needed to develop more sustainable worldviews." Willis Jenkins and Christopher Key Chapple, "Religion and Environment," *Annual Review of Environment and Resources* 36 (2011): 441–463; 443.

30. As we shall see, the cosmological themes of dharma, interdependence, and balance play central roles in ecological reflection in Hindu, Buddhist, and American Indian contexts.

31. Like many theologians, I understand Catholic social thought as distinct from but complementary to Catholic social teaching. Catholic social teaching is the official teaching of the Catholic Church and includes "papal encyclicals and apostolic letters; statements of Vatican offices and commissions and worldwide church councils and synods; and pastoral letters from individual bishops, regional groupings of bishops, or entire Episcopal conferences." Thomas Massaro, *Living Justice: Catholic Social Teaching in Action* (Lanham, MD: Rowman and Littlefield, 2012), 39. Catholic social thought refers to a broader, "related authority readily observable in upstanding Catholics who interpret and put into practice the words of the magisterium" (Massaro, *Living Justice*, 39). In the Catholic Church, teaching bodies are important, and the Church recognizes two: the hierarchical magisterium, composed of bishops, with the pope at the head; and the theological magisterium, composed of theologians. Thus Catholic social teaching is limited to the statements of the hierarchical magisterium, while Catholic social thought includes the reflections of Catholic theologians and ethicists and the work of various Catholic social

organizations. Catholic social thought is in continuity with Catholic social teaching but engages different starting points, dialogue partners, and contexts. I will use the term "Catholic social thought," then, to include and encompass the limited body of documents promulgated by popes and bishops as well as the work of Catholic scholars. While I begin with documents from Catholic social teaching and then turn to theologians for further elucidation, I view the expanded principles I argue for as belonging to Catholic social thought.

32. There is a wealth of literature, both introductory and advanced, on Catholic social teaching and thought. For a comprehensive introduction, see Massaro, *Living Justice*; and J. Milburn Thompson, *Introducing Catholic Social Thought* (Maryknoll, NY: Orbis, 2010). For Catholic social teaching proper, see David J. O'Brien and Thomas A. Shannon, eds., *Catholic Social Thought: The Documentary Heritage* (Maryknoll, NY: Orbis Books, 1992); and the scholarly commentaries on this documentary heritage, Kenneth R. Himes, ed., *Modern Catholic Social Teaching: Commentaries and Interpretations* (Washington, DC: Georgetown University Press, 2005).

33. Joseph Des Jardins, among others, criticizes extending ethics to include non-humans as too narrow, too individualistic, and insufficiently comprehensive to address the multivalent concerns of environmental ethics. Joseph Des Jardins, *Environmental Ethics: An Introduction to Environmental Philosophy* (Boston: Wadsworth Cengage Learning, 2006), 127–128. While I do speak of expanding or extending the common good to include nonhumans, more properly I envision the cosmic common good as a theocentric reorientation that places God as the center of value, so that all that God has created, human and nonhuman, is included within a common moral framework.

34. Paul Tillich, *Systematic Theology*, Volume II (Chicago: University of Chicago Press, 1957), 10.

35. Holmes Rolston also notes the connection between the living ground of Earth and God as the ground of being: "'[G]round' is an earthy enough word to symbolize this dimension of depth where nature becomes charged with the numinous." Holmes Rolston, "Ecology: A Primer for Christian Ethics," *Journal of Catholic Social Thought* 4, no. 2 (2007): 293–312; 311.

36. John Grim and Mary Evelyn Tucker have noted the same concern, as it "conjures up images of exploitation which may cause apprehension," especially for indigenous communities. Mary Evelyn Tucker and John Grim, "Series Foreword," in *Indigenous Traditions and Ecology: The Interbeing of Cosmology and Community*, ed. John Grim, xv–xxxii (Cambridge, MA: Harvard University Press, 2001): xxi–xxii.

37. An alternative way of framing my approach is that I seek to put key insights derived from the Harvard series on Religion and Ecology into constructive dialogue with each other.

CHAPTER 2

1. US Conference of Catholic Bishops, "Seven Themes of Catholic Social Teaching," http://www.usccb.org/beliefs-and-teachings/what-we-believe/catholic-social-teaching/seven-themes-of-catholic-social-teaching.cfm.
2. Pontifical Council for Justice and Peace, *Compendium of the Social Doctrine of the Church*, 107. http://www.vatican.va/roman_curia/pontifical_councils/justpeace/documents/rc_pc_justpeace_doc_20060526_compendio-dott-soc_en.html.
3. Todd Whitmore, "Catholic Social Teaching: Starting with the Common Good," in *Living the Catholic Social Tradition: Cases and Commentary*, ed. Kathleen Weigert (Lanham, MD: Rowman and Littlefield, 2005): 59–85; 61. See also Barbara Wall, "Ethical Considerations for a New Jurisprudence: A Catholic Social Thought Perspective," *Barry Law Review* 11 (Fall 2008): 77–93, at 87.
4. Whitmore, "Catholic Social Teaching," 61.
5. Second Vatican Council, *Gaudium et Spes* (1965), 26. http://www.vatican.va/archive/hist_councils/ii_vatican_council/documents/vat-ii_cons_19651207_gaudium-et-spes_en.html.
6. Hollenbach, *The Common Good and Christian Ethics*, 8.
7. David Hollenbach, "The Common Good Revisited," *Theological Studies* 50 (March 1989): 86.
8. Hollenbach, *The Common Good and Christian Ethics*, 81.
9. Hollenbach, *The Common Good and Christian Ethics*, 83.
10. Hollenbach, *The Common Good and Christian Ethics*, 75.
11. John XXIII, *Pacem in Terris* (1963), 26. http://www.vatican.va/holy_father/john_xxiii/encyclicals/documents/hf_j-xxiii_enc_11041963_pacem_en.html.
12. Francis, *Evangelii Gaudium* (2013), 235. http://w2.vatican.va/content/francesco/en/apost_exhortations/documents/papa-francesco_esortazione-ap_20131124_evangelii-gaudium.html.
13. See Michael Sandel, *Liberalism and the Limits of Justice*, 2nd edition (Cambridge: Cambridge University Press: 1982, 1998).
14. Francis, Twitter post, April 28, 2014, 1:28 a.m., https://twitter.com/Pontifex/status/460697074585980928.
15. Thomas Massaro, *Living Justice: Catholic Social Teaching in Action* (Lanham, MD: Rowman & Littlefield, 2012), 80–82.
16. Pontifical Council for Justice and Peace, *Compendium*, 189.
17. Massaro, *Living Justice*, 86.
18. Massaro, *Living Justice*, 89.
19. Whitmore, "Catholic Social Teaching," 76.
20. *Gaudium et Spes*, 69.
21. John Paul II, *Sollicitudo Rei Socialis* (1987), 42. http://www.vatican.va/holy_father/john_paul_ii/encyclicals/documents/hf_jp-ii_enc_30121987_sollicitudo-rei-socialis_en.html.

22. Massaro, *Living Justice*, 123.

23. John XXIII, *Mater et Magistra* (1961), 59. http://www.vatican.va/holy_father/john_xxiii/encyclicals/ documents/hf_j-xxiii_enc_15051961_mater_en.html.

24. Francis, *Evangelii Gaudium*, 183.

25. Donal Dorr, *Option for the Poor and for the Earth: Catholic Social Teaching* (Maryknoll, NY: Orbis Books, 1983, 1992, 2012), 5–6.

26. Dorr, *Option for the Poor and for the Earth*, 430.

27. Dorr, *Option for the Poor and for the Earth*, 424.

28. Dorr, *Option for the Poor and for the Earth*, 435–436.

29. Francis, *Laudato Si'*, 1, 220, 89, 228, 42. http://w2.vatican.va/content/francesco/en/encyclicals/documents/papa-francesco_20150524_enciclica-laudato-si.html.

30. John Paul II, *Peace with God the Creator, Peace with All Creation*, Message for the Celebration of the World Day of Peace (1990), 8. http://www.vatican.va/holy_father/john_paul_ii/messages/peace/documents/hf_jp-ii_mes_19891208_xxiii-world-day-for-peace_en.html.

31. US Conference of Catholic Bishops, *Renewing the Earth* (1991). http://www.usccb.org/issues-and-action/human-life-and-dignity/environment/renewing-the-earth.cfm.

32. US Conference of Catholic Bishops, *Global Climate Change: A Plea for Dialogue, Prudence, and the Common Good* (2001). http://www.usccb.org/issues-and-action/human-life-and-dignity/environment/global-climate-change-a-plea-for-dialogue-prudence-and-the-common-good.cfm.

33. This story, largely through Thomas Berry, has been influential for many theologians: see Denis Edwards, *Ecology at the Heart of Faith: The Change of Heart that Leads to a New Way of Living on Earth* (Maryknoll, NY: Orbis, 2006); David Toolan, *At Home in the Cosmos* (Maryknoll, NY: Orbis, 2001); Sallie McFague, *The Body of God* (Minneapolis: Fortress Press, 1993); Lutheran theologian Larry Rasmussen remarks how this must impact our conception of God and salvation as well: "Any God-talk . . . that does not include the entire fifteen-billion-year history of the cosmos and does not relate to all its entities . . . speaks of a God too small." Larry Rasmussen, *Earth Community, Earth Ethics* (Maryknoll, NY: Orbis Books, 1996), 266.

34. Brian Thomas Swimme and Mary Evelyn Tucker, *The Journey of the Universe* (New Haven, CT: Yale University Press, 2011).

35. As Chapter 4 explores, Thomas Berry demonstrates the contribution of the scientific story of the cosmos to a functional theological cosmology.

36. John Hart, *Sacramental Commons: Christian Ecological Ethics* (Lanham, MD: Rowman & Littlefield, 2006), 18.

37. Cited in Dorr, *Option for the Poor and for the Earth*, 433.

38. Elizabeth Johnson, *Ask the Beasts: Darwin and the God of Love* (New York: Bloomsbury Publishing, 2014), 63.

39. Stephen Scharper and Andrew J. Weigert, "An Invitation to Inclusive Environmental Reflection," in *Catholic Social Thought: American Reflections on the Compendium*, eds. D. Paul Sullins and Anthony J. Blasi (Lanham, MD: Lexington Books, 2009), 127–142; 135–137.

40. Leonardo Boff, *Cry of the Earth, Cry of the Poor* (Maryknoll, NY: Orbis Books, 1997), 33.

41. John A. Grim and Mary Evelyn Tucker, *Ecology and Religion* (Washington, DC: Island Press), 62.

42. While scientists debate the legitimacy of the term "ecosystem," it remains politically and ethically consequential. *The Convention on Biological Diversity*, an international treaty signed by nearly two hundred countries, defines an ecosystem as a "dynamic complex of plant, animal and micro-organism communities and their non-living environment interacting as a functional unit." *Convention on Biological Diversity*, Article 2, "Use of Terms," http://www.cbd.int/convention/articles.shtml?a=cbd-02.

43. Christiana Peppard, "Denaturing Nature," *The Union Seminary Quarterly Review*, 62, no. 1–2 (Spring/Summer 2011): 97–120, at 109.

44. Russell Butkus and Steven Kolmes, "Ecology and the Common Good: Sustainability and Catholic Social Teaching," *Journal of Catholic Social Thought* 4, no. 2 (2007): 403–436, 430.

45. Butkus and Kolmes, "Ecology and the Common Good," 435.

46. Scharper and Weigert, "An Invitation to Inclusive Environmental Reflection," 130.

47. Scharper and Weigert, "An Invitation to Inclusive Environmental Reflection," 132.

48. Scharper and Weigert, "An Invitation to Inclusive Environmental Reflection," 130.

49. Jame Schaefer, "Environmental Degradation, Social Sin, and the Common Good," in *God, Creation, and Climate Change*, ed. Richard Miller (Maryknoll, NY: Orbis Books, 2010): 69–94; 84.

50. Lisa Sideris, *Environmental Ethics, Ecological Theology, and Natural Selection* (New York: Columbia University Press: 2003), 7.

51. Sideris, *Environmental Ethics*, 12.

52. Sideris, *Environmental Ethics*, 22.

53. The term was first coined by Nobel laureate Paul Crutzen, but since then has become increasingly accepted. See Jan Zalasiewicz, Mark Williams, Will Steffen, and Paul Crutzen, "The New World of the Anthropocene," *Environmental Science & Technology* 44, no. 7 (2010): 2228–2231.

54. Bill McKibben, *Eaarth: Making a Life on a Tough New Planet* (New York: Times Books, 2010), xiii.

55. John Paul II, General Audience Address, 4, January 17, 2001. http://www.vatican.va/holy_father/john_paul_ii/audiences/2001/documents/hf_jp-ii_aud_20010117_en.html. Francis, *Laudato Si'*, 5.

56. Hence Christiana Peppard's concerns about descriptions of "nature" and defenses of "wilderness" in ecological ethics. See Peppard, "Denaturing Nature."

57. Holmes Rolston, "Ecology: A Primer for Christian Ethics," *Journal of Catholic Social Thought* 4, no. 2 (2007): 293–312, at 305.

58. Johnson, *Ask the Beasts*, 242.

59. William French, "Common Ground, Common Skies: Natural Law and Ecological Responsibility," *Journal of Ecumenical Studies* 42, no. 3 (Summer 2007): 373–388; 377.

60. Francis, *Laudato Si'*, 161, 201.

61. Many eco-theologians outline a wide range of biblical and theological principles that lend further support to the concept of a cosmic common good, but I limit myself to the doctrine of creation.

62. J. Milburn Thompson, *Introducing Catholic Social Thought* (Maryknoll, NY: Orbis Books, 2010), 162.

63. Francis, *Laudato Si'*, 75, 83, 76, 77.

64. Francis, *Laudato Si'*, 101, 78, 203.

65. Francis, *Laudato Si'*, 160.

66. Others who made similar proposals for a cosmic common good include Jame Schaefer, "Environmental Degradation," 81; and John Hart, who discusses "cosmic commons goods": *Cosmic Commons: Spirit, Science, & Space* (Eugene, OR: Cascade Books, 2013), 222–223.

67. See Alicia Change, "Stephen Hawking: Space Exploration Is Key to Saving Humanity," *Huffington Post*, April 10, 2013. http://www.huffingtonpost.com/2013/04/11/stephen-hawking-space-exploration-humanity_n_3061329.html.

68. See John Hart's proposal for a "cosmic charter" in *Cosmic Commons*.

69. John Paul II, *Sollicitudo Rei Socialis*, 34.

70. Francis, *Laudato Si'*, 236.

71. Francis, *Laudato Si'*, 115 ff.

72. See Willis Jenkins, *The Future of Ethics: Sustainability, Social Justice, and Religious Creativity* (Washington, DC: Georgetown University Press, 2013).

73. See Larry Rasmussen, *Earth-Honoring Faith: Religious Ethics in a New Key* (New York: Oxford University Press, 2013).

74. I do acknowledge a danger in this formulation. A moral framework oriented around the cosmos stretches the purview of ethics so far, it does seem to institute a new kind of abstraction, divorced from the living realities of Earth and its creatures. In what way can a human have a connection to the cosmos as a whole? I will argue later that the virtue of Earth solidarity helps to combat the danger of assuming a perspective so removed from the messiness and complexity of life.

75. Witness the popular television series "Cosmos: A Personal Voyage," hosted by Carl Sagan, and its contemporary sequel, "Cosmos: A Spacetime Odyssey," hosted by Neil deGrasse Tyson: http://www.cosmosontv.com; and the Emmy

award–winning documentary *Journey of the Universe*: www.journeyoftheuni-verse.org.

76. Hart, *Sacramental Commons*, 17.

77. Paul Knitter, *One Earth, Many Religions: Multi-Faith Dialogue and Global Responsibility* (Maryknoll, NY: Orbis Books, 1995), 79.

78. Francis, *Laudato Si'*, 221.

79. Hart, *Sacramental Commons*, 33.

80. Sacramentality, or the capacity of creation to disclose and be a conduit of the divine, is a crucial factor of a theocentric, Catholic ecological ethic. John Hart combines common good thinking with sacramentality in *Sacramental Commons*, and Jame Schaefer draws on patristic authors to develop five steps for nurturing a sacramental sensibility. Schaefer, *Theological Foundations for Environmental Ethics: Reconstructing Patristic and Medieval Concepts* (Washington, DC: Georgetown University Press, 2009), 65–102. I do not engage it here, in part because I seek to explore the interreligious potential for the cosmic common good, and comparative sacramentology would exceed the scope of the book.

81. Hart, *Sacramental Commons*, 16.

82. Hart, *Sacramental Commons*, 59.

83. Francis, *Laudato Si'*, 17.

84. Schaefer, "Environmental Degradation," 81.

85. See Chapter 3.

86. See, for example, Schaefer, "Solidarity," 413. Rosemary Radford Ruether, *Gaia and God: An Ecofeminist Theology of Earth Healing* (New York: HarperCollins Publishers, 1992), 201; Michael Northcott's call for a "parochial ecology," in *The Environment and Christian Ethics* (New York: Cambridge University Press, 1996), 308–327; and similarities to Kevin J. O'Brien's proposal for "multiscalar ethics," in *An Ethics of Biodiversity* (Washington, DC: Georgetown University Press, 2010), 79–108.

87. Schaefer, *Foundations*, 29–31.

88. Rasmussen, "Human Environmental Rights and/or Biotic Rights," in *Religion and Human Rights: Competing Claims?* ed. Carrie Gustafson and Peter H. Juviler (Armonk, NY: M. E. Sharpe, 1999), 36–52; 43.

89. Rasmussen, "Human Environmental Rights," 43.

90. Hart, *Sacramental Commons*, 151.

91. Aldo Leopold, *A Sand County Almanac* (New York: Ballantine Books, 1970).

92. These terms are Peter Wenz's. See Peter Wenz, *Environmental Justice* (Albany: State University of New York Press, 1988).

93. Francis, *Laudato Si'*, 140.

94. Schaefer, *Foundations*, 27–28.

95. See Peppard, "Denaturing Nature."

96. See "Great Pacific Garbage Patch," *National Geographic*, http://education.nation-
algeographic.com/education/encyclopedia/great-pacific-garbage-patch/?ar_a=1.

97. Edward Schillebeekx, *The Schillebeecks Reader*, ed. Robert J. Schreiter (New York
Crossroad, 1984), 272–274.

98. Similarly, James Gustafson refers to Hans Jonas, who argues that an awareness
of an ethical problem often begins with a sense of the *malum*, with an evil that is
to be avoided, rather than the good to be preserved. James Gustafson, *A Sense of
the Divine: The Natural Environment of a Theocentric Perspective* (Cleveland: The
Pilgrim Press, 1996), 23–24.

99. In light of the ineluctable death and destruction that an evolutionary universe
entails, many Christian theologians develop an eschatological ethic that imag-
ines how God will redeem all of creation, lest attributing intrinsic value to the
evolutionary process sanctions and celebrates inevitable suffering. I do not
include an eschatological ethic because I intend to focus only on a perceptible
cosmic common good that obtains in this world and protects the diversity of
life on an imperiled Earth, and so I stress the value even of those destructive
processes without which the flourishing of life is impossible.

CHAPTER 3

1. Jame Schaefer comments that authors from the Patristic and medieval eras
are "privileged witnesses" to the Catholic tradition and are worth retrieving.
Jame Schaefer, *Theological Foundations for Environmental Ethics: Reconstructing
Patristic and Medieval Concepts* (Washington, DC: Georgetown University Press,
2009), 3. Schaefer's extensive research demonstrates the abundance of ecologically resonant themes in both Augustine and Aquinas.

2. Jaroslav Pelikan contends that "in a manner and to a degree unique for any
Christian thinker outside the New Testament, Augustine has determined the
form and content of church doctrine for most of Western Christian history."
Pelikan, *The Christian Tradition: A History of the Development of Doctrine*, Vol. 1
(Chicago: University of Chicago Press, 1971), 293.

3. For example, Pope Leo XIII, the first to author a document of Catholic social
teaching, also promulgated *Aeterni Patris: Encylical of Pope Leo XIII on the
Restoration of Christian Philosophy* (1879), making the thought of Thomas
Aquinas the official philosophical and theological worldview for the Catholic
Church. http://www.vatican.va/holy_father/leo_xiii/encyclicals/documents/
hf_l-xiii_enc_04081879_aeterni-patris_en.html.

4. H. Paul Santmire regards Augustine as "the flowering of the ecological promise
of classical theology." Santmire, *The Travail of Nature: The Ambiguous Ecological
Promise of Christian Theology* (Philadelphia: Fortress, 1985), 73. Scott Dunham
draws on Augustine's Trinitarian doctrine of creation to explore Augustine's contribution to an ecologically informed theological ethic. *The Trinity and Creation*

in Augustine: An Ecological Analysis (Albany: State University of New York Press, 2008).

5.　There is already a substantial literature of "eco-Thomism," and many others draw on Aquinas to develop their own theological and ethical framework, including Willis Jenkins, *Ecologies of Grace: Environmental Ethics and Christian Theology* (Oxford: Oxford University Press, 2008); Celia Deane-Drummond, *The Ethics of Nature* (Malden, MA: Blackwell Publishing, 2004); Louke van Wensveen, *Dirty Virtues: The Emergence of Ecological Virtue Ethics* (Amherst, NY: Humanity Books, 2000). William French argues that Aquinas offers a "cosmological-ecological" principle that can guide ecological ethics. William C. French, "Catholicism and the Common Good of the Biosphere," in *An Ecology of the Spirit: Religious Reflection and Environmental Consciousness*, ed. Michael H. Barnes (Lanham, MD: University Press of America, 1994), 177–194; 192. For an application of Thomas Aquinas and the cosmic common good to climate change, see my "Thomas Aquinas, the Cosmic Common Good, and Climate Change," in *Confronting the Climate Crisis: Catholic Theological Perspectives*, ed. Jame Schaefer (Milwaukee, WI: Marquette University Press, 2011), 125–144. For a negative assessment of Aquinas's potential contribution to ecological ethics, see Francisco Benzoni, *Ecological Ethics and the Human Soul: Aquinas, Whitehead, and the Metaphysics of Value* (Notre Dame, IN: University of Notre Dame Press, 2007).

6.　Dunham comments that while it is good to recover ancient thinkers, one must note that their concepts of interrelationality, interdependence, etc., differ from our modern, scientific conceptions. Dunham, *The Trinity and Creation in Augustine*, 3.

7.　For this reason Schaefer argues that these authors must be reconstructed in order to be coherent. Schaefer, *Foundations*, 3–5.

8.　In light of my description of intrinsic and instrumental valuation in the previous chapter, an alternative way of framing these would be: (1) theocentrism; (2) intrinsic value of creatures; (3) instrumental value of creatures; (4) intrinsic value of a diversity of creatures; (5) intrinsic value of instrumental ordering—the value of the entirety of creation as it exists.

9.　*Confessions*, translation R. S. Pine-Coffin (New York: Penguin, 1961), 9.10.23.

10.　See Dunham, *The Trinity and Creation in Augustine*, 90; see also *The Literal Meaning of Genesis*, trans. John Hammond Taylor, S.J. (New York: Paulist Press, 1982), 8.26.48.

11.　*Confessions*, 7.13.19.

12.　Similarly, Jame Schaefer identifies in Aquinas an "internal common good" (795–796) or "created common good" (799) of the universe, while God is the "absolute common good" (796) or the "uncreated common good" of creatures (799). Jame Schaefer, "Valuing Earth Intrinsically and Instrumentally: A Theological Framework for Environmental Ethics," *Theological Studies* 66 (2005): 783–814.

13.　See point 5 later in this chapter.

14. *Summa Theologica*, translated by Fathers of the English Dominican Province (Chicago: Benziger Brothers, 1948) 1.60.5. Hereafter referred to as ST.
15. ST 2 | 2.26.3.
16. See Chapter 2, n. 74.
17. On this theme in Augustine, see Dunham, *The Trinity and Creation in Augustine*, 58; in Aquinas, see Schaefer, "Degradation," 81.
18. "But you have disposed all things by measure and number and weight." *The Catholic Study Bible* (New American Bible), eds. Donald Senior and John J. Collins (New York: Oxford University Press, 2006).
19. *Literal Meaning of Genesis*, 4.3.7.
20. Dunham, *The Trinity and Creation in Augustine*, 96. Dunham refers to *Tractates on John* 1.13.3.
21. *Literal Meaning of Genesis*, 4.4.7.
22. Dunham, *The Trinity and Creation in Augustine*, 103.
23. *Literal Meaning of Genesis*, 4.12.23.
24. *Literal Meaning of Genesis*, 4.3.7.
25. *Confessions*, 1.1.1.
26. *Confessions*, 13.9.10.
27. *Literal Meaning of Genesis*, 2.1.2–3.
28. ST 1 | 2.91.2.
29. ST 2 | 2 26.3.
30. Schaefer, *Foundations*, 19.
31. Jenkins calls this a "cosmology of desire" and remarks that we can see a creature's "life practice" as the way it voices its desire for God. There is thus a twofold integrity to creation: (1) a thing's specific difference, its own "life-practice," and (2) a common notion of creatureliness and a shared orientation to the Creator's goodness. Jenkins, *Ecologies of Grace*, 120.
32. *Summa Contra Gentiles*, translated by Fathers of the English Dominican Province (Chicago: Benziger Brothers, 1924), 2.45, n. 2. Hereafter SCG.
33. ST 1.44.4.
34. SCG 2.46.2.
35. Jenkins comments that "the integrity of creation names the common dignity of diverse participations in the eternal law of God's wisdom." *Ecologies of Grace*, 123.
36. *Literal Meaning*, 3.16.25.
37. *Literal Meaning*, 3.16.25.
38. *Literal Meaning*, 3.16.25.
39. SCG 3.22.6.
40. SCG 2.2. Jenkins argues that a primary purpose behind creation's integrity for humans is contemplative because we are made deiform by knowing God through creatures. *Ecologies of Grace*, 128–130.
41. SCG 3.128, cited by Schaefer, *Foundations*, 21.
42. ST 1.22.2.

43. ST 1.22.2, ad 2.
44. ST 1.22.2, ad 2.
45. *The City of God*, translated by Marcus Dods, D.D. Introduction by Thomas Merton (New York: The Modern Library, a division of Random House, 1950), 22.24.
46. *City of God*, 12.5.
47. Indeed, in some ways Aquinas revels most in the sheer fact that anything exists at all. "For Thomas, it is not really the marvelous complexity and ingenuity of things that alerts the mind to the reality of God, it is rather the metaphysical implications of very simple observations about things, beginning with the primary fact of their being at all." Simon Tugwell, "Thomas Aquinas: Introduction," in *Albert and Thomas, Selected Writings*, translated by S. Tugwell (New York: Paulist Press, 1988), 213. Tugwell goes too far, however, since Aquinas clearly expresses an appreciation not only for the fact that creatures exist, but also for the diversity of creatures that inhabit the universe.
48. ST 1.47.1.
49. *Disputed Questions on Truth*, translated by Robert W. Mulligan, S.J. (Chicago: Henry Regnery Company, 1952), 1.5.3 ad 2.
50. In *I Sentences*, 44.1.2 ad 6, quoted in Oliva Blanchette, *The Perfection of the Universe According to Aquinas: A Teleological Cosmology* (University Park: Pennsylvania State University Press, 1992), 125–126.
51. *City of God*, 1.20.
52. *Confessions*, 7.12.
53. *Literal Meaning of Genesis*, 3.20.30.
54. *Literal Meaning of Genesis*, 3.16.25.
55. *City of God*, 19.13.
56. *City of God*, 19.13.
57. *Confessions*, 7.12.
58. *City of God*, 19.12.
59. *City of God*, 12.4.
60. *Confessions*, 4.10.
61. Augustine also remarks that some aspects of creation are oppositional to human interests because of the just punishment following Adam's sin. See *City of God* 11.22.
62. *City of God*, 11.16.
63. *City of God*, 11.22.
64. *Literal Meaning*, 3.16.25.
65. *City of God*, 12.4.
66. ST 1.76.3.
67. SCG 2.39.6.
68. ST 1.93.2.
69. ST 1.93.2.ad 3.
70. ST 1.65.2.

71. ST 1.47.2.
72. ST 1.15.2.
73. *City of God*, 2.44.2.
74. *City of God*, 3.71.2.
75. SCG 2.39.7.
76. ST 1.44.1.
77. ST 1.47.3.
78. SCG 2.42.3. The italicized words come from Aristotle's *Ethics*.
79. SCG 2.44.2.
80. SCG 2.44.17.
81. ST 1.25.6 ad 3.
82. ST 1.65.2.
83. SCG 2:45.10.
84. See also Schaefer, *Foundations*, 22.
85. *The Rule of Augustine*, 5.2, cited by Phyllis Zagano and Thomas C. McGonigle, *The Dominican Tradition* (Collegeville, MN: Liturgical Press, 2006), 134.
86. ST 2 | 2.26.3, ad 2.
87. See *City of God*, 3.24.
88. See ST 1 | 2.19.10.
89. Schaefer develops various models for the human person in this age of ecological degradation that would correspond well to the cosmic common good, including the human as "*intrinsic-instrumental valuer* of the good creation," "the *respecter* of the ways in which creatures and the totality of creation praise God," and "the *companion* of entities that have emerged from the cosmological-biological continuum." She highlights the human as "virtuous cooperator," who, out of love for God, cooperates with God's grace to support the intercooperation of creatures and to enable nonhumans "to achieve their God endowed purposes for existing in the universe." Schaefer, *Foundations*, 267–280, 271.
90. Denis Edwards contends that "Aquinas never knew Darwin's theory of evolution, but he would have had no difficulty in understanding it as the way that God creates." Cited by Elizabeth Johnson, *Ask the Beasts: Darwin and the God of Love* (New York: Bloomsbury Publishing, 2014), 168.
91. This forms part of the basis for Benzoni's rejection of Aquinas as an adequate foundation for ecological ethics.

CHAPTER 4

1. Berry's worldview advanced beyond Teilhard, though in critical ways, such as rejecting an overly optimistic view of progress and human technology, and evincing grave concern for ecological devastation. Mary Evelyn Tucker, "Editor's Afterword: an Intellectual Biography of Thomas Berry," in *Evening*

Thoughts: Reflecting on Earth as a Sacred Community, ed. Mary Evelyn Tucker (San Francisco: Sierra Club Books, 2006), 151–171; 162–164.

2. Peter Ellard draws on various dimensions of Berry to argue for a "dark green" Catholic theology, rather than a shallow inclusion of the environment among other social issues. See "Thomas Berry, Groundwork for a Dark Green Catholic Theology," in *Confronting the Climate Crisis: Catholic Theological Perspectives*, ed. Jame Schaefer (Milwaukee: Marquette University Press), 301–320.

3. Berry's vision was significantly influenced by Augustine and Aquinas, and in fact Berry took the religious name "Thomas" because of his deep affinity with Thomistic thought.

4. Thomas Berry, *The Christian Future and the Fate of the Earth*, edited by Mary Evelyn Tucker and John Grim (Maryknoll, NY: Orbis Books, 2009), 31.

5. Thomas Berry, *The Great Work: Our Way into the Future* (New York: Bell Tower, 1999), 49.

6. Other terms include "originating power," *Christian Future and the Fate of the Earth*, 116; and the "all pervasive mysterious power." Thomas Berry, C.P., and Thomas Clarke, S.J., *Befriending the Earth: A Theology of Reconciliation Between Humans and the Earth* (Mystic, CT: Twenty-Third Publications, 1991), 11.

7. Rudolf Otto, *The Idea of the Holy* (London: Oxford University Press, 1923).

8. *Befriending the Earth*, 10–11.

9. Thomas Berry, "The New Story," *Teilhard Studies* #1, Anima Press, American Teilhard Association, Winter 1978.

10. Mary Evelyn Tucker and Brian Swimme, students of Thomas Berry's, created an Emmy Award–winning documentary that graphically depicts key features of this story. www.journeyoftheuniverse.org.

11. Thomas Berry, *The Dream of the Earth* (San Francisco, CA: Sierra Club Books, 1990), xi.

12. Berry, *Great Work*, 1–3.

13. Berry, *Great Work*, 14.

14. Berry, *Great Work*, 49.

15. Berry, *Dream of the Earth*, 123.

16. A properly Catholic ecological ethics would certainly not dismiss the centrality of the Bible, but Berry rightly points out that for many Christians the Bible alone has failed to spark an ecological conversion.

17. Berry, *Dream of the Earth*, 87.

18. Berry, *Great Work*, 163.

19. Berry, *Great Work*, 31.

20. Matthew Fox comments that evolution was in some ways a vocation for both Teilhard and Berry, such that Berry's work is a "journey with evolution and its profound and meaningful gifts to our sense of the whole." Matthew Fox, "Some Thoughts on Thomas Berry's Contributions to the Western Spiritual Tradition,"

in *Thomas Berry, Dreamer of the Earth,* ed. Ervin Laszlo and Allan Combs, 16–31 (Rochester, VT: Inner Traditions, 2011), 20.

21. Tucker, "Intellectual Biography," 163.

22. Tucker, "Intellectual Biography," 155.

23. Berry, *Great Work,* 190.

24. Thomas Berry and Brian Swimme, *The Universe Story* (New York: Harper-Collins, 1992).

25. Berry, *Dream of the Earth,* 106.

26. Berry, *Great Work,* 52.

27. Berry, *Great Work,* 52.

28. Celia Deanne-Drummond faults Berry for his excessively rosy estimation of the evolutionary development of life, in particular for his insufficient appreciation for the violence, suffering, and death it requires. Celia Deane-Drummond, *Eco-Theology* (Winona, MN: Anselm Academic, 2008), 42. I make a similar criticism of Catholic social thought and Thomas Berry, and I draw on James Nash to propose a model of the human as the creative and altruistic predator. See "Co-Creator or Creative Predator? James Nash's Contributions to Catholic Social Teaching on Ecological Ethics," *Worldviews: Global Religions, Culture, and Ecology* 18, no. 2 (2014): 99–121. Still, I think such a critique is valid only in the context of the overarching primacy of the cosmic story and the need for humanity to view it as good and to incorporate their own self-understanding within it. Thus the criticism is a valid addition and correction to Berry's cosmocentric worldview, but it does not replace it.

29. Berry, *Great Work,* 17.

30. Berry, *Great Work,* 27. Of course, this is a thoroughly Augustinian theme as well. See *Confessions,* Book 4.

31. Berry, *Great Work,* 27.

32. Ellard, "Groundwork for a Dark Green Catholic Theology," 309.

33. Berry, *Great Work,* 33.

34. Ellard, "Groundwork for a Dark Green Catholic Theology," 309.

35. Leonardo Boff discusses a similar threefold scheme. Creation is composed of (1) complexity/differentiation (2) interiority/autopoiesis (3) connectedness/communion. Leonardo Boff, *Cry of the Earth, Cry of the Poor* (Maryknoll, NY: Orbis Books, 1997), 150.

36. Tucker, "Intellectual Biography," 168.

37. Catholics may perceive in these three features an image of the triune God, who is above all a God of relationships. Berry, *Christian Future and Fate of Earth,* 81.

38. Berry, *Dream of the Earth,* 106.

39. Thomas Aquinas, *Summa Theologiae,* 1.47.1.

40. Berry and Swimme, *Universe Story,* 71.

41. Berry, *Great Work,* 163.

42. Berry, *Great Work*, 163.

43. Berry, *Dream of the Earth*, 106.

44. Berry, *Dream of the Earth*, 134.

45. Berry and Swimme, *Universe Story*, 75. Environmental philosopher Holmes Rolston identifies in Genesis the Earth's innate capacity of autopoiesis, "Ecology: A Primer for Christian Ethics," *Journal of Catholic Social Thought* 4, no. 2 (2007): 293–312, at 296.

46. Berry and Swimme, *Universe Story*, 75.

47. Berry, *Great Work*, 19.

48. Berry, *Great Work*, 175.

49. Berry and Swimme, *Universe Story*, 72.

50. Berry and Clarke, *Befriending the Earth*, 14.

51. Berry, *Evening Thoughts*, 17.

52. Berry, *Great Work*, 4.

53. Berry, *Great Work*, 163.

54. Berry, *Great Work*, 48.

55. Berry, *Great Work*, 51.

56. For this reason Berry calls us to "inscendence," the descent into our own evolutionarily developed genetic coding and our natural impulses to come into contact with the living cosmos and discern the paths to a sustainable future that our rational minds cannot conceive. Hence he speaks of reinventing the human, at the species level. *Christian Future and The Fate of Earth*, 117–118. See also Bill Plotkin, "Inscendence—The Key to the Great Work of Time: A Soulcentric View of Thomas Berry's Work," in *Thomas Berry, Dreamer of the Earth*, 42–71.

57. Read the entire account at http://thomasberry.org.

58. Matthew Fox likens Berry to a Moses figure who led humanity "out of a bondage of a land of anthropocentrism to a land of cosmology and ecology." Fox, "Some Thoughts," 23.

59. Berry, *Great Work*, 12.

60. Berry, *Great Work*, 13. This echoes the famous maxim of naturalist Aldo Leopold who argued for a land ethic: "A thing is right when it tends to preserve the integrity, stability, and beauty of the biotic community. It is wrong when it tends otherwise." See Aldo Leopold, *A Sand County Almanac* (New York: Ballantine Books, 1970), 224–225.

61. Berry, *Great Work*, 20.

62. See Chapter 2; and John Hart, *Sacramental Commons: Christian Ecological Ethics* (Lanham, MD: Rowman & Littlefield, 2006), 17.

63. Berry, *Christian Future and The Fate of Earth*, 118.

64. Berry, *Great Work*, 105.

65. Francis, *Laudato Si'*, 76. http://w2.vatican.va/content/francesco/en/encyclicals/documents/papa-francesco_20150524_enciclica-laudato-si.html.

66. Berry, *Christian Future*, 119.

CHAPTER 5

1. Kevin P. Doran, *Solidarity: A Synthesis of Personalism and Communalism in the Thought of Karol Wojtyla/Pope John Paul II* (New York: Peter Lang Publishing, Inc., 1996), 120.

2. US Catholic Bishops, *Economic Justice for All: Pastoral Letter on Catholic Social Teaching and the U.S. Economy* (1986), 248. http://www.usccb.org/upload/economic_justice_for_all.pdf.

3. Thomas Massaro, *Living Justice: Catholic Social Teaching in Action* (Lanham, MD: Rowman & Littlefield, 2012), 115.

4. *Economic Justice for All*, 16.

5. Francis, *Laudato Si'*, 158. http://w2.vatican.va/content/francesco/en/encyclicals/documents/papa-francesco_20150524_enciclica-laudato-si.html.

6. Kenneth Himes, *Responses to 101 Questions on Catholic Social Teaching* (New York: Paulist Press, 2001), 38.

7. John Paul II, *Sollicitudo Rei Socialis*, 26. http://www.vatican.va/holy_father/john_paul_ii/encyclicals/documents/hf_jp-ii_enc_30121987_sollicitudo-rei-socialis_en.html.

8. Pontifical Council for Justice and Peace, *Compendium of the Social Doctrine of the Church*, 195. http://www.vatican.va/roman_curia/pontifical_councils/justpeace/documents/rc_pc_justpeace_doc_20060526_compendio-dott-soc_en.html.

9. Paul VI, *Populorum Progressio: On the Development of Peoples* (1967), 73. http://www.vatican.va/holy_father/paul_vi/encyclicals/documents/hf_p-vi_enc_26031967_populorum_en.html.

10. Paul VI, *Populorum Progressio*, 48.

11. Paul VI, *Populorum Progressio*, 44.

12. US Catholic Bishops, *Economic Justice for All*, 187.

13. John Paul II, *Sollicitudo Rei Socialis*, 38.

14. Meghan Clark, "Anatomy of a Social Virtue: Solidarity and Corresponding Vices," *Political Theology* 15, no. 1 (2014): 26–39, 28.

15. Doran, *Solidarity*, 193.

16. Clark, "Anatomy," 30.

17. Massaro, *Living Justice*, 85.

18. Of course the ultimate end of solidarity would be God as the absolute common good, while the proximate end would be something internal to creation: either the universal common good of humanity or, as I propose, the cosmic common good.

19. Clark, "Anatomy," 38. See Aquinas, *Summa Theologiae*, 2 | 2.58–122, the "Treatise on Justice."

20. See David Hollenbach, *The Common Good and Christian Ethics*, 189.

21. Clark, "Anatomy," 34.

22. Daniel Daly, "Structures of Virtue and Vice," *New Blackfriars* 92 (2011): 355.

23. Gerald J. Beyer, *Recovering Solidarity: Lessons from Poland's Unfinished Revolution* (Notre Dame, IN: University of Notre Dame Press, 2010), 89.

24. Clark, "Anatomy," 36.

25. *Sollicitudo Rei Socialis*, 39.

26. John Paul II, *Centesimus Annus*, 41. http://www.vatican.va/holy_father/ john_paul_ii/encyclicals/documents/hf_jp-ii_enc_01051991_centesimus-annus_en.html.

27. Gerald J. Beyer, "A Theoretical Appreciation of the Ethic of Solidarity in Poland Twenty-Five Years After," *Journal of Religious Ethics* 35, no. 2 (2007): 207–232; 212.

28. Beyer, *Recovering Solidarity*, 99.

29. Beyer, "Theoretical Appreciation," 226.

30. US Catholic Bishops, *Global Climate Change: A Plea for Dialogue, Prudence, and the Common Good* (Washington, DC: US Catholic Conference, 2001).

31. The Indigenous Peoples Climate Change Assessment, http://www.unutki.org/ default.php?doc_id=96#Aims.

32. IPCC, *Climate Change 2014: Impacts, Adaptation, and Vulnerability: Summary for Policymakers*.

33. Francis, *Laudato Si'*, 140.

34. Sarah Wheaton, "People, and Poodles, Contributing to Cleanup," *New York Times* (May 6, 2010: A20). BP later refused to use them, commenting that their products were the best available. http://www.npr.org/templates/story/story. php?storyId=127041062.

35. Francis, *Laudato Si'*, 19.

36. E.g., Louke Van Wensveen, *Dirty Virtues: The Emergence of Ecological Virtue Ethics* (Amherst, NY: Humanity Books, 2000); Nancy Rourke, "The Environment Within: Virtue Ethics," in *Green Discipleship*, 163–182; Celia Deane-Drummond, *The Ethics of Nature* (Malden, MA: Blackwell Publishing, 2004).

37. See Francis, *Laudato Si'*, 115.

38. Francis, *Laudato Si'*, 101.

39. Francis, *Laudato Si'*, 60. Interestingly, at times some conflate these two poles: a view of the human person as so fully a part of creation that we are incapable of radically altering planetary processes, and so therefore humanity bears no responsibility for restoring ecosystems or addressing climate change by limiting our consumption or industrial effluents. It is a perverse form of humility that excuses human exploitation of Earth without accepting the possibility that human activity has become a global and dominant force.

40. Francis, *Laudato Si'*, 219.

41. Jame Schaefer, "Solidarity, Subsidiarity, and Option for the Poor: Extending Catholic Social Teaching in Response to the Climate Crisis," in *Confronting the*

Climate Crisis: Catholic Theological Perspectives, ed., Jame Schaefer (Milwaukee: Marquette University Press), 389–425; 411.

42. Schaefer, "Solidarity," 416–417.

43. Francis, *Laudato Si'*, 49.

44. Jenkins, *Future of Ethics*, 6.

45. Francis, *Laudato Si'*, 85.

46. Mary Evelyn Tucker and Brian Swimme, students of Thomas Berry's, created an Emmy Award–winning documentary with this title whose images of beauty demonstrate the perceptual and affective dimensions of Earth solidarity. See www.journeyoftheuniverse.org.

47. See Chapter 3.

48. Francis, *Laudato Si'*, 12, 246.

49. Schaefer, "Solidarity," 417.

50. Francis, *Laudato Si'*, 211.

51. Rights, as I will show, need not be equal in order to exist, and so rights too can flow from basic creaturely dignity.

CHAPTER 6

1. Pontifical Council for Justice and Peace, *Compendium of the Social Doctrine of the Church*, 193. http://www.vatican.va/roman_curia/pontifical_councils/justpeace/documents/rc_pc_justpeace_doc_20060526_compendio-dott-soc_en.html.

2. Thomas Hoppe, "Human Rights," in *The New Dictionary of Catholic Social Thought*, ed. Judith Dwyer (Collegeville, MN: The Liturgical Press, 1994), 454–470; 455.

3. John XXIII, *Pacem in Terris*, 28. http://www.vatican.va/holy_father/john_xxiii/encyclicals/documents/hf_j-xxiii_enc_11041963_pacem_en.html.

4. John XXIII, *Pacem in Terris*, 60.

5. John XXIII, *Pacem in Terris*, 29.

6. John XXIII, *Pacem in Terris*, 30.

7. John XXIII, *Pacem in Terris*, 11.

8. John XXIII's understanding of rights reflects the general transformation of Catholic social thought from a vision of social order through hierarchy to order based on the equality of all citizens. Thus John XXIII enumerates not only the social and economic rights that earlier popes extolled, but also the political and civil rights, including religious liberty, that other popes were more suspicious of. David O'Brien, "A Century of Catholic Social Teaching," in *One Hundred Years of Catholic Social Teaching: Celebration and Challenge*, ed. John Coleman (Maryknoll, NY: Orbis, 1991), 13–24; 22.

9. Gerald Beyer agrees that "participation in the life of the community" is a new dimension of Catholic social thought that goes beyond economic rights based in

natural law. Gerald J. Beyer, *Recovering Solidarity: Lessons from Poland's Unfinished Revolution* (Notre Dame, IN: University of Notre Dame Press, 2010), 139.

10. Meghan Clark, "Anatomy of a Social Virtue: Solidarity and Corresponding Vices," *Political Theology* 15, no. 1 (2014): 26–39; 36.

11. Michael Himes and Kenneth Himes, "Creation and an Environmental Ethic," in *Fullness of Faith: The Public Significance of Theology* (New York: Paulist, 1993), 104–124; 116.

12. Hoppe, "Human Rights," 466.

13. See, for example, the debates in *Religion and Human Rights: Competing Claims?* ed. Carrie Gustafson and Peter H. Juviler (Armonk, NY: M. E. Sharpe, 1999).

14. Thomas Sieger Derr, "Environmental Ethics and Christian Humanism," in *Environmental Ethics and Christian Humanism*, ed. Thomas Sieger Derr with James A. Nash and Richard John Neuhaus (Nashville, TN: Abingdon Press, 1996), 30.

15. Holmes Rolston, III, *Environmental Ethics: Duties to and Values in the Natural World* (Philadelphia: Temple University Press, 1988), 52.

16. Richard Watson, "Self-Consciousness and the Rights of Nonhuman Animals and Nature," in *The Animal Rights/Environmental Ethics Debate*, ed. Eugene Hargrove (Albany: State University of New York Press, 1992), 2.

17. Bryan Norton, "Environmental Ethics and Nonhuman Rights," in *The Animal Rights/Environmental Ethics Debate*, 176.

18. John Passmore, *Man's Responsibility for Nature*, quoted by Gunther Wittenberg, "Plant and Animal Rights – an Absurd Idea or Ecological Necessity. Perspectives from the Hebrew Torah," *Journal of Theology for Southern Africa* 131 (July, 2008), 74.

19. Roderick Nash's comprehensive analysis of the development of rights language applied to nature demonstrates that there has been a strand in Western philosophical thought that has sought to do this for some time. See Roderick Nash, *The Rights of Nature: A History of Environmental Ethics* (Madison: University of Wisconsin Press, 1989).

20. Similarly, Andrew Linzey, arguably the most prominent Christian promoter of rights for nonhumans, describes them as "theos-rights." Rights are grounded in the fact that creation owes its existence to the Creator and that the Creator values it. *Christianity and the Rights of Animals* (New York: Crossroad, 1987), 9. Linzey adopts an "exclusive view" of theos-rights that includes only "flesh and blood" creatures and thus excludes nonanimals (84). Theos-rights mean that animals, however, can make a moral claim on us, because it is in fact God's claim on us (69).

21. John Hart, *Sacramental Commons: Christian Ecological Ethics* (Lanham, MD: Rowman & Littlefield, 2006), 130–131.

22. Hart, *Sacramental Commons*, 133.

23. James Nash, "In Flagrant Dissent: An Environmentalist's Contentions" in *Environmental Ethics and Christian Humanism*, 111.

24. James Nash, "Biotic Rights and Human Ecological Responsibilities," *The Annual of the Society of Christian Ethics* 13 (1993): 137–162; 147.

25. Hart, *Sacramental Commons*, 129.

26. Thomas Berry, *Evening Thoughts: Reflecting on Earth as Sacred Community* (San Francisco: Sierra Club Books, 2006), 149–150.

27. James Nash also invokes these principles. *Loving Nature: Ecological Integrity and Christian Responsibility* (Nashville, TN: Abingdon Press, 1991), 189–191.

28. Hart, *Sacramental Commons*, 130.

29. Nash, "Biotic Rights and Human Ecological Responsibilities," 145.

30. Hart, *Sacramental Commons*, 137.

31. See Cormac Cullinan, *Wild Law: A Manifesto for Earth Justice*, 2nd ed. (White River Junction, VT: Chelsea Green Publishing, 2011); Peter Burdo, ed., *Exploring Wild Law: The Philosophy of Earth Jurisprudence* (Kent Town, South Australia: Wakefield Press, 2011); and the Earth Law Center: http://earthlawcenter.org.

32. Cited by Cass Sunstein, "Introduction: What Are Animal Rights?" in *Animal Rights: Current Debates and New Directions*, ed. Cass R. Sunstein and Martha C. Nussbaum (Cary, NC: Oxford University Press, 2004), 3–21; 4.

33. See Sunstein, "Introduction," 6–7.

34. *Kootenai Tribe of Idaho v. Veneman*, 313 F.3d 1094 (9th Cir. 2002).

35. Begonia Filgueira and Ian Mason (2009). *Wild Law: Is There Any Evidence of Earth Jurisprudence in Existing Law and Practice?*, 42–44. Accessed at http://www.ukela.org/content/page/1090/Wild%20Law%20Research%20Report%20published%20March%202009.pdf.

36. See John Vidal, "Bolivia Enshrines Natural World's Rights with Equal Status for Mother Earth," *The Guardian*, April 10, 2011. http://www.theguardian.com/environment/2011/apr/10/bolivia-enshrines-natural-worlds-rights.

37. See http://therightsofnature.org/wp-content/uploads/pdfs/Rights-for-Nature-Articles-in-Ecuadors-Constitution.pdf.

38. http://www.earthcharterinaction.org/content/.

39. Francis, *Laudato Si'*, 207. http://w2.vatican.va/content/francesco/en/encyclicals/documents/papa-francesco_20150524_enciclica-laudato-si.html.

40. John A. Grim and Mary Evelyn Tucker, *Ecology and Religion* (Washington, DC: Island Press, 2014), 157.

41. Francis, *Laudato Si'*, 53.

42. Francis, *Laudato Si'*, 211.

43. Here I build off the work primarily of Thomas Berry, John Hart, and James Nash.

44. Nash, *Loving Nature*, 186.

45. Note the concern among some local residents in West Virginia about the process of mountain top removal to access coal. They mourn not only the effects

on their health and on other creatures, but also on the integrity of the streams, the vegetation, and the mountain as a whole. See "Leveling Appalachia: The Legacy of Mountaintop Removal Mining," at http://e360.yale.edu/feature/ leveling_appalachia_the_legacy_of_mountaintop_removal_mining/2198/.

46. This becomes poignant and complex in the Hindu tradition, where rivers are often described as gods and goddesses and have sacred functions in the lives of millions of people. See Lance Nelson, "Ecology," in *Studying Hinduism: Key Concepts and Methods*, ed. Sushil Mittal and Gene Thursby (New York: Routledge, 2008), 97–111; 102.

47. Thomas Berry, *Dream of the Earth* (San Francisco: Sierra Club Books, 1990), 166–168.

48. See Nash, "Biotic Rights," 155.

49. This must always be distinguished, however from the enormous and unprecedented activity of human beings, such as anthropogenic climate change, which poses a threat to species, ecosystems, and the well-being of the Earth as a whole.

50. Holmes Rolston, "Ecology: A Primer for Christian Ethics," *Journal of Catholic Social Thought* 4, no. 2 (2007): 293–312; 307.

51. This should probably already be expanded to include Earth's immediate orbit, the moon, and, possibly, Mars. As calls to "terraform" and re-create Mars increase, we need serious reflection on why and how that may ever be justified.

52. The term "mixed community" is from Mary Midgely, "The Mixed Community," in *The Animal Rights/Environmental Ethics Debate*, ed. Eugene Hargrove (Albany: State University of New York Press, 1992), 211–226.

CHAPTER 7

1. Francis X. Clooney, S.J., "Comparative Theology," in *The Oxford Handbook of Systematic Theology*, eds. Kathryn Tanner, John Webster, and Iain Torrance (Oxford: Oxford University Press, 2007), 653–669. Clooney traces the term "comparative theology" back to 1700 and he notes a tradition of comparative theology in the nineteenth century, but one that differs considerably from what is known as comparative theology today. "Comparative Theology," 656.

2. James Fredericks, "Introduction," in *The New Comparative Theology: Interreligious Insights from the Next Generation*, ed. Francis X. Clooney, S.J. (New York: Continuum, 2010), ix–xix.

3. Francis X. Clooney, S.J., *Comparative Theology: Deep Learning across Religious Borders* (Malden, MA: Wiley-Blackwell, 2010), 7.

4. Clooney, "Comparative Theology," 653–654.

5. See David Tracy, "Comparative Theology," in *The Encyclopedia of Religion* (New York: Macmillan, 1987), 14:446–455; 446.

6. Clooney, "Comparative Theology," 660.
7. Clooney, *Deep Learning*, 13.
8. Fredericks, "Introduction," xi.
9. Clooney, *Deep Learning*, 10.
10. Francis X. Clooney, S.J., "The Study of Non-Christian Religions in the Post-Vatican II Church," *Journal of Ecumenical Studies* 28, no. 3 (1991): 488.
11. Fredericks, "Introduction," xiii.
12. Francis X. Clooney, S.J., "The Emerging Field of Comparative Theology: A Bibliographical Review (1989–95)," *Theological Studies* 56, no. 3 (September 1995): 521–550; 522.
13. Clooney, "Emerging Field," 522.
14. Kristin Beise Kiblinger argues that Fredericks and Clooney are critiquing an older and outdated form of theology of religions. The field has advanced considerably, and in fact comparative theology exemplifies these new approaches. For Kiblinger, comparative theology depends on some cogent theology of religions, and it is better to admit our locations and presuppositions. See Kiblinger, "Relating Theology of Religions and Comparative Theology," in *The New Comparative Theology: Interreligious Insights from the Next Generation*, ed. Francis X. Clooney, S.J. (New York: Continuum, 2010), 21–42.
15. Fredericks, "Introduction," xiv.
16. Fredericks, "Introduction," xv.
17. See Francis X. Clooney, *Beyond Compare: St. Francis de Sales and Sri Vedanta Desika on Loving Surrender to God* (Washington, DC: Georgetown University Press, 2008), 16, 19; and *Theology after Vedanta: An Experiment in Comparative Theology* (Albany: State University of New York Press, 1993), 4–6.
18. Fredericks, "Introduction," xiii.
19. Clooney, "Comparative Theology," 661.
20. Fredericks, "Introduction," xiii.
21. Clooney, *Deep Learning*, 11.
22. Clooney, "Comparative Theology," 664.
23. Clooney, "Comparative Theology," 667. Elsewhere Clooney describes how comparative theology must look outward to be "intelligently engaged" with others, and to look inward and to attend to the "well-being of our faith in our community." Clooney, *Deep Learning*, 7–8.
24. Clooney, *Deep Learning*, 15.
25. Clooney, "Comparative Theology," 659.
26. Clooney, *Deep Learning*, 4.
27. Clooney, *Deep Learning*, 4.
28. For example, Clooney focuses his work on Hindu-Christian comparisons, while Fredericks's work engages Buddhist thinkers.
29. Sometimes this is further limited to one or a narrow set of texts that are chosen as representative of each thinker, rather than the entirety of their corpora.

30. E.g., Lee Yearley, *Mencius and Aquinas: Theories of Virtue and Conceptions of Courage* (Albany: State University of New York Press, 1990); John Sheveland, *Piety and Responsibility: Patterns of Unity in Karl Rahner, Karl Barth, and Vedanta Desika* (Burlington, VT: Ashgate, 2011).

31. E.g., John Thatamanil, *The Immanent Divine: God, Creation and the Human Predicament* (Minneapolis: Fortress Press, 2006); Thomas Cattoi, *Divine Contingency: Theologies of Divine Embodiment in Maximos the Confessor and Tsong Kha Pa* (Piscataway, NJ: Gorgias Press, 2008).

32. E.g., Francis X. Clooney, S.J., *Hindu God, Christian God: How Reason Helps Break Down the Boundaries Between Religions* (New York: Oxford, 2001).

33. Obviously, classical theological concepts in dialogue may be employed for eco- logical ethics, such as my comparative theology of creation in Thomas Aquinas and Hindu theologian Vedānta Deśika. See Daniel Scheid, "Vedānta Deśika and Thomas Aquinas on the Intrinsic Value of Nature," *Journal of Vaishnava Studies* 18 (2010): 27–42.

34. Donald K. Swearer, "An Assessment of Buddhist Ecophilosophy," *Harvard Theological Review* 99, no. 2 (2006): 123–137.

35. See, for example, Larry Rasmussen, who hopes that other religious traditions will explore Earth faith and Earth ethics "from their own turf" because "Earth's distress, after all, is the most ecumenical of issues. As such it requires a religious response of corresponding scope. No one religious tradition will suffice." Larry Rasmussen, *Earth Community, Earth Ethics* (Maryknoll, NY: Orbis Books, 1996), 271. At the same time, Lance Nelson has also suggested that it would be ideal if people within each tradition undertook their own analysis, but in light of press- ing ecological problems, it is permissible for non-Hindus to pose "respectful questions" to classic Hindu texts. Lance Nelson, "Reading the *Bhagavadgita* from an Ecological Perspective," *Hinduism and Ecology: The Intersection of Earth, Sky, and Water*, ed. Christopher Key Chapple and Mary Evelyn Tucker (Cambridge, MA: Harvard University Press, 2000), 135–150; 128. Happily, enough work has been done by "insiders" within these traditions that Christian "outsiders" need not rely solely on their own interpretation of non-Christian concepts and texts.

36. This term stems from John Rawls. See John Rawls, *Political Liberalism* (New York: Columbia University Press, 1993), 134–149.

CHAPTER 8

1. For an overview, see Gavin Flood, *An Introduction to Hinduism* (New York: Cambridge University Press, 1996).

2. For a sense of the multitudinous ways in which the Hindu tradition can apply to ecology, see *Hinduism and Ecology: The Intersection of Earth, Sky, and Water* ed. Christopher Key Chapple and Mary Evelyn Tucker (Cambridge, MA: Harvard University Press, 2000); *Purifying the Earthly Body of God: Religion and Ecology*

in Hindu India, ed. Lance Nelson (Albany: State University of New York Press, 1998); Klaus Klostermaier, "Hinduism and Ecology," in *A Survey of Hinduism* (Albany: State University of New York Press, 2007), 476–489; Lance Nelson, "Ecology," in *Studying Hinduism: Key Concepts and Methods*, ed. Sushil Mittal and Gene Thursby (New York: Routledge, 2008), 97–111; Vasudha Narayanan, "'One Tree Is Equal to Ten Sons': Hindu Responses to the Problems of Ecology, Population, and Consumption," *Journal of the American Academy of Religion* 65: 291–332.

3. See Chapple, "Toward an Indigenous Indian Environmentalism," in *Purifying the Earthly Body*, 13–28.

4. Jain also observes a difference between Hindus and Jains on this account. For most Jains, the ideal is to be an ascetic, and their behavior more closely matches the austere practices of ascetics; for most Hindus, on the other hand, the goal of life is to become a perfect devotee. Pankaj Jain, *Dharma and Ecology of Hindu Communities: Sustenance and Sustainability* (Burlington, VT: Ashgate, 2011), 117.

5. While my summary of dharmic ecology is based on the constructive work of Hindu theologians such as O. P. Dwivedi, Pankaj Jain, and Vasudha Narayanan, I supplement their vision with the work of Hindu scholars, "sympathetic outsiders" who know the tradition deeply and wish to explore its ecological relevance.

6. Conceptually, the present usage of dharma has its roots in an older term, *Ṛta*. In the *Vedas*, the most ancient Hindu texts, the term *Ṛta* is used as a celebration of cosmic order. In the famous "Purusha Sukta" of the Rig Veda (10:90), *Ṛta* is reworded and reinterpreted as dharma. Arnold Kunst distinguishes *ṛtam* (cosmic order), dharma (social and worldly order), and *vrata* (the duties necessary to maintain social order). Later, dharma includes these dimensions: it represents cosmic, social, and personal order. See Arnold Kunst, "Use and Misuse of Dharma," in *The Concept of Duty in South Asia*, eds. W. D. O'Flaherty and J. Duncan M. Derrett (Delhi: Vikas, 1979), 3–17. While *ṛta* and dharma both contain the idea of cosmic order that sustains the universe, there is a shift away from the physical sacrifice of animals in Vedic rituals for *ṛta* to metaphorical sacrifices of a cosmic person for dharma. This parallels the shift away from rituals as necessary for material prosperity to the Upaniṣadic focus on metaphysical pursuits. Jain, *Dharma and Ecology*, 107.

7. Klostermaier, *A Survey of Hinduism*, 30.

8. Bruce Sullivan, *The A to Z of Hinduism* (London: The Scarecrow Press, 2001), 76.

9. "In Hinduism, law, ethics, and soteriology are always tied together." Arti Dhand, "The *Dharma* of Ethics, the Ethics of *Dharma*: Quizzing the Ideals of Hinduism," *Journal of Religious Ethics* 30, no. 3 (2002): 347–372; 351.

10. Arvind Sharma, *Modern Hindu Thought: An Introduction* (New York: Oxford University Press, 2005), 90. See also Jain, *Dharma and Ecology*, 106.

11. Gavin Flood, *An Introduction to Hinduism*, 53.

12. Narayanan, "A Tree," 323.
13. Vasudha Narayanan, "Water, Wood, and Wisdom: Ecological Perspectives from the Hindu Traditions," *Daedalus* 130, no. 4 (Fall 2001): 179–206; 181.
14. Cf. Jain, *Dharma and Ecology*, 124.
15. Narayanan, "A Tree," 295.
16. Narayanan, "A Tree," 296.
17. John A. Grim and Mary Evelyn Tucker, *Ecology and Religion* (Washington, DC: Island Press, 2014), 57.
18. Nelson, "Ecology," 99.
19. Nelson, "Ecology," 104.
20. Narayanan, "A Tree," 299.
21. Narayanan, "A Tree," 297.
22. Jain, *Dharma and Ecology*, 117.
23. Narayanan, "A Tree," 299.
24. Narayanan, "A Tree," 291–292.
25. Meera Nanda, "Dharmic Ecology and the Neo-Pagan International: The Dangers of Religious Environmentalism in India." Cited by Nelson, "Ecology," 108.
26. Jain, *Dharma and Ecology*, 127.
27. Jain, *Dharma and Ecology*, 130–131.
28. Swami Vibudhesha Teertha, "Sustaining the Balance." Found at Alliance for Religions and Conservation, http://www.arcworld.org/faiths.asp?pageID=77.
29. Narayanan, "A Tree," 311–312.
30. O. P. Dwivedi, "Dharmic Ecology," in *Hinduism and Ecology*, 5.
31. Though this is a modern development, it is now considered to be the main scripture of Hinduism. Sharma, *Modern Hindu Thought*, 29.
32. *Bhagavad Gītā*, trans. R. C. Zaehner (New York: Oxford University Press, 1966). All in text citations come from Zaehner.
33. Flood, *An Introduction to Hinduism*, 126.
34. Lance Nelson, "Cows, Elephants, Dogs, and Other Lesser Embodiments of *Ātman*: Reflections on Hindu Attitudes Toward Nonhuman Animals," in *A Communion of Subjects: Animals in Religion, Science, and Ethics*, ed. Paul Waldau and Kimberly Patton (New York: Columbia University Press, 2006), 179–193; 181.
35. Dwivedi, "Dharmic Ecology," 5.
36. Cited by O. P. Dwivedi, "Hindu Religion and Environmental Well-being," in *The Oxford Handbook of Religion and Ecology*, ed. Roger Gottlieb (New York: Oxford, 2006), 160–183; 165.
37. Dwivedi, "Dharmic Ecology," 13.
38. Jain, *Dharma and Ecology*, 125.
39. Dwivedi, "Dharmic Ecology," 12.
40. Dwivedi, "Dharmic Ecology," 13.
41. Mary McGee, "State Responsibility for Environmental Management: Perspectives from Hindu Texts on Polity," in *Hinduism and Ecology*, 59–100. Ann Grodzins

Gold recounts how this ethos was embodied, albeit imperfectly, in the rule of Vansh Pradip Singh in Rajasthan, who was accustomed to saying, "If you cut a branch, you cut my finger." See Gold, "'If You Cut a Branch You Cut My Finger': Court, Forest, and Environmental Ethics in Rajasthan," in *Hinduism and Ecology*, 317–336.

42. Dwivedi, "Dharmic Ecology," 6, 13.

43. The dedication of the Bishnois became an inspiration to the Chipko movement in Uttar Pradesh, which protested the destruction of a local forest from government contractors by forming circles around trees and hugging them. See George A. James, "Ethical and Religious Dimensions of Chipko Resistance," in *Hinduism and Ecology*, 499–530.

44. Jain, *Dharma and Ecology*, 9.

45. Jain, *Dharma and Ecology*, 120.

46. Nelson "Ecology," 109.

47. Jain, *Dharma and Ecology*, 119.

48. Jain, *Dharma and Ecology*, 130.

49. Jain, *Dharma and Ecology*, 120.

50. See Vijaya Rettakudi Nagarjan, "The Earth as Goddess Bhu Devi: Toward a Theory of 'Embedded Ecologies' in Folk Hinduism," in *Purifying the Earthly Body*, 270.

51. Jain conjectures that perhaps ancient nature worship, long practiced by indigenous groups, was "traditionalized" into Brahmanical texts. Jain, *Dharma and Ecology*, 123–124.

52. Jain, *Dharma and Ecology*, 126.

53. See Harold Coward, "The Ecological Implications of Karma Theory," in *Purifying the Earthly Body*, 39–49.

54. Mahābhārata 18:116:37–41. Cited by Christopher Key Chapple, "Ecological Nonviolence and the Hindu Tradition," reprinted in *Many Heavens, One Earth: Readings on Religion and the Environment*, ed. Clifford Chalmers Cain (Lanham, MD: Lexington Books, 2013), 125.

55. Albertina Nutgeren, "From Cosmos to Commodity . . . and Back: A Critique of Hindu Environmental Rhetoric in Educational Programs," in *Religion and Sustainable Development: Opportunities and Challenges for Higher Education*, eds. Cathrien de Pater and Irene Dankelman (Münster: LIT Verlag, 2009), 159–168; 164.

56. Jain, *Dharma and Ecology*, 125.

57. Jain, *Dharma and Ecology*, 121.

58. Jain, *Dharma and Ecology*, 122.

59. Nelson, "Cows," 181.

60. Yet, as Nelson notes, for many conservative teachers, one must be a "twice-born" Hindu male, that is, a member of the upper three castes. *Śankara* even teaches

that one must be a Brahmin, and then in addition a *sannyasin* (world-renouncer). Nelson, "Cows," 184.

61. Nelson, "Cows," 189.

62. Edwin Bryant, "Strategies of Vedic Subversion," in *A Communion of Subjects*, 194–203, 194.

63. Bryant, "Strategies," 197–198.

64. Bryant, "Strategies," 202.

65. Chapple recounts two anecdotes that express the persistent cultural force of *ahiṃsā* and the Hindu reverence for life. When an American development worker proposed using poison to save grain from rats in India, his coworker was shocked and responded that this solution would be culturally unacceptable due to *ahiṃsā*. Instead, they elevated the grain off the ground, saving the grain and sparing the rats. In another instance, a local temple was overrun by ants, so they built a shrine to the ants to lure them away. In time, this second shrine became nearly more popular! See Chapple, "Ecological Nonviolence," 123–124.

66. For background, see Patrick Olivelle, "Introduction," in *The Law Code of Manu*, trans. Olivelle (New York: Oxford University Press, 2004), xvi–xlv. All in-text citations come from Olivelle.

67. Patricia Mumme, "Models and Images for a Vaisnava Environmental Theology," in *Purifying the Earthly Body of God*, 133–161; 146.

68. Discussed by Narayanan, "Water, Wood, and Wisdom," 190.

69. Some modern Hindus understand passages like this figuratively, so that it is not that we are reborn as animals, but that bad actions lead to an irrational existence. Sharma, *Modern Hindu Thought*, 34.

70. Olivelle notes that Vedic literature includes such an idea in reference to plants and grains as well. Olivelle, n.5.55, 254. See also Bryant, 198.

71. Ryan McLaughlin argues for an ethic of preservation and protest on these grounds. *Preservation and Protest: Theological Foundations for an Eco-Eschatological Ethics* (Minneapolis: Fortress, 2014).

72. Nagarjan, "The Earth as Goddess," 277–280.

CHAPTER 9

1. Among the many examples, see *Dharma Gaia: A Harvest of Essays in Buddhism and Ecology*, ed. Allan Hunt Badiner (Berkeley: Parallax Press, 1990); *Dharma Rain: Sources of Buddhist Environmentalism*, eds. Stephanie Kaza and Kenneth Kraft (Boston: Shambhala Press, 2000); and *Buddhism and Ecology: The Interconnection of Dharma and Deeds*, eds. Mary Evelyn Tucker and Duncan Ryuken Williams (Cambridge, MA: Harvard University Press, 1997).

2. Simon P. James, *Zen Buddhism and Environmental Ethics* (Burlington, VT: Ashgate, 2004).

3. David Loy, *Money Sex War Karma: Notes for a Buddhist Revolution* (Somerville, MA: Wisdom Publications, 2008).

4. Christopher Key Chapple, "Animals and Environment in the Buddhist Birth Stories," in *Buddhism and Ecology*, 131–148.

5. Graham Parkes, "Voices of Mountains, Trees, and Rivers: Kūkai, Dōgen, and a Deeper Ecology," in *Buddhism and Ecology*, 111–128.

6. For consistency's sake I will translate *pratītyasamutpāda* as "dependent origination" when discussing it as a metaphysical statement about reality, and as "interdependence" when discussing how it is applied ecologically.

7. This principle functions differently in various Buddhist traditions, but there is a common thread between them.

8. Thich Nhat Hanh, *The Heart of the Buddha's Teaching: Transforming Suffering into Peace, Joy, and Liberation* (Berkeley, CA: Parallax Press, 1998), 221. I spell his name without diacritics, rather than Thích Nhất Hạnh, since it appears this way on most of his books.

9. Peter Harvey, *An Introduction to Buddhist Ethics* (New York: Cambridge University Press, 2004), 39.

10. Cited by Hanh, *Heart of the Buddha's Teaching*, 221. More precisely, this verse expresses *idaṃpratyayatā/idappaccayata*, the principle of specific conditionality that is a key formulation of dependent origination.

11. Harvey, *An Introduction*, 33.

12. Harvey, *An Introduction*, 124.

13. David Clairmont, "Why Does the Buddha Close His Eyes in My Eden? A Buddhist Ecological Challenge and Invitation to Christians," in *Green Discipleship: Catholic Theological Ethics and the Environment*, ed. Tobias L. Winright (Winona MN: Anselm Academic, 2011), 340–358; 346.

14. Walpola Rahula, *What the Buddha Taught*, rev. ed. (New York: Grove Press, 1974), 51.

15. Sallie King, *Socially Engaged Buddhism* (Honolulu: University of Hawaiʻi Press, 2009), 45–46.

16. Dependent origination was meant to explain the karmic origin of how beings exist as they are, and as such it does not have an implication for ecological ethics. For this reason Andrew Olendzki disparages positive appeals to dependent origination: "The more interconnected we become, the more bound in the net of conditioned phenomena we may find ourselves." In David McMahan, *The Making of Buddhist Modernism* (Oxford: Oxford University Press, 2008), 181–182.

17. Similar to my use of Augustine and Aquinas, many contemporary Buddhists do not presume that the ancient doctrine of dependent origination had an immediate ecological application but see promising similarities between this doctrine and the kind of interdependence that ecologists describe.

18. King, *Socially Engaged Buddhism*, 119.

19. King, *Socially Engaged Buddhism*, 1.

20. King, *Socially Engaged Buddhism* 2.

21. Harvey, *An Introduction*, 113, 185. See also King, *Socially Engaged Buddhism*, 4.

22. Thich Nhat Hanh, *The World We Have: A Buddhist Approach to Peace and Ecology* (Berkeley, CA: Parallax Press, 2008), 43–44.

23. Hanh, *Heart of the Buddha's Teaching* 226.

24. Hanh, *Heart of the Buddha's Teaching*, 225.

25. Hanh, *Heart of the Buddha's Teaching*, 231.

26. Hanh, *Heart of the Buddha's Teaching*, 232–234.

27. Hanh, *Heart of the Buddha's Teaching*, 236.

28. Hanh, *Heart of the Buddha's Teaching*, 231.

29. Thich Nhat Hanh, *The Sun My Heart: From Mindfulness to Insight Contemplation* (Berkeley, CA: Parallax Press, 1988), 68.

30. Hanh, *The Sun My Heart*, 70.

31. Hanh, *The Blooming of the Lotus*, 2nd edition (Boston: Beacon Press, 2009), 27.

32. Hanh, *Blooming of the Lotus*, chapter 7.

33. Hanh, *Blooming of the Lotus*, 121.

34. Thich Nhat Hanh, *Essential Writings*, ed. Robert Ellsberg (Maryknoll, NY: Orbis Books, 2001), 62–63.

35. Hanh, *The Sun My Heart*, 84.

36. Hanh, *The World We Have*, 46.

37. Hanh, *Heart of the Buddha's Teaching*, 222.

38. Hanh, *Heart of the Buddha's Teaching*, 234.

39. Hanh, *Heart of the Buddha's Teaching*, 238.

40. Hanh, *Heart of the Buddha's Teaching*, 238.

41. Thich Nhat Hanh, "The Moment Is Perfect," *Shambhala Sun*, May 2008, 64–67.

42. Hanh, *The World We Have*, 21.

43. Hanh, *Blooming of the Lotus*, 40–42.

44. Hanh, *Blooming of the Lotus*, 45.

45. Hanh, *Essential Writings*, 55.

46. Hanh, *Essential Writings*, 63.

47. Hanh, *The Sun My Heart*, 72.

48. Hanh, *For a Future to Be Possible*, 19.

49. Hanh, *For a Future to Be Possible*, 14.

50. Hanh, *Essential Writings*, 67–68.

51. Steve Odin, "The Japanese Concept of Nature in Relation to the Environmental Ethics and Conservation Aesthetics of Aldo Leopold," in *Buddhism and Ecology*, 89–110, 103.

52. Joanna Macy, *World as Lover, World as Self* (Berkeley CA: Parallax Press, 1991), 38.

53. Macy, *World as Lover, World as Self*, 53–58.

54. Macy, *World as Lover, World as Self*, 56.
55. Macy, *World as Lover, World as Self*, 58.
56. Macy, *World as Lover, World as Self*, 53.
57. Macy, *World as Lover, World as Self*, 13.
58. Macy, *World as Lover, World as Self*, 13–14.
59. Macy, *World as Lover, World as Self*, 68.
60. Macy, *World as Lover, World as Self*, 42.
61. Macy, *World as Lover, World as Self*, 74.
62. Macy, *World as Lover, World as Self*, 58–59.
63. Macy, *World as Lover, World as Self*, 83.
64. Macy, *World as Lover, World as Self*, 61–62.
65. Ian Harris specifically criticizes Joanna Macy for extending the net of Indra image too far. Ian Harris, "Buddhism and the Discourse of Environmental Concern: Some Methodological Problems Considered," in *Buddhism and Ecology*, 377–402.
66. Francis H. Cook, *Hua-yen Buddhism: The Jewel Net of Indra* (University Park: Pennsylvania State University Press, 1977), 2.
67. Odin, "The Japanese Concept of Nature," 98.
68. David R. Loy, *The Great Awakening: A Buddhist Social Theory* (Boston: Wisdom Publications, 2003), 183.
69. David Loy, *The Great Awakening*, 184.
70. Cook, *Hua-Yen Buddhism*, 2.
71. David Loy, *The Great Awakening*, 183.
72. Cook, *Hua-Yen Buddhism*, 2.
73. Stephanie Kaza, "The Greening of Buddhism: Promise and Perils," in *The Oxford Handbook of Religion and Ecology*, ed. Roger Gottlieb (New York: Oxford, 2006), 184–206; 193.
74. For this reason Nhat Hanh and Macy would likely reject a proposal for Earth rights, on the basis that there is no substantial self in any species who can possess that right. Still, given the centrality of "rights" discourse in the West in defending the dignity of the weak and adjudicating conflicts, I maintain that Earth rights are a meaningful expression of commitment to the cosmic common good in these contexts.

CHAPTER 10

1. Francis agrees, saying "it is essential to show special care for indigenous communities and their cultural traditions. They are not merely one minority among others, but should be the principal dialogue partners." *Laudato Si'*, 146. http://w2.vatican.va/content/francesco/en/encyclicals/documents/papa-francesco_20150524_enciclica-laudato-si.html.

2. So charges eco-feminist Rosemary Radford Ruether, cited by Willis Jenkins and Christopher Key Chapple, "Religion and Environment," *Annual Review of Environment and Resources* 36 (2011): 441–463; 447.

3. There lurk dangers of hegemonic use in my turn to Hindu and Buddhist traditions as well, but I associate the greatest power differential between White americans and indigenous peoples.

4. Cynthia Moe-Lobeda, *Resisting Structural Evil: Love as Ecological and Economic Vocation* (Minneapolis: Fortress, 2013), 10, 15.

5. Tinker, an Osage citizen through his father and an amer-european descendant through his mother, knows how to bridge the divisions between Western Christianities and indigenous traditions. He earned a doctorate in theology and is a past president of the Native American Theological Association, as well as a director of Four Winds American Indian Survival Project in Denver, where he acts as a traditional American Indian spiritual leader.

6. When I describe Western and Christian theologians from my perspective, I will use the conventional capitalized form; when I describe them from an American Indian perspective, I will use lower case, following Tinker's orthography. Tinker explains that while one might capitalize Christian (or Muslim) out of respect for persons, utilizing the lower case for "christian" and "american" helps readers avoid making these dominant worldviews seem normative and universal. Similarly, Tinker capitalizes "White" to demonstrate a cultural investment in Whiteness that americans prefer to ignore. George Tinker, *American Indian Liberation: A Theology of Sovereignty* (Maryknoll, NY: Orbis Books, 2008), 1–2.

7. Tinker, *American Indian Liberation*, 8.

8. Francis, *Evangelii Gaudium*, 222. http://w2.vatican.va/content/francesco/en/apost_exhortations/documents/papa-francesco_esortazione-ap_20131124_evangelii-gaudium.html.

9. Francis, *Evangelii Gaudium*, 223.

10. Tinker, *American Indian Liberation*, 9.

11. John Grim depicts this in the sweat-lodge experience of Daniel Cardinal, a Canadian Blackhawk. John A. Grim, "Indigenous Traditions: Religion and Ecology," in *The Oxford Handbook of Religion and Ecology*, ed. Roger Gottlieb (New York: Oxford, 2006), 283–309; 296.

12. George Tinker, "American Indians' Religious Traditions," in *The Hope of Liberation in World Religions*, ed. Miguel A. De La Torre (Waco, TX: Baylor University Press, 2008), 257–274; 258.

13. Tinker, *American Indian Liberation*, 9.

14. Tinker, *American Indian Liberation*, 9.

15. Tinker, "An American Indian Theological Response to Ecojustice," 163.

16. Vine Deloria, *God Is Red* (New York: Grosset & Dunlap, 1973), 91.

17. Grim, "Indigenous Traditions," 301.

18. Tinker, *American Indian Liberation*, 10.

19. Grim, "Indigenous Traditions," 287.

20. In mathematics, a reciprocal stands for a quantity divided into one; in a similar way, an ethic of reciprocity acknowledges the relationship between and among multiple parties who are part of a larger indivisible whole.

21. "Any disruption of the community's balance ... called for attention to whatever ceremony needed to be done in order to restore balance." George Tinker, "American Indians' Religious Traditions," 262.

22. Tinker, "American Indians' Religious Traditions," 264.

23. Achiel Peelman similarly contrasts *mitakuye oyasin*, which stresses the relatedness of the speaker to everything that surrounds her, to "amen" in Christian prayers, which accentuates the speaker. Peelman, *Christ Is a Native American* (Toronto: Novalis, 1995), 42.

24. George Tinker, "For All My Relations: Justice, Peace and the Integrity of Christmas Trees," *Sojourners* 20, no. 1 (1991): 19–21; 20.

25. Tinker, "American Indians and the Arts of the Land: Spatial Metaphors and Contemporary Existence," in *Voices from the Third World: 1990* (Sri Lanka: Ecumenical Association of Third World Theologians, 1991), 171–193; 185.

26. Tinker, "An American Indian Theological Response to Ecojustice," 163.

27. Tinker, "Arts of the Land," 186.

28. Tinker, "Arts of the Land," 186.

29. Tinker, "Arts of the Land," 185.

30. Tinker, *American Indian Liberation*, 155.

31. Larry Rasmussen, *Earth Community, Earth Ethics* (Maryknoll, NY: Orbis Books, 1996), 241.

32. Tinker, *American Indian Liberation*, 155–156.

33. Tinker, "An American Indian Theological Response to Ecojustice," 166–167.

34. Grim, "Indigenous Traditions," 292.

35. Grim, "Indigenous Traditions," 307.

36. Aldo Seoane and Wica Agli, "House Vote in Favor of the Keystone XL Pipeline an Act of War," http://www.lakotavoice.com/2014/11/15/house-vote-in-favor-of-the-keystone-xl-pipeline-an-act-of-war/.

37. Tinker, "For All My Relations," 21.

38. Vine Deloria, *God Is Red*, 101. Again, spatiality seems to be key. Deloria points to the Navajo, for example, who can identify the particular mountain from which their ancestors emerged. "No one can say when the creation story of the Navajo happened, but everyone is fairly certain where the emergence took place." *God Is Red*, 138.

39. Deloria, *God Is Red*, 114.

40. Tinker, "Ecojustice," 109.

41. Aaron Huey, "America's Native Prisoners of War," 2010. http://www.ted.com/talks/aaron_huey.html.
42. http://www.ted.com/talks/aaron_huey.html.
43. Tinker, *American Indian Liberation*, 156.
44. Tinker, *American Indian Liberation*, 10–15.
45. Tinker's critique of temporal thinking and his promotion of spatiality could also inform doctrines such as creation or Christology, or liturgical practices like the Mass, which could be vastly different if they were articulated or celebrated with an emphasis on space, rather than or in addition to the already overriding concern with time.
46. George Tinker, "For All My Relations," 20.
47. See John Paul II, *Centesimus Annus*, 36. http://www.vatican.va/holy_father/john_paul_ii/encyclicals/documents/hf_jp-ii_enc_01051991_centesimus-annus_en.html.
48. See http://esa.un.org/wpp.

CONCLUSION

1. Francis, *Evangelii Gaudium*, 235. http://w2.vatican.va/content/francesco/en/apost_exhortations/documents/papa-francesco_esortazione-ap_20131124_evangelii-gaudium.html.
2. Francis, *Laudato Si'*, 220. http://w2.vatican.va/content/francesco/en/encyclicals/documents/papa-francesco_20150524_enciclica-laudato-si.html.

Bibliography

Abram, David. *The Spell of the Sensuous: Perception and Language in a More-Than-Human World*. New York: Vintage Books, 1996.

Agliardo, Michael. "Restoring Creation and Redressing the Public Square," in *Green Discipleship: Catholic Theological Ethics and the Environment*, edited by Tobias L. Winright, 37–59.

Aristotle. *The Nichomachean Ethics*. Book 2: Section 9, translated by J. A. K. Thompson. New York: Penguin Books, 1953, 1976, 2004.

Aquinas, St. Thomas. *Disputed Questions on Truth*, translated by Robert W. Mulligan, S.J. Chicago: Henry Regnery, 1952.

Aquinas, St. Thomas. *Summa Contra Gentiles*, translated by Fathers of the English Dominican Province. Chicago: Benziger Brothers, 1924.

Aquinas, St. Thomas. *Summa Theologica*, translated by Fathers of the English Dominican Province. Chicago: Benziger Brothers, 1948.

Augustine, St. *Confessions*, translated by R. S. Pine-Coffin. New York: Penguin, 1961.

Augustine, St. *Expositions of the Psalms 121–150*, translated by M. Boulding. *Works of St. Augustine*, part 3, volume 20. Hyde Park, NY: New City Press, 2004.

Augustine, St. *The City of God*, translated by Marcus Dods, D.D. Introduction by Thomas Merton. New York: The Modern Library, a division of Random House, 1950.

Augustine, St. *The Literal Meaning of Genesis*, Volumes 1 and 2, translated by John Hammond Taylor, S.J. New York: Paulist Press, 1982.

Badiner, Allan Hunt, ed. *Dharma Gaia: A Harvest of Essays in Buddhism and Ecology*. Berkeley, CA: Parallax Press, 1990.

Benedict XVI. *Caritas in Veritate*, Encyclical Letter on Integral Human Development in Charity and Truth. 2009. http://www.vatican.va/holy_father/benedict_xvi/encyclicals/documents/hf_ben-xvi_enc_20090629_caritas-in-veritate_en.html.

Benedict XVI. *If You Want to Cultivate Peace, Protect Creation*, Message of His Holiness Pope Benedict XVI for the Celebration of the World Day of Peace. 2010.

http://www.vatican.va/holy_father/benedict_xvi/messages/peace/documents/hf_ben-xvi_mes_20091208_xliii-world-day-peace_en.html.

Benzoni, Francisco. *Ecological Ethics and the Human Soul: Aquinas, Whitehead, and the Metaphysics of Value*. Notre Dame, IN: University of Notre Dame Press, 2007.

Berry, Thomas. *The Christian Future and the Fate of the Earth*. Edited by Mary Evelyn Tucker and John Grim. Maryknoll, NY: Orbis Books, 2009.

Berry, Thomas. *Evening Thoughts: Reflecting on Earth as a Sacred Community*. Edited by Mary Evelyn Tucker. San Francisco: Sierra Club Books, 2006.

Berry, Thomas. *The Dream of the Earth*. San Francisco: Sierra Club Books, 1990.

Berry, Thomas. *The Great Work: Our Way into the Future*. New York: Bell Tower, 1999.

Berry, Thomas, and Thomas Clarke, S.J. *Befriending the Earth: A Theology of Reconciliation Between Humans and the Earth*. Mystic, CT: Twenty-Third Publications, 1991.

Berry, Thomas, and Brian Swimme. *The Universe Story*. New York: HarperCollins, 1992.

Beyer, Gerald J. "A Theoretical Appreciation of the Ethic of Solidarity in Poland Twenty-Five Years After." *Journal of Religious Ethics* 35, no. 2 (2007): 207–232.

Beyer, Gerald J. *Recovering Solidarity: Lessons from Poland's Unfinished Revolution*. Notre Dame, IN: University of Notre Dame Press, 2010.

Blanchette, Oliva. *The Perfection of the Universe According to Aquinas: A Teleological Cosmology*. University Park: Pennsylvania State University Press, 1992.

Boff, Leonardo. *Cry of the Earth, Cry of the Poor*. Maryknoll, NY: Orbis Books, 1997.

Brady, Bernard V. *Essential Catholic Social Thought*. Maryknoll NY: Orbis Books, 2008.

Bryant, Edwin. "Strategies of Vedic Subversion," in *A Communion of Subjects*, edited by Paul Waldau and Kimberly Patton, 194–203.

Burdo, Peter, ed. *Exploring Wild Law: The Philosophy of Earth Jurisprudence*. Kent Town, South Australia: Wakefield Press, 2011.

Butkus, Russell, and Steven Kolmes. "Ecology and the Common Good: Sustainability and Catholic Social Teaching." *Journal of Catholic Social Thought* 4, no. 2 (2007): 403–436.

Callicott, J. Baird. "Intrinsic Value in Nature: A Metaethical Analysis." http://ejap.louisiana.edu/EJAP/1995.spring/callicott.1995.spring.html.

Cattoi, Thomas. *Divine Contingency: Theologies of Divine Embodiment in Maximos the Confessor and Tsong Kha Pa*. Piscataway, NJ: Gorgias Press, 2008.

Change, Alicia. "Stephen Hawking: Space Exploration Is Key to Saving Humanity," *Huffington Post*, April 10, 2013. http://www.huffingtonpost.com/2013/04/11/stephen-hawking-space-exploration-humanity_n_3061329.html.

Chapple, Christopher Key. "Animals and Environment in the Buddhist Birth Stories," in *Buddhism and Ecology: The Interconnection of Dharma and Deeds*, edited by Mary Evelyn Tucker, 131–148. Cambridge, MA: Harvard University Press, 1998.

Chapple, Christopher Key. "Ecological Nonviolence and the Hindu Tradition," reprinted in *Many Heavens, One Earth: Readings on Religion and the Environment*, edited by Clifford Chalmers Cain, 123–130. Lanham, MD: Lexington Books, 2013.

Chapple, Christopher Key. "Toward an Indigenous Indian Environmentalism," in *Purifying the Earthly Body of God*, edited by Lance Nelson, 13–28.

Chapple, Christopher Key, and Mary Evelyn Tucker, eds. *Hinduism and Ecology: The Intersection of Earth, Sky, and Water*. Cambridge, MA: Harvard University Press, 2000.

Clairmont, David. "Why Does the Buddha Close His Eyes in My Eden? A Buddhist Ecological Challenge and Invitation to Christians," in *Green Discipleship: Catholic Theological Ethics and the Environment*, edited by Tobias L. Winright, 340–358.

Clark, Meghan. "Anatomy of a Social Virtue: Solidarity and Corresponding Vices." *Political Theology* 15, no. 1 (2014): 26–39.

Clippard, Seth. "The Lorax Wears Saffron: Toward a Buddhist Environmentalism." *Journal of Buddhist Ethics* 18 (2011): 212–248.

Clooney, Francis, S.J. *Beyond Compare: St. Francis de Sales and Sri Vedanta Desika on Loving Surrender to God*. Washington, DC: Georgetown University Press, 2008.

Clooney, Francis, S.J. *Comparative Theology: Deep Learning across Religious Borders*. Wiley-Blackwell, 2010a.

Clooney, Francis, S.J., ed. *The New Comparative Theology: Interreligious Insights from the Next Generation*. New York: Continuum, 2010b.

Clooney, Francis, S.J. "Comparative Theology," in *The Oxford Handbook of Systematic Theology*, edited by Kathryn Tanner, John Webster, and Iain Torrance, 653–669. New York: Oxford University Press, 2007.

Clooney, Francis, S.J. *Divine Mother, Blessed Mother: Hindu Goddesses and the Virgin Mary*. New York: Oxford University Press, 2005.

Clooney, Francis, S.J. *Hindu God, Christian God: How Reason Helps Break Down the Boundaries Between Religions*. New York: Oxford University Press, 2001.

Clooney, Francis, S.J. "The Emerging Field of Comparative Theology: A Bibliographical Review (1989–95)." *Theological Studies* 56, no. 3 (1995): 521–550.

Clooney, Francis, S.J. "The Study of Non-Christian Religions in the Post-Vatican II Roman Catholic Church." *Journal of Ecumenical Studies* 28, no. 3 (1991): 482–494.

Clooney, Francis, S.J. *Theology after Vedanta: An Experiment in Comparative Theology*. Albany: State University of New York Press, 1993.

Convention on Biological Diversity, Article 2, "Use of Terms," http://www.cbd.int/convention/articles.shtml?a=cbd-02.

Cook, Francis H. *Hua-yen Buddhism: The Jewel Net of Indra*. University Park: Pennsylvania State University Press, 1977.

Coward, Harold. "The Ecological Implications of Karma Theory," in *Purifying the Earthly Body of God*, edited by Lance Nelson, 39–49.

Cullinan, Cormac. *Wild Law: A Manifesto for Earth Justice*, 2nd ed. White River Junction, VT: Chelsea Green Publishing, 2011.

Curran, Charles. "Catholic Social Teaching and Human Morality," in *One Hundred Years of Catholic Social Thought: Celebration and Challenge*, edited by John Coleman, 72–87. Maryknoll, NY: Orbis Books, 1991.

Daly, Daniel. "Structures of Virtue and Vice." *New Blackfriars* 92 (2011): 341–357.

Deane-Drummond, Celia. *Eco-Theology*. Winona, MN: Anselm Academic, 2008.

Deane-Drummond, Celia. "Joining in the Dance: Catholic Social Teaching and Ecology." *New Blackfriars* 93, no. 1044 (2012): 193–212.

Deane-Drummond, Celia. *The Ethics of Nature*. Malden, MA: Blackwell Publishing, 2004.

Deloria, Vine. *God Is Red*. New York: Grosset & Dunlap, 1973.

DeMallie, Raymond J. "Lakota Belief and Ritual in the Nineteenth Century," in *Sioux Indian Religion*, edited by Raymond J. DeMallie and Douglas R. Parks, 25–44. Norman: University of Oklahoma Press, 1987.

Derr, Thomas Sieger. "Environmental Ethics and Christian Humanism," in *Environmental Ethics and Christian Humanism*, edited by Thomas Sieger Derr with James A. Nash and Richard John Neuhaus, 17–104. Nashville, TN: Abingdon Press, 1996.

De Silva, Padmasiri. "Buddhist Environmental Ethics," in *Dharma Gaia*, edited by Allan Hunt Badiner, 14–19.

Des Jardins, Joseph. *Environmental Ethics: An Introduction to Environmental Philosophy*. Boston: Wadsworth Cengage Learning, 2006.

Dhand, Arti. "The *Dharma* of Ethics, the Ethics of *Dharma*: Quizzing the Ideals of Hinduism." *Journal of Religious Ethics* 30, no. 3 (2002): 347–372.

Dorr, Donal. *Option for the Poor and for the Earth: Catholic Social Teaching*. Maryknoll, NY: Orbis Books, 1983, 1992, 2012.

Doran, Kevin P. *Solidarity: A Synthesis of Personalism and Communalism in the Thought of Karol Wojtyla/Pope John Paul II*. New York: Peter Lang, 1996.

Dunham, Scott. *The Trinity and Creation in Augustine: An Ecological Analysis*. Albany: State University of New York Press, 2008.

Dwivedi, O. P. "Hindu Religion and Environmental Well-being," in *The Oxford Handbook of Religion and Ecology*, edited by Roger Gottlieb, 160–183. New York: Oxford, 2006.

Dwivedi, O. P. "Dharmic Ecology," in *Hinduism and Ecology*, edited by Christopher Key Chapple and Mary Evelyn Tucker, 3–22.

Earth Charter. http://www.earthcharterinaction.org/content.

Earth Law Center. http://earthlawcenter.org.

Edwards, Denis. *Ecology at the Heart of Faith: The Change of Heart That Leads to a New Way of Living on Earth*. Maryknoll, NY: Orbis, 2006.

Ellard, Peter. "Thomas Berry, Groundwork for a Dark Green Catholic Theology," in *Confronting the Climate Crisis: Catholic Theological Perspectives*, edited by Jame Schaefer, 301–320. Milwaukee: Marquette University Press, 2011.

Fabian, Johannes. *Time and the Other*. New York: Columbia University Press, 1983.

Fergusson, David. "Creation," in *The Oxford Handbook of Systematic Theology*, edited by Kathryn Tanner, John Webster, and Iain Torrance, 72–90. New York: Oxford University Press, 2007.

Filgueira, Begonia, and Ian Mason. 2009. *Wild Law: Is There Any Evidence of Earth Jurisprudence in Existing Law and Practice?* http://www.ukela.org/content/page/1090/Wild%20Law%20Research%20Report%20published%20March%202009.pdf.

Forum on Religion and Ecology at Yale University. http://fore.yale.edu/.

Forum on Religion and Ecology at Yale University. "Leveling Appalachia: The Legacy of Mountaintop Removal Mining." http://e360.yale.edu/feature/leveling_appalachia_the_legacy_of_mountaintop_removal_mining/2198/.

Fox, Matthew. "Some Thoughts on Thomas Berry's Contributions to the Western Spiritual Tradition," in *Thomas Berry, Dreamer of the Earth*, edited by Ervin Laszlo and Allan Combs, 16–31. Rochester, VT: Inner Traditions, 2011.

Flood, Gavin. *An Introduction to Hinduism*. New York: Cambridge University Press, 1996.

Francis [Pope]. *Evangelii Gaudium*. Apostolic Exhortation on the Proclamation of the Gospel in Today's World, November 24, 2013. http://w2.vatican.va/content/francesco/en/apost_exhortations/documents/papa-francesco_esortazione-ap_20131124_evangelii-gaudium.html.

Francis [Pope]. *Laudato Si'*. May 24, 2015. http://w2.vatican.va/content/francesco/en/encyclicals/documents/papa-francesco_20150524_enciclica-laudato-si.html.

Francis [Pope]. Twitter post, April 28, 2014, 1:28 a.m., https://twitter.com/Pontifex/status/460697074585980928.

Fredericks, James. "Introduction," in *The New Comparative Theology: Interreligious Insights from the Next Generation*, edited by Francis X. Clooney S.J., ix–xix. New York: Continuum, 2010:.

French, William C. "Catholicism and the Common Good of the Biosphere," in *An Ecology of the Spirit: Religious Reflection and Environmental Consciousness*, edited by Michael H. Barnes, 177–194. Lanham, MD: University Press of America, 1994.

French, William C. "Common Ground, Common Skies: Natural Law and Ecological Responsibility." *Journal of Ecumenical Studies* 42, no. 3 (Summer 2007): 373–388.

French, William C. "Natural Law and Ecological Responsibility: Drawing on the Thomistic Tradition." *University of St. Thomas Law Journal* 5, no. 1 (2008): 20.

Gold, Ann Grodzins. "'If You Cut a Branch You Cut My Finger': Court, Forest, and Environmental Ethics in Rajasthan," in *Hinduism and Ecology*, edited by Christopher Key Chapple and Mary Evelyn Tucker, 317–336.

Grim, John A., and Mary Evelyn Tucker. *Ecology and Religion*. Washington, DC: Island Press, 2014.

Grim, John A. "Indigenous Traditions: Religion and Ecology," in *The Oxford Handbook of Religion and Ecology*, edited by Roger Gottlieb, 283–309. New York: Oxford, 2006.

Gustafson, Carrie, and Peter H. Juviler, eds. *Religion and Human Rights: Competing Claims?* Armonk, NY: M.E. Sharpe, 1999.

Gustafson, James. *A Sense of the Divine: The Natural Environment of a Theocentric Perspective*. Cleveland: The Pilgrim Press, 1996.

Hanh, Thich Nhat. *Call Me by My True Names: The Collected Poems of Thich Nhat Hanh*. Berkeley CA: Parallax Press, 1999.

Hanh, Thich Nhat. *The Blooming of the Lotus*, 2nd edition. Boston: Beacon Press, 2009.

Hanh, Thich Nhat. *The Heart of the Buddha's Teaching: Transforming Suffering into Peace, Joy, and Liberation*. Berkeley, CA: Parallax Press, 1998.

Hanh, Thich Nhat. *The Sun My Heart: From Mindfulness to Insight Contemplation*. Berkeley, CA: Parallax Press, 1988.

Hanh, Thich Nhat. *The World We Have: A Buddhist Approach to Peace and Ecology*. Berkeley, CA: Parallax Press, 2008.

Hargrove, Eugene. *The Animal Rights/Environmental Ethics Debate*. Albany: State University of New York Press, 1992.

Harris, Ian. "Buddhism and the Discourse of Environmental Concern: Some Methodological Problems Considered," in *Buddhism and Ecology*, edited by Mary Evelyn Tucker and Duncan Ryuken Williams, 377–402.

Hart, John. *Cosmic Commons: Spirit, Science, and Space*. Eugene, OR: Cascade Books, 2013.

Hart, John. *Sacramental Commons: Christian Ecological Ethics*. Lanham, MD: Rowman & Littlefield, 2006.

Hart, John. *What Are They Saying about Environmental Theology?* New York: Paulist Press, 2004.

Harvey, Peter. *An Introduction to Buddhist Ethics*. New York: Cambridge University Press, 2004.

Haught, John. *The Promise of Nature: Ecology and Cosmic Purpose*. Eugene, OR: Wipf & Stock Publishers, 2004.

Hessel, Dieter. "Notes on Moral Theology." *Theological Studies* 51, no. 1 (1990): 64–81.

Himes, Michael, and Kenneth Himes. *Fullness of Faith: The Public Significance of Theology*. New York: Paulist Press, 1993.

Himes, Kenneth R., ed. *Modern Catholic Social Teaching: Commentaries and Interpretations*. Washington, DC: Georgetown University Press, 2005.

Himes, Kenneth R., ed. *Responses to 101 Questions on Catholic Social Teaching*. New York: Paulist Press, 2001.

Hollenbach, David. "The Common Good Revisited." *Theological Studies* 50 (March 1989): 86.

Hollenbach, David. *The Common Good and Christian Ethics*. Cambridge: Cambridge University Press, 2002.

Hornsby-Smith, Michael P. *An Introduction to Catholic Social Thought*. New York: Cambridge University Press, 2006.

Hoppe, Thomas. "Human Rights," in *The New Dictionary of Catholic Social Thought*, edited by Judith Dwyer, 454–470. Collegeville, MN: The Liturgical Press, 1994.

Huey, Aaron. "America's Native Prisoners of War." 2010. http://www.ted.com/talks/ aaron_huey.html.

Intergovernmental Panel on Climate Change. *Fifth Assessment Report*. 2014. http:// www.ipcc.ch/.

Jain, Pankaj. *Dharma and Ecology of Hindu Communities: Sustenance and Sustainability*. Burlington, VT: Ashgate, 2011.

James, George A. "Ethical and Religious Dimensions of Chipko Resistance," in *Hinduism and Ecology*, edited by Christopher Key Chapple and Mary Evelyn Tucker, 499–530.

James, Simon P. *Zen Buddhism and Environmental Ethics*. Burlington, VT: Ashgate, 2004.

Jenkins, Willis, and Christopher Key Chapple. "Religion and Environment." *Annual Review of Environment and Resources* 36 (2011): 441–463.

Jenkins, Willis. "After Lynn White: Religious Ethics and Environmental Problems," *Journal of Religious Ethics* 37, no. 2 (2009): 283–309.

Jenkins, Willis. *Ecologies of Grace: Environmental Ethics and Christian Theology*. Oxford: Oxford University Press, 2008.

Jenkins, Willis. *The Future of Ethics: Sustainability, Social Justice, and Religious Creativity*. Washington, DC: Georgetown University Press, 2013.

John Paul II, St. *Centesimus Annus*. January 5, 1991. http://www.vatican.va/holy_father/ john_paul_ii/encyclicals/documents/hf_jp-ii_enc_01051991_centesimus-annus_en.html.

John Paul II, St. General Audience Address. January 17, 2001. http://www. vatican.va/holy_father/john_paul_ii/audiences/2001/documents/ hf_jp-ii_aud_20010117_en.html.

John Paul II, St. *Peace with God the Creator, Peace with All Creation*, Message for the celebration of the World Day of Peace. January 1, 1990. http:// www.vatican.va/holy_father/john_paul_ii/messages/peace/documents/ hf_jp-ii_mes_19891208_xxiii-world-day-for-peace_en.html.

John Paul II, St. *Sollicitudo Rei Socialis*. December 30, 1987. http:// www.vatican.va/holy_father/john_paul_ii/encyclicals/documents/ hf_jp-ii_enc_30121987_sollicitudo-rei-socialis_en.html.

John Paul II, St. and the Ecumenical Patriarch His Holiness Bartholomew I. *Common Declaration on Environmental Ethics*. June 10, 2002. http://www. vatican.va/holy_father/john_paul_ii/speeches/2002/june/documents/ hf_jp-ii_spe_20020610_venice-declaration_en.html.

John XXIII, St. *Mater et Magistra*, Encyclical Letter on Christianity and Social Progress. May 15, 1961. http://www.vatican.va/holy_father/john_xxiii/encyclicals/ documents/hf_j-xxiii_enc_15051961_mater_en.html.

John XXIII, St. *Pacem in Terris*, Encyclical Letter on Establishing Universal Peace in Truth, Justice, Charity, and Liberty. April 11, 1963. http://www.vatican.va/holy_father/ john_xxiii/encyclicals/documents/hf_j-xxiii_enc_11041963_pacem_en.html.

Johnson, Elizabeth. *Ask the Beasts: Darwin and the God of Love*. New York: Bloomsbury Publishing, 2014.

Kaza, Stephanie, and Kenneth Kraft. *Dharma Rain: Sources of Buddhist Environmentalism*. Boston: Shambhala Press, 2000.

Kaza, Stephanie. "The Greening of Buddhism: Promise and Perils," in *The Oxford Handbook of Religion and Ecology*, edited by Roger Gottlieb, 184–206. New York: Oxford, 2006.

Kiblinger, Kristin Beise. "Relating Theology of Religions and Comparative Theology," in *The New Comparative Theology: Interreligious Insights from the Next Generation*, edited by Francis X. Clooney, S.J., 21–42.

King, Sallie. *Socially Engaged Buddhism*. Honolulu: University of Hawai'i Press, 2009.

Klostermaier, Klaus. *A Survey of Hinduism*. Albany: SUNY Press, 2007.

Knitter, Paul. *One Earth, Many Religions: Multi-Faith Dialogue and Global Responsibility*. Maryknoll, NY: Orbis Books, 1995.

Kootenai Tribe of Idaho v. Veneman. 313 F.3d 1094. 9th Cir. 2002.

Kunst, Arnold. "Use and Misuse of Dharma," in *The Concept of Duty in South Asia*, edited by W. D. O'Flaherty and J. Duncan M. Derrett, 3–17. London: School of Oriental and African Studies, 1978.

Linzey, Andrew. *Christianity and the Rights of Animals*. New York: Crossroad, 1987.

Leo XIII. *Aeterni Patris*. http://www.vatican.va/holy_father/leo_xiii/encyclicals/documents/hf_l-xiii_enc_04081879_aeterni-patris_en.html.

Leopold, Aldo. *A Sand County Almanac*. New York: Ballantine Books, 1970.

Longwood, Merle. "Common Good and Environmental Issues." *Theological Studies* 34, no. 03 (1973): 468–480.

Loy, David R. *Money Sex War Karma: Notes for a Buddhist Revolution*. Somerville MA: Wisdom Publications, 2008.

Loy, David R. *The Great Awakening: A Buddhist Social Theory*. Boston: Wisdom Publications, 2003.

Macy, Joanna. *World as Lover, World as Self*. Berkeley, CA: Parallax Press, 1991.

Magesa, Laurenti. *African Ethics: The Moral Traditions of Abundant Life*. Maryknoll, NY: Orbis Books, 1997.

Massaro, Thomas. *Living Justice: Catholic Social Teaching in Action*. Lanham, MD: Rowman & Littlefield, 2012.

McFague, Sallie. *The Body of God: An Ecological Theology*. Minneapolis: Augsburg, 1993.

McFague, Sallie. *Super, Natural Christians: How We Should Love Nature*. Minneapolis: Fortress Press, 1997.

McGee, Mary. "State Responsibility for Environmental Management: Perspectives from Hindu Texts on Polity," in *Hinduism and Ecology*, edited by Christopher Key Chapple and Mary Evelyn Tucker, 59–100.

McKibben, Bill. *Eaarth: Making a Life on a Tough New Planet*. New York: Times Books, 2010.

McLaughlin, Ryan Patrick. *Preservation and Protest: Theological Foundations for an Eco-Eschatological Ethics*. Minneapolis: Fortress Press, 2014.

McMahan, David. *The Making of Buddhist Modernism*. Oxford: Oxford University Press, 2008.

McNeill, J. R. *Something New Under the Sun: An Environmental History of the Twentieth Century*. New York: W. W. Norton, 2000.

Midgely. Mary. "The Mixed Community," in *The Animal Rights/Environmental Ethics Debate*, edited by Eugene Hargrove, 211–226.

Millennium Ecosystem Assessment. *Living beyond Our Means: Natural Assets and Human Well-Being*: http://www.maweb.org/en/boardstatement.aspx.

Moe-Lobeda, Cynthia. *Resisting Structural Evil: Love as Ecological and Economic Vocation*. Minneapolis: Fortress, 2013.

Mumme, Patricia. "Models and Images for a Vaisnava Environmental Theology," in *Purifying the Earthly Body of God*, edited by Lance Nelson, 133–161.

Nagarjan, Vijaya Rettakudi. "The Earth as Goddess Bhu Devi: Toward a Theory of 'Embedded Ecologies' in Folk Hinduism," in *Purifying the Earthly Body of God*, edited by Lance Nelson, 269–296.

Narayanan, Vasudha. "'One Tree Is Equal to Ten Sons': Hindu Responses to the Problems of Ecology, Population, and Consumption." *Journal of the American Academy of Religion* 65 (1997): 291–332.

Narayanan, Vasudha. "Water, Wood, and Wisdom: Ecological Perspectives from the Hindu Traditions." *Daedalus* 130, no. 4 Fall (2001): 179–206.

Nash, James. "Biotic Rights and Human Ecological Responsibilities." *The Annual of the Society of Christian Ethics* (1993): 137–162.

Nash, James. "In Flagrant Dissent: An Environmentalist's Contentions," in *Environmental Ethics and Christian Humanism*, edited by Thomas Sieger Derr, 105–124.

Nash, James. *Loving Nature: Ecological Integrity and Christian Responsibility*. Nashville, TN: Abingdon Press, 1991.

Nash, Roderick. *The Rights of Nature: A History of Environmental Ethics*. Madison: The University of Wisconsin Press, 1989.

National Geographic. "Great Pacific Garbage Patch." (2015). http://education.nationalgeographic.com/education/encyclopedia/great-pacific-garbage-patch/?ar_a=1.

Nelson, Lance. "Reading the *Bhagavadgita* from an Ecological Perspective," in *Hinduism and Ecology: The Intersection of Earth, Sky, and Water*, edited by Christopher Key Chapple and Mary Evelyn Tucker, 135–150.

Nelson, Lance. "Cows, Elephants, Dogs, and Other Lesser Embodiments of Ātman: Reflections on Hindu Attitudes Toward Nonhuman Animals," in *A Communion of Subjects*, edited by Paul Waldau and Kimberly Patton, 179–193.

Nelson, Lance. "Ecology," in *Studying Hinduism: Key Concepts and Methods*, edited by Sushil Mittal and Gene Thursby, 97–111. New York: Routledge, 2008.

Nelson, Lance. "The Dualism of Nondualism: Advaita Vedānta and the Irrelevance of Nature," in *Purifying the Earthly Body of God*, 61–88.

Nelson, Lance, ed. *Purifying the Earthly Body of God: Religion and Ecology in Hindu India*. Albany: State University of New York Press, 1998.

Northcott, Michael. *The Environment and Christian Ethics*. New York: Cambridge University Press, 1996.

Norton, Bryan. "Environmental Ethics and Nonhuman Rights," in *The Animal Rights/Environmental Ethics Debate*, edited by Eugene Hargrove, 71–94.

Nutgeren, Albertina. "From Cosmos to Commodity . . . and Back: A Critique of Hindu Environmental Rhetoric in Educational Programs," in *Religion and Sustainable Development: Opportunities and Challenges for Higher Education*, edited by Cathrien de Pater and Irene Dankelman, 159–168. Münster: LIT Verlag, 2009.

O'Brien, David J., and Thomas A. Shannon, eds. *Catholic Social Thought: The Documentary Heritage*. Maryknoll, NY: Orbis Books, 1992.

O'Brien, David. "A Century of Catholic Social Teaching," in *One Hundred Years of Catholic Social Teaching: Celebration and Challenge*, edited by John Coleman, 13–24. Maryknoll, NY: Orbis, 1991.

O'Brien, Kevin J. *An Ethics of Biodiversity*. Washington, DC: Georgetown University Press, 2010.

O'Keefe, John. "Pope Benedict's Anthropocentrism: Is it a Deal Breaker?" *The Greening of the Papacy*, edited by Ronald A. Simkins and John J. O'Keefe, *Journal of Religion & Society Supplement* 9 (2013): 85–93. http://moses.creighton.edu/JRS/2013/2013-13.pdf.

Olivelle, Patrick, translator. *The Law Code of Manu*. New York: Oxford University Press, 2004.

Olivelle, Patrick. "Introduction," in *The Law Code of Manu*, translated by Patrick Olivelle, xvi–xlv.

Odin, Steve. "The Japanese Concept of Nature in Relation to the Environmental Ethics and Conservation Aesthetics of Aldo Leopold," in *Buddhism and Ecology*, edited by Mary Evelyn Tucker and Duncan Ryuken Williams, 89–110.

Parkes, Graham. "Voices of Mountains, Trees, and Rivers: Kūkai, Dōgen, and a Deeper Ecology," in *Buddhism and Ecology*, edited by Mary Evelyn Tucker and Duncan Ryuken Williams, 111–128.

Paul VI. "A Hospitable Earth for Future Generations," issued at the opening of the United Nations Conference on the Environment at Stockholm on June 1, 1972. http://conservation.catholic.org/pope_paul_vi.htm.

Paul VI. *Gaudium et Spes: Pastoral Constitution on the Church in the Modern World*. 1965. http://www.vatican.va/archive/hist_councils/ii_vatican_council/documents/vat-ii_cons_19651207_gaudium-et-spes_en.html.

Paul VI. *Populorum Progressio: On the Development of Peoples*. 1967. http://www.vatican.va/holy_father/paul_vi/encyclicals/documents/hf_p-vi_enc_26031967_populorum_en.html.

Pawlikowski, John, and Richard Fragomeni. *The Ecological Challenge*. Collegeville, MN: Liturgical Press, 1994.

Peelman, Achiel. *Christ Is a Native American*. Toronto: Novalis, 1995.

Pelikan, Jaroslav. *The Christian Tradition: A History of the Development of Doctrine*, Vol. 1. Chicago: University of Chicago Press, 1971.

Peppard, Christiana. "Denaturing Nature." *The Union Seminary Quarterly Review* 63, no. 1–2 (2011): 97–120.

Pinchot, Gifford. *Breaking New Ground*. Washington, DC: Island Press, 1998.

Pieper, Josef. *Guide to Thomas Aquinas*, translated by Richard Winston and Clara Winston. San Francisco: Ignatius Press, 1991.

Plotkin, Bill. "Inscendence—The Key to the Great Work of Time: A Soulcentric View of Thomas Berry's Work," in *Thomas Berry, Dreamer of the Earth*, edited by Ervin Laszlo and Allan Combs, 42–71. Rochester, VT: Inner Traditions, 2011.

Pontifical Council for Justice and Peace. *Compendium of the Social Doctrine of the Church*. http://www.vatican.va/roman_curia/pontifical_councils/justpeace/documents/rc_pc_justpeace_doc_20060526_compendio-dott-soc_en.html.

Rahula, Walpola. *What the Buddha Taught*, 2nd rev. ed. New York: Grove Press, 1974.

Rasmussen, Larry. *Earth Community, Earth Ethics*. Maryknoll, NY: Orbis Books, 1996.

Rasmussen, Larry. *Earth-Honoring Faith: Religious Ethics in a New Key*. New York: Oxford University Press, 2013.

Rasmussen, Larry. "Human Environmental Rights and/or Biotic Rights," in *Religion and Human Rights: Competing Claims?* edited by Carrie Gustafson and Peter H. Juviler, 36–52. Armonk, NY: M. E. Sharpe, 1999.

Ratzinger, Joseph. *'In the Beginning . . .' A Catholic Understanding of Creation and the Fall*, translated by Boniface Ramey, O.P. New York: Continuum, 1986.

Ratzinger, Joseph. *Gospel, Catechesis, Catechism: Sidelights on the Catechism of the Catholic Church*. San Francisco: Ignatius Press, 1997.

Rawls, John. *Political Liberalism*. Columbia University Press, 1993.

Rolston, Holmes. "Ecology: A Primer for Christian Ethics." *Journal of Catholic Social Thought* 4, no. 2 (2007): 293–312.

Rolston, Holmes. *Environmental Ethics: Duties to and Values in the Natural World*. Philadelphia: Temple University Press, 1988.

Rourke, Nancy. "The Environment Within: Virtue Ethics," in *Green Discipleship*, edited by Tobias Winright, 163–182.

Ruether, Rosemary Radford. *Gaia and God: An Ecofeminist Theology of Earth Healing*. New York: HarperCollins, 1992.

Sandel, Michael. *Liberalism and the Limits of Justice*, 2nd Edition. Cambridge: Cambridge University Press, 1982, 1998.

Santmire, H. Paul. *The Travail of Nature: The Ambiguous Ecological Promise of Christian Theology*. Philadelphia: Fortress, 1985.

Schaefer, Jame. "Environmental Degradation, Social Sin, and the Common Good," in *God, Creation, and Climate Change*, edited by Richard Miller, 69–94. Maryknoll NY: Orbis Books, 2010.

Schaefer, Jame. "Solidarity, Subsidiarity, and Option for the Poor: Extending Catholic Social Teaching in Response to the Climate Crisis," in *Confronting the Climate Crisis*, edited by Jame Schaefer, 389–425. Milwaukee: Marquette University Press. 2011.

Schaefer, Jame. *Theological Foundations for Environmental Ethics: Reconstructing Patristic and Medieval Concepts*. Washington, DC: Georgetown University Press. 2009.

Schaefer, Jame. "Valuing Earth Intrinsically and Instrumentally: A Theological Framework for Environmental Ethics." *Theological Studies* 66 (2005): 783–814.

Schaefer, Jame, ed. *Confronting the Climate Crisis: Catholic Theological Perspectives*. Milwaukee: Marquette University Press. 2011.

Schaefer, Jame, and Tobias Winright, eds. *Environmental Justice and Climate Change: Assessing Pope Benedict XVI's Ecological Vision for the Catholic Church in the United States*. New York: Lexington Books, 2013.

Scharper, Stephen, and Andrew J. Weigert. "An Invitation to Inclusive Environmental Reflection," in *Catholic Social Thought: American Reflections on the Compendium*, edited by D. Paul Sullins and Anthony J. Blasi, 127–142. Lanham, MD: Lexington Books, 2009.

Scheid, Daniel. "Co-Creator or Creative Predator? James Nash's Contributions to Catholic Social Teaching on Ecological Ethics" in *Worldviews: Global Religions, Culture, and Ecology* 18, no. 2 (2014): 99–121.

Scheid, Daniel. "Just Peacemaking Theory and the Promotion of Dignified Subsistence," in *Violence, Transformation, and the Sacred: They Shall Be Called Children of God* (College Theology Society Annual Volume 2011), edited by Margaret R. Pfeil and Tobias L. Winright, 175–189. Maryknoll, NY: Orbis, 2012.

Scheid, Daniel. "Thomas Aquinas, the Cosmic Common Good, and Climate Change," in *Confronting the Climate Crisis: Catholic Theological Perspectives*, edited by Jame Schaefer, 125–144.

Scheid, Daniel. "Vedānta Deśika and Thomas Aquinas on the Intrinsic Value of Nature." *Journal of Vaishnava Studies* 18 (2010): 27–42.

Schillebeeckx, Edward. *The Schillebeeckx Reader*, edited by Robert J. Schreiter. New York: Crossroad, 1984.

Senior, Donald, and John J. Collins, eds. *The Catholic Study Bible*. New York: Oxford University Press, 2006.

Seoane, Aldo and Wica Agli. "House Vote in Favor of the Keystone XL Pipeline an Act of War." 2014. http://www.lakotavoice.com/2014/11/15/house-vote-in-favor-of-the-keystone-xl-pipeline-an-act-of-war.

Sharma, Arvind. *Modern Hindu Thought: An Introduction.* New York: Oxford University Press, 2005.

Sheveland, John. *Piety and Responsibility: Patterns of Unity in Karl Rahner, Karl Barth, and Vedanta Desika.* Burlington, VT: Ashgate, 2011.

Sideris, Lisa. *Environmental Ethics, Ecological Theology, and Natural Selection.* New York: Columbia University Press. 2003.

Silecchia, Lucia A. "Discerning the Environmental Perspective of Pope Benedict XVI." *Journal of Catholic Social Thought* 4, no. 2 (Summer 2007): 271–292.

Singh, Timon. "Vatican City Crowned the 'Greenest State in the World.' " *Inhabitat—Sustainable Design Innovation,* December 10, 2010. http://inhabitat.com/the-vatican-city-is-the-greenest-state-in-the-world/.

Speth, James Gustave. *Red Sky at Morning: America and the Crisis of the Global Environment.* New Haven, CT: Yale University Press, 2004.

Stone, Daniel. "How Green Was the 'Green Pope'?" National Geographic News, February 28, 2013. http://news.nationalgeographic.com/news/2013/02/130228-environmental-pope-green-efficiency-vatican-city/.

Sullivan, Bruce. *The A to Z of Hinduism.* London: The Scarecrow Press, 2001.

Sunstein, Cass. "Introduction: What Are Animal Rights?" in *Animal Rights: Current Debates and New Directions,* edited by Cass R. Sunstein and Martha C. Nussbaum, 3–21. Cary, NC: Oxford University Press, 2004.

Swearer, Donald K. "An Assessment of Buddhist Ecophilosophy." *Harvard Theological Review* 99, no. 2 (2006): 123–137.

Taylor, Bron. "Earth and Nature-Based Spirituality, Part I: From Deep Ecology to Radical Environmentalism." *Religion* 31, no. 2 (2001): 175–193.

Taylor, Bron. "Earth and Nature-Based Spirituality, Part II: From Earth First! and Bioregionalism to Scientific Paganism and the New Age." *Religion* 31, no. 3 (2001): 225–245.

Taylor, Sarah M. *Green Sisters: A Spiritual Ecology.* Cambridge, MA: Harvard University Press, 2008.

Teertha, Swami Vibudhesha. "Sustaining the Balance." Alliance for Religions and Conservation. http://www.arcworld.org/faiths.asp?pageID=77.

Thatamanil, John. *The Immanent Divine: God, Creation and the Human Predicament.* Minneapolis: Fortress Press, 2006.

The Catholic Bishops Conference of the Philippines. "What Is Happening to Our Beautiful Land?" 1987. http://www.cbcponline.net/documents/1980s/1988-ecology.html.

The Forum on Religion and Ecology at Yale University. http://fore.yale.edu/.

The National Religious Partnership for the Environment. http://www.nrpe.org/.

Thompson, J. Milburn. *Introducing Catholic Social Thought.* Maryknoll, NY: Orbis Books, 2010.

Tierney, Brian. *The Idea of Natural Rights: Studies on Natural Rights, Natural Law, and Church Law 1150–1625.* Atlanta: Scholars Press, 1997.

Tillich, Paul. *Systematic Theology*, Volume II. Chicago: University of Chicago Press, 1957.

Tinker, George. *American Indian Liberation: A Theology of Sovereignty.* Maryknoll, NY: Orbis Books, 2008.

Tinker, George. "American Indians and the Arts of the Land: Spatial Metaphors and Contemporary Existence," in *Voices from the Third World: 1990*, 171–193. Sri Lanka: Ecumenical Association of Third World Theologians, 1991.

Tinker, George. "American Indians' Religious Traditions," in *The Hope of Liberation in World Religions*, edited by Miguel A. De La Torre, 257–274. Waco, TX: Baylor University Press, 2008.

Tinker, George. "An American Indian Theological Response to Ecojustice," in *Defending Mother Earth: Native American Perspectives on Environmental Justice*, edited by Jace Weaver, 153–176. Maryknoll, NY: Orbis Books, 1996.

Tinker, George. "For All My Relations: Justice, Peace and the Integrity of Christmas Trees." *Sojourners* 20, no. 1 (1991): 19–21.

Tinker, George. "Native Americans and the Land: The End of Living, and the Beginning of Survival." *Word & World* VI, no. 1 (1986): 66–74.

Toolan, David. *At Home in the Cosmos.* Maryknoll, NY: Orbis Books, 2001.

Tracy, David. "Comparative Theology," in *The Encyclopedia of Religion*, 14:446–455. New York: Macmillan.

Tucker, Mary Evelyn. "Editor's Afterword: An Intellectual Biography of Thomas Berry," in *Evening Thoughts: Reflecting on Earth as a Sacred Community*, edited by Mary Evelyn Tucker, 151–171. San Francisco: Sierra Club Books, 2006.

Tucker, Mary Evelyn, and John Grim. "Series Foreword." In *Indigenous Traditions and Ecology: The Interbeing of Cosmology and Community*, edited by John Grim, xv–xxxii. Cambridge, MA: Harvard University Press, 2001.

Tucker, Mary Evelyn, and Duncan Ryuken Williams, eds. *Buddhism and Ecology: The Interconnection of Dharma and Deeds.* Cambridge, MA: Harvard University Press, 1997.

Swimme, Brian Thomas and Mary Evelyn Tucker. *The Journey of the Universe.* New Haven, CT: Yale University Press, 2011. www.journeyoftheuniverse.org.

Tugwell, Simon. "Thomas Aquinas. Introduction." *Albert and Thomas, Selected Writings.* New York: Paulist Press, 1988.

Tyson, Neil deGrasse. "Cosmos: A Spacetime Odyssey." http://www.cosmosontv.com/.

United Nations Environment Programme, *Global Environment Outlook 5:* 2012. http://www.unep.org/geo/pdfs/geo5/GEO5_report_full_en.pdf.

US Conference of Catholic Bishops. Catholic Campaign for Human Development. "2013–2014 List of Awardees." http://www.usccb.org/about/catholic-campaign-for-human-development/upload/grantee-list-2013-2014.pdf.

US Conference of Catholic Bishops. Catholic Relief Services. "Climate Change." (2015). http://www.crs.org/pope-francis-climate/.

US Conference of Catholic Bishops. *Economic Justice for All: Pastoral Letter on Catholic Social Teaching and the U.S. Economy.* 1986. http://www.usccb.org/upload/economic_justice_for_all.pdf.

US Conference of Catholic Bishops. *Global Climate Change: A Plea for Dialogue, Prudence, and the Common Good.* June 15, 2001. http://www.usccb.org/issues-and-action/human-life-and-dignity/environment/global-climate-change-a-plea-for-dialogue-prudence-and-the-common-good.cfm.

US Conference of Catholic Bishops. *Renewing the Earth.* 1992. http://www.usccb.org/issues-and-action/human-life-and-dignity/environment/renewing-the-earth.cfm.

US Conference of Catholic Bishops. "Seven Themes of Catholic Social Teaching." (2005). http://www.usccb.org/beliefs-and-teachings/what-we-believe/catholic-social-teaching/seven-themes-of-catholic-social-teaching.cfm.

van Wensveen, Louke. *Dirty Virtues: The Emergence of Ecological Virtue Ethics.* Amherst, NY: Humanity Books, 2000.

Vidal, John. "Bolivia Enshrines Natural World's Rights with Equal Status for Mother Earth." *The Guardian.* April 10, 2011. http://www.theguardian.com/environment/2011/apr/10/bolivia-enshrines-natural-worlds-rights.

Waldau, Paul, and Kimberly Patton, eds. *A Communion of Subjects: Animals in Religion, Science, and Ethics.* New York: Columbia University Press, 2006.

Wall, Barbara. "Ethical Considerations for a New Jurisprudence: A Catholic Social Thought Perspective." *Barry Law Review* 11 (Fall 2008): 77–93.

Watson, Richard. "Self-Consciousness and the Rights of Nonhuman Animals and Nature," in *The Animal Rights/Environmental Ethics Debate,* edited by Eugene Hargrove, 1–36.

Wenz, Peter. *Environmental Justice.* Albany: State University of New York Press, 1988.

Wheaton, Sarah. "People, and Poodles, Contributing to Cleanup." *New York Times.* May 6, 2010: A20.

White, Lynn, Jr. "The Historical Roots of Our Ecological Crisis." *Science* 155, no. 3767 (1967): 1203–1207.

Whitmore, Todd. "Catholic Social Teaching: Starting with the Common Good," in *Living the Catholic Social Tradition: Cases and Commentary,* edited by Kathleen Weigert, 59–85. Lanham, MD: Rowman and Littlefield, 2005.

Winright, Tobias L. *Green Discipleship: Catholic Theological Ethics and the Environment.* Winona, MN: Anselm Academic, 2011.

Wittenberg, Gunther. "Plant and Animal Rights—an Absurd Idea or Ecological Necessity? Perspectives from the Hebrew Torah." *Journal of Theology for Southern Africa* 131 (July 2008): 72–83.

Worldwatch Institute. 2015. http://www.worldwatch.org.

Yearley, Lee. *Mencius and Aquinas: Theories of Virtue and Conceptions of Courage.* Albany: State University of New York Press, 1990.

Zaehner, R. C., translator. *Bhagavad Gītā.* New York: Oxford University Press, 1966.

Zagano, Phyllis, and Thomas C. McGonigle. *The Dominican Tradition.* Collegeville, MN: Liturgical Press, 2006.

Zalasiewicz, Jan, Mark Williams, Will Steffen, and Paul Crutzen. "The New World of the Anthropocene." *Environmental Science & Technology* 44, no. 7 (2010): 2228–2231.

Index

CPSIA information can be obtained
at www.ICGtesting.com
Printed in the USA
BVHW041256291221
625137BV00002B/4